Access 2003 for Starters

THE MISSING MANUAL

Access 2003 for Starters
THE MISSING MANUAL

Exactly what you need to get started

Kate J. Chase and Scott Palmer

POGUE PRESS™
O'REILLY®

Beijing · Cambridge · Farnham · Köln · Paris · Sebastopol · Taipei · Tokyo

Access 2003 for Starters: THE MISSING MANUAL

by Kate J. Chase and Scott Palmer

Published by O'Reilly Media, Inc., 1005 Gravenstein Highway North, Sebastopol, CA 95472.

O'Reilly books may be purchased for educational, business, or sales promotional use. Online editions are also available for most titles (*safari.oreilly.com*). For more information, contact our corporate/institutional sales department: (800) 998-9938 or *corporate@oreilly.com*.

Printing History:
October 2005:   First Edition.

 This book uses RepKover™, a durable and flexible lay-flat binding.

ISBN: 0-596-00665-9
[M]

TABLE OF CONTENTS

THE MISSING CREDITS

About The Authors

 Kate J. Chase is a Microsoft MVP in Office Systems as well as the author/co-author or editor of more than 30 technical reference books, including several books and training modules devoted to Office products. She has developed and managed vibrant online support communities for industry leaders like America Online, The Microsoft Network, and ZDnet. In addition, she frequently uses the tools in Office to work collaboratively with partners throughout the U.S. and the world.

 **Scott Palmer, Ph.D.** (co-author) has done database design and programming since 1985. He is the author of 21 books, including three bestsellers. He was computer columnist for The Washington DC Business Journal and has written for *The Wall Street Journal, Federal Computer Week, InfoWorld, PC World, Cato Policy Report, Reason Magazine,* and many other publications. He studied at Indiana University, the State University of New York, and the University of London, and is a member of the Mathematical Association of America and the American Economic Association.

About the Creative Team

Nan Barber (editor) is O'Reilly's associate editor for the Missing Manual series and has worn every hat from copy editor to co-author. She works in O'Reilly's Cambridge office and never doubted for a moment that the Commissioner's Trophy would someday come back home to Boston. Email: *nanbarber@mac.com*.

Michele Filshie (editor) is O'Reilly's assistant editor for Missing Manuals and editor of four Personal Trainers (another O'Reilly series). Before turning to the world of computer-related books, Michele was all literature, all the time, and spent many happy years at Black Sparrow Press. Email: *mfilshie@oreilly.com*.

Babette Bloch (technical reviewer) has used computers since the late 80s, starting with DOS database programs and word processors. She now teaches Quicken to teenagers and adults and leads a Quicken SIG for the Golden Gate Computer Society. Email: *babette.bloch@ggcs.org*.

Tim Hinton (technical reviewer) works in the operations department at O'Reilly. He also enjoys doing art, studying history, and sharing laughs. Email: *hinton@oreilly.com*.

Michael Schmalz (technical reviewer) is the author of *Integrating Excel and Access* (O'Reilly) and has done technical reviews on a number of O'Reilly titles. Michael has a degree in Finance from Penn State and currently works in financial services and business and technology consulting. Email: *mschmalz@infoadvising.com*.

Jill Steinberg (copy editor) is a freelance writer and editor based in Seattle, and has produced content for O'Reilly, Intel, Microsoft, and the University of Washington. Jill was educated at Brandeis University, Williams College, and Stanford University. Email: *saysjill@gmail.com*.

Rose Cassano (cover illustration) has worked as an independent designer and illustrator for 20 years. Assignments have ranged from the nonprofit sector to corporate clientele. She lives in beautiful Southern Oregon, grateful for the miracles of modern technology that make working there a reality. Email: *cassano@usi.net*. Web: *www.rosecassano.com*.

Acknowledgements

I would like to thank the admirable team of Sarah Milstein, Nan Barber, Michele Filshie, who helped keep this project on schedule; and Babette, Michael, and Tim, who kept the book technically accurate as well as highly readable. Thanks also go to my dynamic agent, David Fugate of Waterside Productions.

—Kate Chase

The Missing Manual Series

The Missing Manuals are conceived as superbly written guides to computer products that don't come with printed manuals (which is just about all of them). Each book features a handcrafted index, cross-references to specific page numbers (not just "see Chapter 9"), and an ironclad promise never to use an apostrophe in the possessive word its. Current and upcoming titles include:

AppleScript: The Missing Manual by Adam Goldstein

AppleWorks 6: The Missing Manual by Jim Elferdink and David Reynolds

Creating Web Sites: The Missing Manual by Matthew MacDonald

Dreamweaver 8: The Missing Manual by David Sawyer McFarland

eBay: The Missing Manual by Nancy Conner

Excel: The Missing Manual by Matthew MacDonald

Excel for Starters: The Missing Manual by Matthew MacDonald

FileMaker Pro 8: The Missing Manual by Geoff Coffey and Susan Prosser

FrontPage 2003: The Missing Manual by Jessica Mantaro

GarageBand 2: The Missing Manual by David Pogue

Google: The Missing Manual, 2nd Edition by Sarah Milstein and Rael Dornfest

Home Networking: The Missing Manual by Scott Lowe

iLife '05: The Missing Manual by David Pogue

iMovie HD & iDVD 5: The Missing Manual by David Pogue

iPhoto 5: The Missing Manual by David Pogue

iPod & iTunes: The Missing Manual, 3rd Edition by Jude Biersdorfer *iWork '05: The Missing Manual* by Jim Elferdink

Mac OS X Power Hound, Panther Edition by Rob Griffiths

Mac OS X: The Missing Manual, Tiger Edition by David Pogue

Office 2004 for Macintosh: The Missing Manual by Mark H. Walker and Franklin Tessler

Photoshop Elements 4: The Missing Manual by Barbara Brundage

QuickBooks: The Missing Manual by Bonnie Biafore

Quicken for Starters: The Missing Manual by Bonnie Biafore

Switching to the Mac: The Missing Manual, Tiger Edition by David Pogue and Adam Goldstein

Windows 2000 Pro: The Missing Manual by Sharon Crawford

Windows XP Power Hound by Preston Gralla

Windows XP for Starters: The Missing Manual by David Pogue

Windows XP Home Edition: The Missing Manual, 2nd Edition by David Pogue

Windows XP Pro: The Missing Manual, 2nd Edition by David Pogue, Craig Zacker, and Linda Zacker

INTRODUCTION

▶ **What's a Database?**

▶ **About Access Databases**

▶ **About This Book**

▶ **The Very Basics**

▶ **Example Databases**

▶ **About MissingManuals.com**

▶ **Safari Enabled**

TOO MUCH INFORMATION. Seemingly simple tasks like banking and shopping these days require you to have multiple account numbers, credit card numbers, screen names, and passwords at your fingertips. Even a simple address list isn't so simple anymore, now that folks have multiple phone numbers for cell phones, pagers, and fax machines.

Information is good. If you know how to store, retrieve, and control information, you can manage your own stock portfolio, keep an archive of form letters and documents so that you never have to reinvent the wheel, or print catalogs for your business at great savings over hiring an outside company.

All you need to make information work for you is a computer and Microsoft Access 2003. With Access, you can take thousands or millions of pieces of information, organize them, and retrieve them easily when you need them. Whether you're keeping track of inventory and customer orders for a business, statistical data for a research project, or even the types and colors of a closet full of shoes, you can do it with Access.

Access is perhaps the most misunderstood member of the Microsoft Office suite. It may look and act like Excel at times, but it's much more than spreadsheet software. As you'll see in this introduction, Access is a relational database program, with similarities to software from companies like FileMaker and Oracle. If you've never used a database before, there's no need to be intimidated: Access makes it easy to get started.

What's a Database?

A database is an organized collection of information, but it includes more than just the information itself. A database also groups, indexes, and catalogs the information so that it's easy to find when you need it. It stores and displays information in a standard format so you can immediately know which and what kind of information you're looking at.

Whether computerized or not, a database makes it easy both to find existing information and to add new information. A filing cabinet is an example of a non-computerized database:

▶ It divides information among drawers, each of which has a label indicating what it contains.

▶ Within each drawer, file folders contain specific types of information, like receipts, bills, and individual employee records.

▶ Just like the drawers, each file folder is labeled to show what it contains.

▶ Within each folder, forms and reports follow a standard format that organizes their content. When you pull out a certain kind of form or report, you know in advance where on the page to find the information you need and what it will be called.

Imagine trying to find the same information without a filing cabinet or file folders. Instead of being organized for easy retrieval, the papers are simply scattered on the floor. It would take at least five times longer to find the information—if you could find it at all.

Database Management Software

Database management software like Microsoft Access organizes computer data just as a filing cabinet organizes paper data. Using database software, you can add, check, and retrieve information with a speed and efficiency that would otherwise be impossible. Database software accomplishes this in much the same way as a filing cabinet:

▶ It divides information among databases, each of which has a name indicating what it contains.

▶ Within each database, tables contain specific types of information, like customer records and order records.

▶ Within each table, information follows a consistent format. When you open a table, you know in advance where to find the information you need and what it will be called.

An example of database management software at work is the airways database maintained by the U.S. National Flight Data Center, as shown in Figure I-1. With more than 500 airways between cities, the number of possible routes exceeds the number of stars in our galaxy. Without database management software, it would be impossible to store, check, and retrieve airplane routing information quickly. This image also demonstrates that information doesn't have to look like columns of words and numbers. Access may not be able to create a map like this one, but it lets you present your information in an enormous variety of ways.

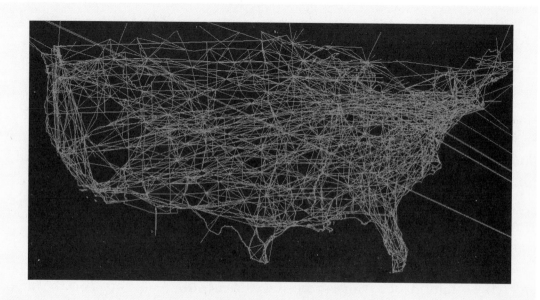

Figure I-1.

This computer map shows airways in American airspace. The U.S. National Flight Data Center uses MySQL, a database manager similar to Access, to manage information about the routes that airplanes are allowed to take in the United States.

When *Not* to Use a Database Manager

Database management software is best for handling large amounts of complex information. However, if your data is simple and your database is small, then database management software—even Microsoft Access—may waste your time. Its extra database features give you more power when you need it, but if you don't need it, a simpler approach is usually better.

If your database has fewer than 100 records and the information doesn't change very often, consider keeping it in a Word document or Excel spreadsheet instead of in Access. A personal Rolodex file is an example of this kind of database.

Many newspaper reporters keep their contact lists in Word files, with a separate paragraph for each contact. In addition to contact names, each paragraph includes keywords about the contact's expertise. When reporters need to find a contact, they can quickly search for names or keywords by using Word's search feature. If they start each paragraph with the contact's last name, they can even sort the contact records in alphabetical order.

That kind of solution isn't appropriate for more complex or rapidly changing data. But for simple databases, use a simple solution.

About Access Databases

Access takes a modular approach to organizing information: It's a kind of wrapper to hold—and connect—individual parts like tables, forms, and reports. This approach is very powerful because you can add as many items as you need, reprocessing and repurposing your data in infinite ways. For lack of a better term, Access calls these database parts *objects* (much more on that in Chapter 1). All Access databases have one thing in common—a Database window, where you can switch between objects and create new ones.

An Access database is also *relational,* which simply means that you can *link* tables together to combine their data. As you'll see later in this book, connecting tables of fundamentally different information is what gives you the power to create invoices and statements, sort direct mail lists, and generate reports that Excel never dreamed of.

About This Book

As database managers go, Access 2003 is, well, quite accessible. Like all Microsoft Office programs, it comes with tons of built-in help screens and a wealth of online assistance. Microsoft—like most software companies—seems to believe that as a result, you don't need any printed documentation.

But sometimes you need a handy reference that's written with *you* in mind. You want a book that puts information you need at your fingertips, that you can mark up and pepper with sticky notes. Most of all, you need a friendly guide to walk you through the procedures, whispering insider secrets and commonsense advice along the way.

Access 2003 for Starters: The Missing Manual is meant to do just that. It gets you started creating your first database in Chapter 1. Step-by-step instructions show you how to build a simple table and progress to a complex, query-based report. You'll master the features you use most of the time, find out which ones to disregard, and learn how to call on more advanced features when you're ready.

 Note: For highly advanced features beyond the scope of this book, you'll see notes like this one referring you to *other* books where you can learn more. Sometimes these books are published by the Missing Manual series' parent company, O'Reilly Media, but not always! If there's a great book on the subject by *any* publisher, the Missing Manual believes you have a right to know.

About the Outline

Access 2003 for Starters: The Missing Manual has eight chapters, progressing from basic techniques into early intermediate territory. Along the way, real-life examples and step-by-step tutorials help you apply what you're learning. Three appendixes supplement the main material and give you a launch pad for learning more.

▶ **Part One: Building A Database** shows you how to create the fundamental parts of any database: tables to hold data, and forms to enter or display data. You'll learn both how to use Access's Database Wizard and start from scratch. Chapters 2 and 3 cover designing your own tables and forms in great detail. Finally, Chapter 4 introduces you to relational database work. You'll learn not only how to understand relationships, but also how easy it is to make them.

▶ **Part Two: Organizing Information** helps you sift through the information you've amassed using Access's many options for sorting and filtering. In Chapters 6 and 7, you'll learn how to use queries to take sorting and filtering to the next level. With a query, you can apply more powerful filtering features and save them for use in other parts of your database. Chapter 8 is a primer on generating reports that present your database to the world.

▶ **Part Three: Appendixes** provides references and resources for your ongoing Access career. Appendix A walks you through installing Access (if you haven't already) and takes you on a tour of the program's many built-in and online help features, so you can look up any information you need. Appendix B deals with Frequently Asked Questions about hot topics like sharing Access information with other Office programs and how to post your data on the Internet. Last but not least, Appendix C lists and explains most of the commands in Access's menu bar. It's a great way to figure out how to do something in a hurry.

 Note: Don't be surprised if you find some obscure Access menu commands that aren't included in Appendix C. Frankly, Access has so many commands, not even Bill Gates can find them all.

About → These → Arrows

Throughout this book, and throughout the Missing Manual series, you'll find sentences like this one: "Open the Program Files → Microsoft Office → Templates folder." That's shorthand for a much longer instruction that directs you to open three nested folders in sequence, like this: "On your hard drive, you'll find a folder called Program Files. Open that. Inside the Program Files window is a folder called Microsoft Office; double-click it to open it. Inside *that* folder is yet another one called Templates. Double-click to open it, too." See Figure I-2 for an example.

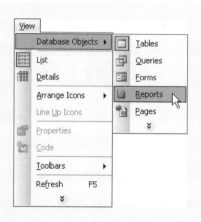

Figure I-2.
When this book says "Choose View → Database Objects → Reports," it means: "Click the View menu to open it. Next, click Database Objects in that menu. Finally, choose Reports from the resulting submenu."

The Very Basics

This book avoids the nerd terminology and jargon that pollute so many computer books. However, you need to know a few terms:

▶ **Clicking.** In this book, you'll find three kinds of instructions for clicking the mouse. To *click* a screen object (such as a button) means to point the mouse pointer at it, and then quickly press and release the left mouse button. *Right-clicking* means the same, except that you press the right mouse button instead. *Double-clicking* a screen object means to point the mouse pointer at it, and then quickly press and release the left mouse button twice, making a "click-click" sound. *Dragging* an object means to

When *Not* to Use a Database Manager

Database management software is best for handling large amounts of complex information. However, if your data is simple and your database is small, then database management software—even Microsoft Access—may waste your time. Its extra database features give you more power when you need it, but if you don't need it, a simpler approach is usually better.

If your database has fewer than 100 records and the information doesn't change very often, consider keeping it in a Word document or Excel spreadsheet instead of in Access. A personal Rolodex file is an example of this kind of database.

Many newspaper reporters keep their contact lists in Word files, with a separate paragraph for each contact. In addition to contact names, each paragraph includes keywords about the contact's expertise. When reporters need to find a contact, they can quickly search for names or keywords by using Word's search feature. If they start each paragraph with the contact's last name, they can even sort the contact records in alphabetical order.

That kind of solution isn't appropriate for more complex or rapidly changing data. But for simple databases, use a simple solution.

point the mouse pointer at it, hold down the left mouse button, move the pointer to a new position for the object, and then release the left mouse button.

▶ **Choosing menu items.** This book uses very compact terminology for talking about menus. When you're told to *Choose View → Database Objects → Reports,* for example, it means "Open the View menu, click Database Objects on the menu, and then click Tables on the submenu."

▶ **Keyboard shortcuts.** The mouse is a mixed blessing. It makes computers easier to use, but it can also be a time-waster. Every time you use the mouse, you must take one hand off the keyboard for a few seconds. Do that a hundred or more times a day, and you're burning up some serious time. Where *keyboard shortcuts* exist that work faster than the mouse, this book gives them to you. For example, the keyboard shortcut for opening an Access database is Ctrl+S, which means you hold down the Ctrl key and press the S key. You can still use the mouse if you prefer; keyboard shortcuts simply give you another option.

Example Databases

As you work through the tutorials in this book, you'll see a number of example databases that demonstrate Access features and good database-building techniques. You can download these files to work in, or to check your work against if you prefer. Just surf to the "Missing CDs" page at *www.missingmanuals.com/cds* using Internet Explorer (or any Web browser). Then click the link next to the title of this book to view these files organized by chapter. Simply click a file's blue, underlined link to download it to your PC.

About MissingManuals.com

At the Missing Manuals Web site (*www.missingmanuals.com*) you'll find articles, tips, and updates for the book. In fact, if you have feedback about the book— whether suggestions, kudos, or corrections—you're invited to submit it on the Web site. Any time we update the book, we'll include any confirmed corrections you've suggested. We'll also note the corrections on the Web site.

In the meantime, we'd love to hear your suggestions for new books in the Missing Manual line. There's a place for that on the Web site, too, as well as a place to go for free email notifications of new titles in the series.

Safari Enabled

 When you see a Safari® Enabled icon on the cover of your favorite technology book, that means the book is available online through the O'Reilly Network Safari Bookshelf.

Safari offers a solution that's better than e-books. It's a virtual library that lets you easily search thousands of top tech books, cut and paste code samples, download chapters, and find quick answers when you need the most accurate, current information. Try it for free at *http://safari.oreilly.com*.

PART ONE: BUILDING A DATABASE

CHAPTER 1:
CREATING DATABASES

▶ A Tour of an Access Database

▶ Creating a New Database

▶ Starting with a Wizard

▶ Modifying the Wizard's Database

▶ Starting from a Blank Database

IN THIS CHAPTER, YOU'LL CREATE YOUR FIRST DATABASE, from the initial concept to a full-fledged Access file. Using Access's Order Entry template as an example, you'll learn how to set up all the types of database fields to give you the information you want, when you want it, and in exactly the way you want it. You'll also learn how to put information into your database and print a simple report.

A Tour of an Access Database

As you read in the introduction to this book, a *database* typically refers to any organized collection of information. In Access, however, a database is much more than that: it's a kind of wrapper to hold other database objects like tables, forms, and reports. An Access database is also *relational,* which means (among other things) that you can link tables together to combine their information.

A computerized database must let you add, store, find, display, and print information. Access does all these things and more. For each task, Access has different database objects.

The Access Window

When you start Access, a large window opens on your desktop. When you open a database, its window appears inside this outer one. You can have any number of individual database windows open in Access, so in effect, the Access window is like a desktop-within-a-desktop. As shown in Figure 1-1, all of Access's toolbars and the task pane also reside in the same window, so it can get pretty busy in there. You can make more room by closing the task pane (click the close button in the upper-right corner) and minimizing any windows you're not currently using.

Tables

Access tables hold the information you store in the database (see Figure 1-2), and you can also use them for data entry. In a table, each row contains one *record* with information about a specific item, like a customer, sales order, or inventory

Database Objects Defined

When you read about Access on the Web or visit a user group, you'll hear much talk about *database objects*. Database objects are somewhat similar to objects in the real world, like dogs, trees, ice cream cones, and books.

All objects have *properties*. A dog, for example, has the properties of color, breed, height, weight, and age. An Access report has the properties of a certain number of columns, a certain content in each column, a certain placement of page numbers, and so forth.

When it comes to databases, the word "object" refers to specific database elements like tables, reports, and forms, all of which are defined in this chapter. The simplest database has only one object—a table. But most databases have many different objects for each function: two or more tables to hold information, forms for various kinds of data entry, several reports for printing, and so on.

item. Each column contains a *field* with information about a specific feature of the record in that row, like a customer's first name, the date of a sales order, or the part number of an inventory item.

Forms

Forms are windows that you can use to enter or display database information (see Figure 1-3). You lay out a form on the screen by dragging text boxes, labels, list boxes, and other controls onto the form window. You get a fill-in-the-blanks window that resembles a paper form. You'll learn how to create your own forms in Chapter 3.

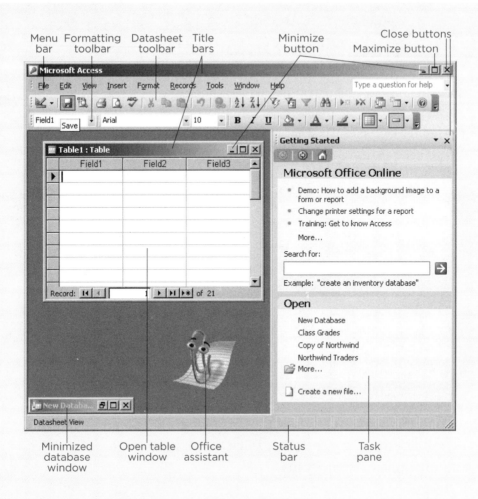

Figure 1-1. Access's window holds all the windows you create in your database, and all the tools you need to work with them. To make room for it all, click the Maximize button in the upper-right.

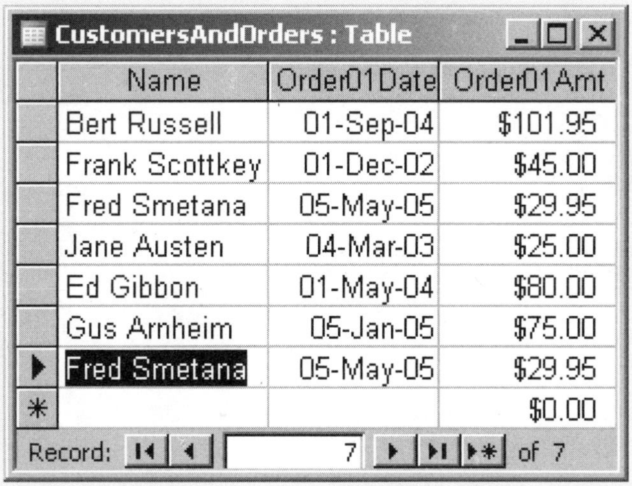

Figure 1-2. An Access table consists of rows (records) and columns (fields). Each row contains information about a particular item, like a customer, a sales order, or an inventory item. Each column has information about one feature of the item. Here, the first column stores text; the second and fourth columns store dates; and the third column stores dollar amounts.

Queries

A *query* is simply a question you ask Access about the information in your database, like "What are the names and addresses of our customers in Chicago?" or "What are our 10 most expensive products?" Access then searches through your database, finds the information to answer your question, and displays it in an easy-to-read format. Access lets you create queries quickly and easily by dragging table fields with your mouse and clicking a button.

Surprisingly, Access queries can do more than just answer your questions. You can use queries to update or change your data, add new records to a table, create cross tab reports, ask people for information, or connect to other database management systems, like Microsoft SQL Server. You'll learn how to create queries in Chapters 6 and 7. See Figure 1-4 for an example.

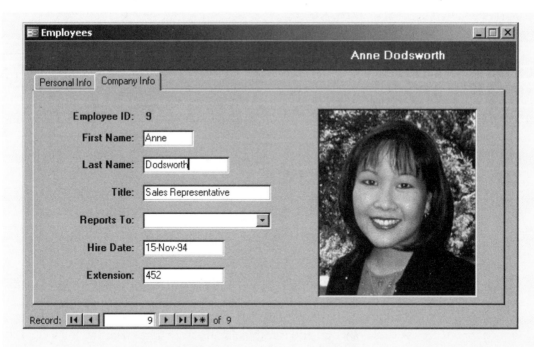

Figure 1-3. Forms let you easily enter or display database information. When you create your own databases, you can use forms to explain database fields and to prevent people from entering the wrong type of information, as you'll learn later in this chapter.

Reports

You can use reports to print your database information or display it onscreen (see Figure 1-5). You can group the information by city or sort the information by last name, for example. You can include totals and other calculations. You can even include graphics.

Access lets you tailor reports so that they not only show the information you want but show it exactly the way you want it. For simple lists, you can create reports with plain columns. For grouped information, you can create columns that stair-step through each group. You can create reports that group together blocks of information or present information in outline format. You can apply

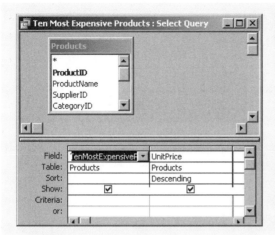

Figure 1-4. In your query design (shown on the left), you drag table fields into a grid to tell Access what information you want. In the query result (shown on the right), Access shows the answer to your query in the format and order you chose. If you want, you can also tell Access to sort the query result or even do calculations based on the result.

any of six predefined styles to give your reports a professional appearance. And, of course, you can either print reports or display them on your screen.

Just as with forms, you design reports by dragging fields into a grid on your screen. If you need a fairly standard report format, you can also have the Access Report Wizard create your report for you. You'll learn how to create reports in Chapter 8.

Putting It All Together

Your own needs determine which forms, reports, and other database objects you'll put into your database. You can add, take away, and edit objects at any time as your skills increase and your needs grow and change. As you become more familiar with Access, you'll develop a keener sense of what you can do. The

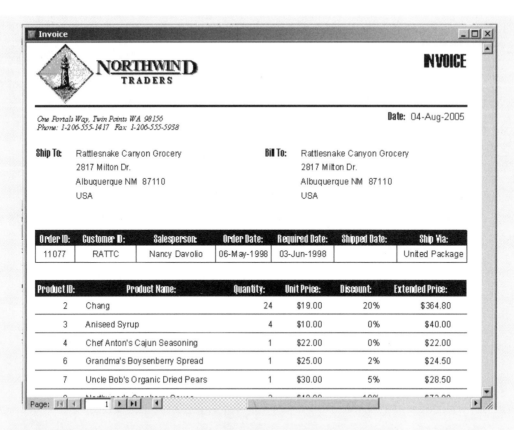

Figure 1-5. Use reports to print database information or display it on your screen. Note that the onscreen preview, like the one shown here, is only approximate. Depending on your printer, the page breaks, formatting, and type fonts may differ slightly from the preview.

possibilities are endless! Here are some examples of objects you may want to build into your database:

▶ Onscreen data-entry forms that check data for accuracy and make sure it's in the correct format.

▶ Saved queries that let you quickly see, for example, only the new customers added in the past week.

▶ A form that lets you create mailing labels.

▶ Reports that include calculated values, like totals, or that group records based on city, Zip code, or account balance.

You can always add more features to your database later on, but when you start out it's good to have an idea where you want to end up. You may find some of the forms you need, for example, in one of Access's templates, so knowing what you want helps save time right from the beginning.

Take a piece of paper (or a blank screen) and make a list of the information you want in your database. Names and addresses? Products and orders? Even if you don't yet know *how* the information fits in, get it down in writing. Where to put it will become clear as you learn about Access. Also think about how you need to use your information. Do you plan to look at long lists of items, for example, or do you need to store large volumes of information, like the standard documents your company uses? When you've jotted down some notes, your database begins to take shape. You're ready to launch Access and get to work.

Creating a New Database

Now that you've got some lists or diagrams of the information you need to track and how you're going to organize it (you did read the previous section, didn't you?), you can launch Access and start building your database. You can start Access two ways:

▶ Click the Windows Start button, and then choose Program Files → Microsoft Office → Microsoft Office Access 2003.

▶ In Windows Explorer, double-click an Access database you want to open.

 Tip: Just like a text document or a spreadsheet, you can close an Access file and pick up where you left off when you return. To close Access, choose File → Exit, or click the close button at the top-right corner of the Access window.

Where Forms Come In

A database is a collection of individual records organized in a way that makes it easy to add, edit, or update records as well as search for and retrieve information.

Using a *form* is the easiest way to add records or modify existing ones. Forms—either on paper or computerized—offer a way to collect information and often become an actual record. You probably already have a fair amount of experience with forms because you've had to fill out medical questionnaires, tax and insurance documents, and credit and employment applications.

Each part of a form—called a *form field*—asks for very specific details, like your last name, your Social Security number, your phone number, your street address, your city, and so on. These form fields usually correspond to individual fields found within an individual record in a database. As you begin to work with databases, you'll see that forms play a role in Access as well: You often use them to enter information into a database. Thinking about something you know fairly well—those pesky forms you have to fill out—helps you appreciate how to design a database so you can obtain and enter all the required details.

Access gives you two main ways to create a database. The method you choose depends on your specific database needs. You can create a database:

- **With the Access Database Wizard.** Access includes 10 predefined databases (templates) designed for common purposes, like tracking customer orders or managing expenses. With this method you use one of the templates as a rough draft of your database. If the template's database fits your needs perfectly, you can then use it without modification; otherwise, you can change it as you wish.

- **From a blank database.** With this method you design and create all the database tables, forms, reports, and other objects yourself. (For more detail on creating a database from scratch, see page 49.)

The easiest way to create a database is to use the Database Wizard with one of Access's database templates. Each database template includes tables, forms, reports, and links that are custom-tailored for a specific kind of database.

 Note: The tutorial on the following pages uses an image file, RoyalQuiet-Deluxe.jpg, which you can download from this book's "Missing CD" page as described on page 10. You can also find an example of the completed Typewriter Orders database there.

Starting with a Wizard

When you use a template to create a database, the Access Database Wizard asks you questions about what you need. The wizard gives you more choices with some templates than it does with others, but you always use the same process:

▶ The wizard asks questions—and you answer them—in a series of windows.

▶ The wizard builds a database based on your answers.

▶ You either use the database as the wizard created it, or you modify it further.

Phase 1: Choosing Your Template

Templates are predesigned database files that let you get started with ease because someone's already done part of the work for you. Templates include common elements, like name and address, so you won't have to spend time creating them. (See the box on page 27 for a tour of Access's templates.)

To start the Access Database Wizard:

1. **Choose File → New.**

   Access displays the New File task pane at the right side of your screen (Figure 1-6).

Figure 1-6. The New File task pane has three sections: the New section, Templates section, and Recently Used Templates section. In the Templates section, you can choose a template on your computer or from Microsoft's Web site.

2. **In the Templates section of the New File task pane, click "On my computer."**

   Access displays the Templates dialog box.

3. **Near the top of the Templates dialog box, click the Databases tab.**

   The dialog box moves the Databases tab to the front and shows the database templates available on your computer (Figure 1-7).

Database Templates

Access includes 10 ready-to-use templates, each designed for a specific database need.

To use one of the database templates included with Access, choose File → New, and in the New dialog box click On My Computer. Access includes these templates:

* **Asset Tracking.** This database keeps information about your company's assets, like computers, printers, desks, and phones. It also keeps information about your company's employees, departments, and vendors.

* **Contact Management.** This database keeps information about contacts, including names, addresses, phone numbers, email, phone call logs, and your notes about each contact.

* **Event Management.** This database keeps information about events your company sponsors, like trade shows, seminars, and parties. It includes information about events, event pricing, attendees, and your employees.

* **Expenses.** This database keeps information about employee expense reports, including expense details and expense categories.

* **Inventory Control.** This database keeps information about your company's inventory, including products, suppliers, purchase orders, and shipping.

* **Ledger.** This database keeps information about your company's finances, including transactions, accounts, and account classifications.

* **Order Entry.** This database keeps information about customer orders, including orders, payments, payment methods, and shipping methods.

* **Resource Scheduling.** This database keeps information for project planning, including resource availability, scheduling, and due dates.

* **Service Call Management.** This database keeps information about customer service requests, including work orders, labor required, parts, and payments.

* **Time and Billing.** This database keeps information for billing clients, including projects, time cards, work codes, and payments.

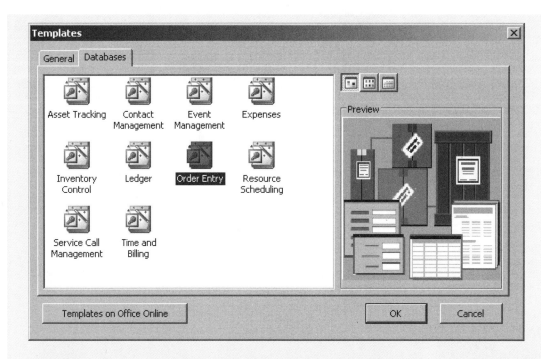

Figure 1-7. The Templates dialog box lets you choose the database template on which to model your new database. If you pick the wrong template, you can start over with a different template. When you click Cancel, Access throws away all the design choices you made.

4. **On the Databases tab, click the Order Entry template, and then click OK.**

   Access displays the New Database dialog box. In this example, you're creating an order entry database. Depending on the template you pick, the steps may differ slightly from the ones you see here.

5. **In the New Database dialog box, browse to where you want to save the file and type *TypewriterOrders* as the filename.**

   To keep the examples in this book organized, you may want to create a folder in My Documents called, for example, Practice Databases and save this database there. Access creates the new database and then displays the first Access Database Wizard screen, as shown in Figure 1-8.

Online Templates

In addition to the templates that Access installs on your computer (see the box on page 27), you can find more on Microsoft's Web site. To browse and download online templates:

1. Make sure that your computer is connected to the Internet.

2. Choose File → New. In the New dialog box, click Templates on Office Online.

3. On Microsoft's Template Web page, click Microsoft Office Programs.

4. Under Access, click the template category you want to see (Business, for example).

5. Click the name of the template you want.

6. Click the Download Now button.

People who've used Access have rated the popularity of the templates on Microsoft's Web site on a scale of zero to five stars. Some of the templates require a specific version of Access, like Access 2000. (The Web site warns you about that if you try to download a template for an Access version different from the one you have.)

6. **Click Next.**

Access displays the second Access Database Wizard screen.

You've created the database file. Next, you'll choose the fields to include in your database tables.

Phase 2: Choosing Table Fields

In the second screen, you can choose the fields for the wizard to include in each table. On the left side of the second Database Wizard screen (see Figure 1-9), Access lists the tables that the wizard can create. On the right side, Access lists the

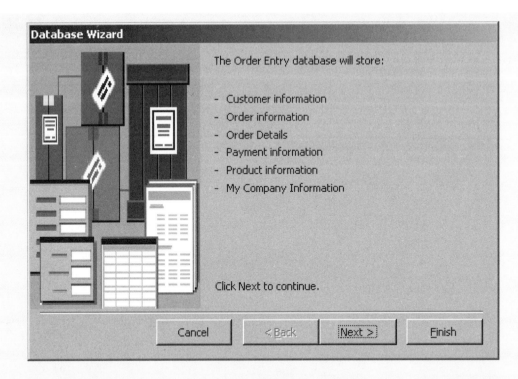

Figure 1-8. The first Access Database Wizard screen shows you the general categories of information that the new database stores. In this case, the database stores information about customers, orders, payments, products, and company information like employee records.

fields that you can put into the currently selected table. Every field that will be in the table has a checkmark in the box next to it.

You can sometimes remove a field from the selected table by clicking its box to uncheck it. However, the wizard requires certain tables to have specific fields because without those fields, the tables wouldn't serve their intended purposes. For example, Access requires the Customer Information table to have a Customer ID field, because without one, the table would lack a foolproof way to identify each customer. If you try to turn off a required field, the wizard politely but firmly refuses.

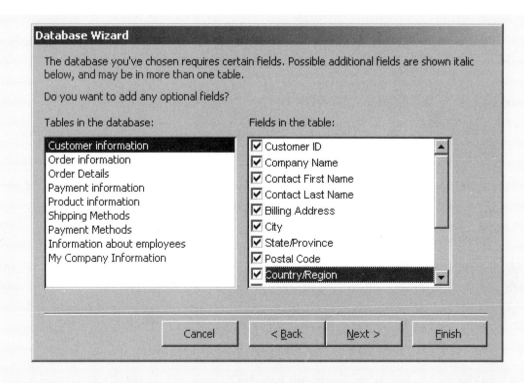

Figure 1-9. The second Access Database Wizard screen lists the tables in the new database and the fields in each table. The Order Entry template, shown here, includes tables that keep information about orders, customers, payments, and shipping.

To add a field to the selected table, click the box next to it.

Try clicking different tables in the "Tables in the Database" list and notice how the "Fields in the Table" list changes to show only the fields in the selected table. The template usually has all the fields you need preselected for a particular table. However, if you want to keep extra information, like each customer's email address, you need to turn on these fields in the template.

Tip: To add, change, or delete fields after you've created your database, you can use the Table Design window (page 45).

To choose table fields:

1. **In the "Tables in the Database" list, click the Information About Employees table.**

   In the "Fields in the Table" list, the wizard shows the fields it plans to put in the table. The box next to the Home Phone field is turned off.

2. **Click the box next to the Home Phone field.**

   The wizard turns on the field's box. When the wizard creates the Information About Employees table, it now includes the Home Phone field.

3. **In the Tables list, click the Customer Information table.**

   The wizard shows the fields it plans to put in the table.

4. **In the Fields list, drag the scroll bar down to see the rest of the field list. Click the box next to the Email Address field to turn it on.**

   The wizard adds Email Address to the list of fields it'll put in the Customer Information table.

    Note: If you've completely abandoned the telephone in favor of email, you may be tempted to turn off the Phone Number field. But if you try it, the wizard displays a message box saying it's a required field and can't be removed. As discussed on page 30, some fields are integral to a database's design, so the wizard's trying to protect them.

5. **Click Next.**

   Access displays the third Database Wizard screen. You've chosen the fields for your tables.

Next you'll choose the visual styles of forms and reports.

Phase 3: Choosing Styles for Forms and Reports

In the third screen, you can control the colors, type fonts, and overall look of onscreen data-entry forms in your new database. On the left side of the third Access Database Wizard screen (see Figure 1-10), Access shows a preview of what your database forms will look like with the currently selected style. The program automatically shows the Standard style. It's a bit drab but won't ruffle the feathers of upper management.

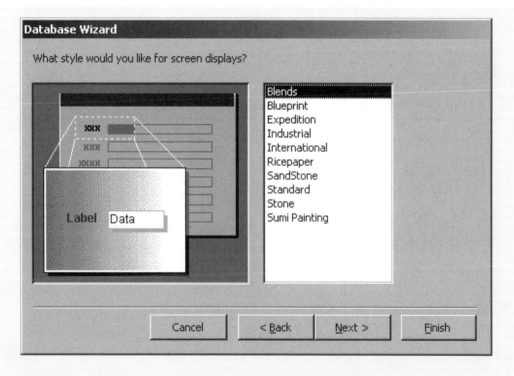

Figure 1-10. The third Access Database Wizard screen lets you choose a style for forms in your database. In the list on the right, you click a style to select it. On the left side of the screen, the wizard shows a preview of what screens will look like with that style.

Tip: To change a form design after you've created your database, use the Form Design window. You'll learn more about that in Chapter 3 (page 115).

To choose styles for forms and reports:

1. **In the Style list, click Blends.**

   The wizard shows a preview of what the style looks like, as shown in Figure 1-10. You can click some others to get an idea of what they look like.

2. **Click Next.**

   Access displays the fourth Database Wizard screen (see Figure 1-11) where you choose a style for reports. This screen works the same way as the previous one, except that styles are now applied to reports instead of to forms.

3. **In the Style list, click the style you want.**

   For this example, choose Bold.

4. **Click Next.**

   Access displays the fifth—and final—Database Wizard screen.

You've chosen styles for your onscreen forms and reports. Next you'll add the final touches: a title for your database and, if you wish, a picture to jazz up the appearance of your reports.

Phase 4: Adding a Title and a Picture

In the last screen (see Figure 1-12), you finish your work by naming your database. If you wish, you can choose to add a picture file to your database reports. As in earlier cases, a preview appears on the left side of the screen. In this case, however, the preview doesn't change as you type a new title or choose a picture; it simply gives you a general idea of what reports will look like.

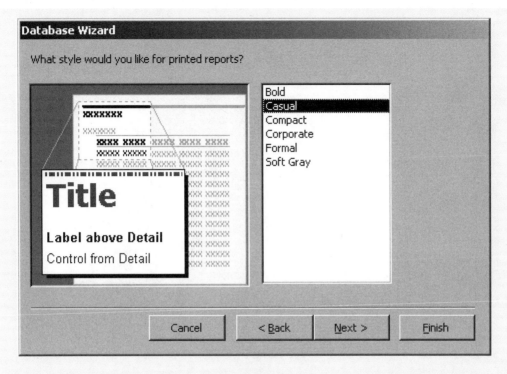

Figure 1-11. The fourth Access Database Wizard screen lets you choose a style for reports. On the left side of the screen, the wizard shows a preview of what reports will look like with the style you select. Unless you're using a color printer, though, the colors print as shades of gray.

 Tip: Keep your database title descriptive but as short as possible. If you use a long title, it may not fit in some onscreen windows. Your database still works just fine, but the last few letters of your database title may not be visible onscreen.

To add a title and picture:

1. **In the title text box, delete the title Access suggests and type the title you want. For this example, type *Customers and Orders*.**

   If you like the title Access suggested, you can skip this step.

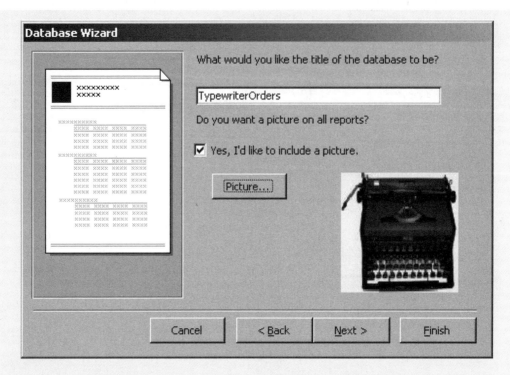

Figure 1-12. On the fifth Access Database Wizard screen you can type a title for your database and choose a picture. If you choose a picture file, the screen shows a preview of the picture in the lower-right corner of the screen. This picture shows a 1947-model Royal Quiet Deluxe typewriter.

2. **Turn on the checkbox labeled "Yes, I'd like to include a picture." Click the Picture button.**

   Access displays the Insert Picture dialog box.

3. **Browse to and select the file RoyalQuietDeluxe1947.jpg, and then click OK.**

   The wizard adds the picture to your report design and shows a preview in the dialog box. If everything looks good, click Next.

   Access displays the final Database Wizard screen.

4. **Click Finish.**

   The wizard creates your database. Access cranks for a few moments while a message box displays its progress in creating the database.

5. **Click OK.**

   The wizard prompts you to enter information about your company (see Figure 1-13).

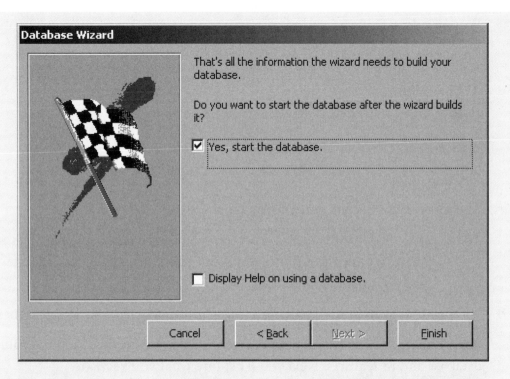

Figure 1-13. If you leave the "Yes, start the database" radio button turned on, when you click Finish, Access asks you to fill in some basic information—like your company name and address—then launches your new database so you can get to work.

6. **In the form boxes, type the appropriate information. For this example, type:**

   Company: *Cambridge Typewriters*

   Address: *123 Font Street*

   City: *Cambridge*

   State/Province: *MA*

   Postal Code: *02138*

   Country/Region: *USA*

   Sales Tax Rate: *0.05*

   Default Terms: *Net 30*

   Invoice Descr: *For Items Ordered*

   Phone Number: *617-555-9876*

7. **At the top-right corner of the form, click Close.**

   The wizard starts your database. Onscreen you see a *switchboard* (see Figure 1-14), which is a panel with buttons you can click to open tables, generate reports, and do other database tasks.

8. **On the Main Switchboard panel, click the button labeled Exit This Database.**

   Access closes the TypewriterOrders database. You've finished creating your database and its features. Next you'll explore what you've made.

Modifying the Wizard's Database

Congratulations! You've created your first database in Access. You made all the big decisions, but the Database Wizard handled the details. You can learn a lot about Access databases by exploring and modifying a database similar to what you and the wizard have just designed. (If you haven't downloaded the example database as discussed on page 10, do so now and then read on.)

Opening a Database

Before you can explore a database, you have to open it. To open a database:

1. **Choose File → Open.**

   The Open dialog box appears. Just as if you were opening any document in Windows, you can use this box to locate and open Access databases anywhere on your PC.

2. **Browse to and select TypewriterOrders_example.mdb. Then click Open.**

   Before opening the database, Access displays a warning box. This message merely means that Access databases may contain programming code that *could* harbor computer viruses, not necessarily that it *does* contain them. The box has three buttons: Cancel, Open, and More Info. If you created a database yourself or obtained it from a trusted source, the database is probably safe.

    Tip: To defend yourself against computer viruses, use up-to-date virus detection software and scan any database files you receive.

3. **Click Open one more time.**

   Access opens the database. The TypewriterOrders database reveals a menu panel called a switchboard. By clicking buttons on the panel, you can do things in your database: view tables, enter data, print reports, and so forth. See Figure 1-14.

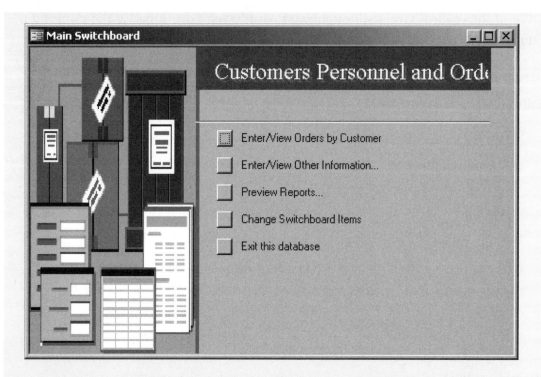

Figure 1-14. Switchboards, like the one shown here, let people who don't know Access do a number of common database tasks simply by clicking buttons. Notice the button at the bottom labeled "Exit this database." It closes the current database but leaves Access open so you can keep working.

 Tip: If you recently worked with a database, Access lists it at the bottom of the File menu. You can open the database by clicking its name on the File menu. That way's faster than browsing to the folder.

Navigating with the Switchboard

You can click around a database switchboard to get a good tour of the database and familiarize yourself with how switchboards work. Each switchboard button either performs a task, like displaying an order list, or opens another panel of switchboard buttons that you can click to do something else, like generate a report.

Here's how to use the switchboard to get to tables, forms, and other objects in your database:

1. **Click the Enter/View Orders by Customer button.**

   Access opens the Orders by Customer form, in which you can view order records or add new records. Notice that the top of the form has information about one customer, while the bottom of the form has a table showing all the orders that the customer has placed. (For more about forms, see Chapter 3.)

2. **In the Orders by Customer form, click the Orders button.**

   Access opens a new form window that shows the details of orders placed by the customer whose record you were viewing. Click the Close button at the top of the Orders window, and then use the same method to close the Orders by Customer window.

3. **Click the Enter/View Other Information button.**

   Access displays another switchboard with buttons for entering and viewing information. See Figure 1-15 for the full story.

4. **Click the Return to Main Switchboard button.**

   You've learned how to click switchboard buttons to do database tasks or to display subswitchboards. This skill may lack the excitement of bungee-jumping, but it's a more useful skill in real life.

5. **From the Window menu, choose 1 TypewriterOrders_example: Database.**

   Access closes the switchboard and displays the Database window.

The switchboard is handy, but it limits what you can do to what's available in its menu buttons. The Database window, on the other hand, lets you get "under the hood" of your database to create, edit, view, and add information to tables and other database objects. In the sections coming up, you'll use the Database window to change a table design, use a form, and print a report (see Figure 1-16).

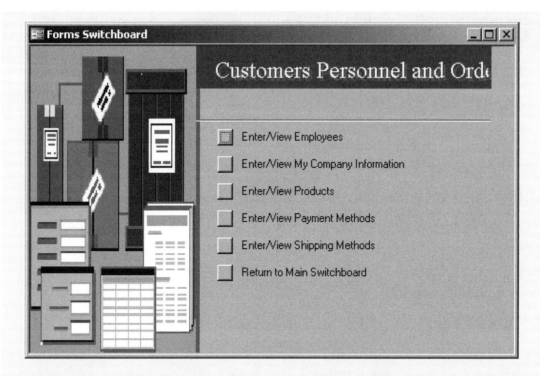

Figure 1-15. Some switchboard buttons perform database actions directly, while others open subswitchboards. For example, the Enter/View Employees button does an action (opening a form window), while the Return to Main Switchboard button simply takes you back to the main switchboard panel, where you can click more buttons.

 Note: In Figure 1-16 you see the Forms list because you've been looking at the switchboard, which is itself simply a type of form (see page 17). You'll learn how to create and modify forms, including switchboard forms, in Chapter 3.

Adjusting Table Designs

When you created your database with the wizard, you chose fields for your tables. But what does that really mean? To understand tables, fields, rows, columns, and

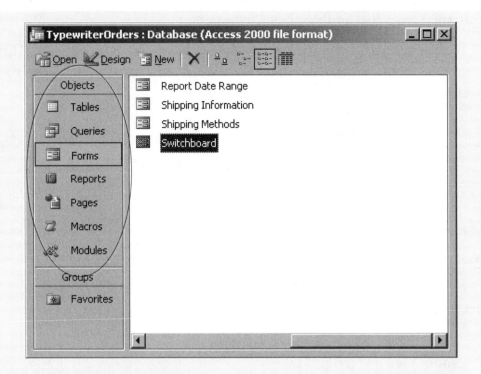

Figure 1-16. You'll see the Database window almost every time you open a database in Access. The only time you may not see it is if your database has a switchboard. Even then, the Database window is present; it's just minimized to the bottom of the Access window. The Objects bar is on the left; you click it to work with a particular type of database object.

records, you should practice working with them. Already, you can make simple adjustments to a table easily:

1. **At the left side of the Database window, on the Objects bar, click Tables.**

    The Database window shows a list of the tables in the database. Notice that the top of the list shows three ways to create a table: in Design view, by using a wizard, or by entering data. (In Chapter 2, you'll learn how to create tables with these methods.)

2. **In the Tables list, double-click Customers.**

Access displays the table in Datasheet view, as shown in Figure 1-17. This table is the correct one, but to add or delete fields, you have to switch to Design view.

Customers : Table				
Customer ID	Company Name	Contact First Name	Contact Last Name	Billing Address
1	ABC Letter Co.	Joe	Letter	123 Blastoff Circle
2	DEF Lettering Co.	Jim	Lettering	456 Apogee Point
3	GHI Cursive Corp.	Francine	Cursive	789 Script Avenue
(AutoNumber)				

Figure 1-17. Here's the Customers table in Datasheet view. A datasheet shows a table's data in row and column format. Each row is a record, like information about one customer. Each column is a field, like the customer's first name, last name, phone number, and so forth.

3. **Choose View → Design View.**

Access displays the table in Design view (as shown in Figure 1-18). Here you can make changes to the table the wizard built for you. Suppose you never use fax machines to communicate with customers, so you can delete the fax number field from the Customers table.

4. **In the top half of the Design window, click the gray button to the left of the Fax Number field.**

Access highlights the row and puts an arrow at the left end of the row.

5. **Choose Edit → Delete Rows, and then click Yes.**

Access deletes the Fax Number field from the table. Next, you'll tell Access to give you more space to display your customers' names.

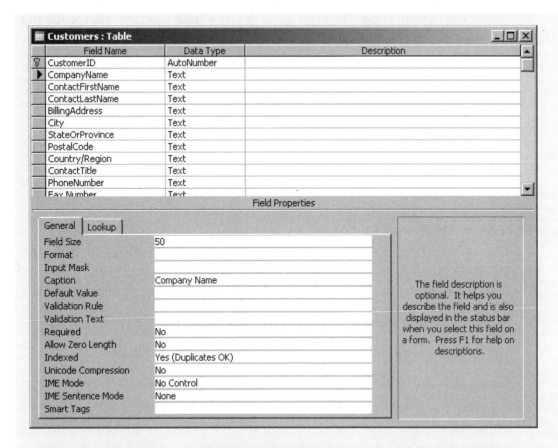

Figure 1-18. In the top half of the window, Design view shows each field's name and the type of information it contains, like Text, Number, and Date/Time. In the bottom half of the window, called the Field Properties pane, you can set the size of the field, give it a default value, and so on.

6. **Click in the row of the ContactFirstName field. In the bottom half of the Design window (the Field Properties pane), click in the Field Size row.**

This box shows how many characters the field can hold.

7. **Delete the default field size, type *20* as the new field size, and then click in a different row.**

   Access changes the field size to 20 characters (letters, digits, and so on).

8. **At the top-right corner of the Design window, click the Close button, and then click Yes.**

   Access closes the table.

You just deleted one field and changed the properties of another.

Adding Records Using a Form

Forms give you a way to enter and display your database information. They hide the technical details of the database and let computer-challenged people focus on entering the information. To understand how it works, look at a simple form:

1. **On the Database window's Objects bar, click Forms.**

   The Database window shows a list of the forms in the database.

   Sometimes, the object list in the Database window is too long to fit in the window. You'll know this is the case in List view if you see a horizontal scroll bar at the bottom of the Database window. When you see that scroll bar, you can click it to scroll left and see the rest of the list.

2. **In the Forms list, double-click Employees.**

   Access displays the form in Data view (see Figure 1-19).

3. **At the bottom of the Form window, click the Next Record button several times.**

   Access moves forward from record to record in the table.

4. **At the bottom of the Form window, click the First Record button.**

   Access displays the first record in the table.

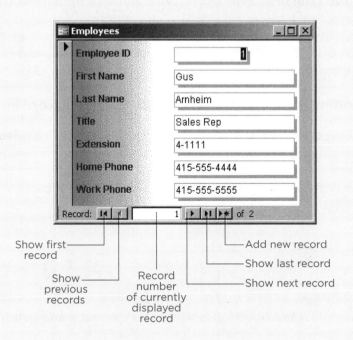

Figure 1-19. With a form in Data view, you can view information that's already in a table or add new data. The navigation buttons at the bottom of the window let you display the first, last, previous, or next record in the table. By clicking the far-right button, you can display an empty form to add a new record to the table.

5. **At the bottom of the Form window, click the Add New Record button.**

   Access displays a blank form in which you can add a new record.

6. **Press the Tab key to move to the First Name field. Type *Benny*, press Tab again, and type *Goodman* in the Last Name field.**

   Notice that Access automatically put the number 3 in the Customer ID field. That's because Customer ID is an Autonumber field.

7. **Click in the Title field, type *Music Director*, and then press the tab.**

   Fill in the rest of the form, pressing Tab after each field. Type *4-9999* in the Extension field, *408-555-9999* in the Home Phone field, and *415-555-9999* in the Work Phone field.

8. **At the bottom of the Form window, click the First Record button.**

   Access moves to the first record in the table and saves your data. If you click the Last Record button, you can see your new record.

When you're done, click the Close button at the top-right corner of the Form window to close it.

Printing a Report

You can use database reports to print your information and also to display it on the computer screen. In a report design, you can group data by city, sort it by last name, and do totals and other calculations. Try viewing and printing a simple report:

1. **On the Objects bar, click Reports.**

   The Database window shows a list of the reports in the database. Notice at the top of the list the two ways you can create a report: in Design view and by using a wizard. Any time you want to design a report, you can use either of these methods by starting from the Database window.

2. **In the Reports list, double-click Customers.**

   Access displays a print preview of the report (see Figure 1-20).

3. **Make sure that your printer is ready to print, and then choose File → Print and click OK.**

   Access prints your report.

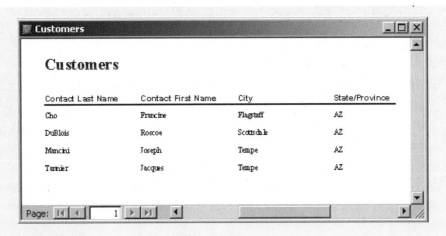

Figure 1-20. As in the Table and Form windows, you can use controls at the bottom of the Report Preview window to move forward and backward in the report. Here, however, you don't move from record to record: you move from page to page. This report has only one page, so the forward and backward buttons are "grayed out," that is, unavailable.

4. **At the left end of the Access toolbar, click the Design View button.**

   Access displays the report in Design view. Design view lets you modify your report design by adding or moving fields and controls. You can also add grouping, sorting, totals, and other features. You'll learn about designing reports in Chapter 8.

When you're done, you can close the Report window, or choose File → Close to close the Order Entry database.

Starting from a Blank Database

If your database needs are unusual—or if you're an incorrigible do-it-yourselfer—you may not want to use one of Access's database templates. As an alternative you can create a blank database. You can then manually design all your tables, forms, reports, and other database objects. That's how the developers of

Access created the templates you use with the Database Wizard: they started with a blank database and added one piece at a time.

On the plus side, creating a blank database gives you freedom: you can design everything just as you want it from the get-go. On the minus side, it's more work, but as database guru Kahlil Gibran said, "Work is love made visible." If you love what you're doing—or even just like it a bit—then it's never a burden to put in a little extra work.

It's easy to create a blank database. Here are the steps:

1. **Start Access, and then choose File → New.**

   At the right side of your screen, Access displays the New File task pane. It's just like the one in Figure 1-6 that you used to open a template. This time, however, you're going to use the New section to create a fresh, empty database document.

2. **Near the top of the Getting Started dialog box, click Blank Database.**

   Access displays the File → New Database dialog box.

3. **In the File → New Database dialog box, choose a folder to save the database in, and then type a filename of your choice.**

   If you're just practicing, you can keep all your work for this chapter in one folder, as described on page 28.

4. **Click Create.**

   Access creates a blank database (see Figure 1-21). You can now add tables (as you'll do in Chapter 2), forms (covered in Chapter 3), and other database objects.

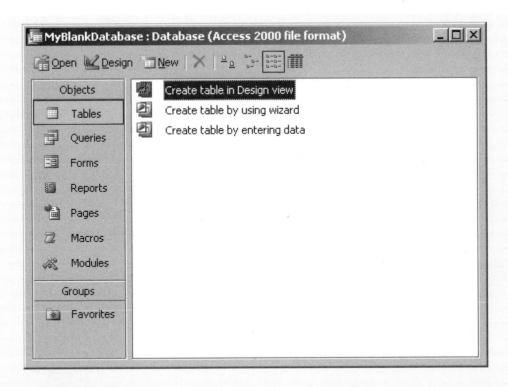

Figure 1-21. A database is a wrapper for tables and other database objects. When you create a blank database, you start with just the wrapper. Notice that the title bar of the Database window reads "Access 2000 file format." Access 2003 automatically uses the older Access 2000 file format so that other people can use your database even if they don't have an up-to-date version of Access.

CHAPTER 2: CREATING TABLES TO HOLD DATA

▶ Planning Your Tables

▶ Creating Tables with the Wizard

▶ Creating Tables in the Design Window

▶ Adding and Editing Table Data

▶ Changing How a Table Displays Data

TABLES DO THE MOST IMPORTANT JOB IN A DATABASE: They actually store your information. They're the foundation for all of Access's other features. Accordingly, when you start a new, blank database, the first thing you do is create tables to hold your data. This chapter walks you through the two ways you can build tables in Access—the Table Wizard and Design view. At the end, you'll learn how to enter records into your newly created tables the quick and dirty way, without the help of a form—in Datasheet view.

In the previous chapter, you started your database with the Order Entry template, which came equipped with a number of tables. A database designer somewhere, sometime, figured out which tables the database would need and then created them. When you create your own tables, you're starting to design the structure of your own database. So dig out any notes you jotted down when you first started planning your database and read the box on the next page for more information on good database design to get a clearer idea of the tables you want to create.

 Note: As your database grows in size and function, you can add new tables to any existing database at any time, including those you've created with a wizard. For example, if you start by keeping only customer information in a database, you can add a new table for order information a year or two down the road.

Planning Your Tables

Start by thinking about the kind of information your database will contain and what you need to do with the information. For example, will your database contain customer, order, and supplier information? Will you sometimes need to combine different types of information, such as connecting customers to their orders or inventory items to their suppliers? Each major type of information should get its own table, with the smaller bits of information going into fields. Some points to consider are listed on page 56.

Good vs. Bad Database Design

The difference between good and bad database design isn't aesthetic. Instead, where a bad database design hits home is in use: A poorly planned database may make it tougher to enter or update new records or it may allow many mistakes to get in. You also see this difference when you're trying to pull information from the database, which, of course, is the whole reason you're going to the trouble of creating and managing that database in the first place.

Utilize the kind of planning discussed both in this chapter and the next one, and you're probably going to do fine. But start the database without such advance work, and you're going to expend a great deal of time later on trying to troubleshoot problems you could've avoided.

* Think ahead of your database needs for the next six months to one year. All too often, people in charge of databases discover after the fact that they're not collecting all the information they'll ultimately need for reports and analyses weeks or months later. While Access lets you go back and modify a database later, it's more work to go back to the information source to obtain the additional details.

* Don't create a database only you can understand.

* Store individual bits of information (like a name or a phone number) in the smallest logical units that make sense, such as dividing a customer's name into last name, first name, and middle initial, or keeping the area code separate from the rest of a phone number.

* Create a logical flow to a record entry. For example, you wouldn't normally put the entry for the customer's last name in one place and the entry for the first name several spots away.

* Make changes as needed rather than waiting until you hit a problem pulling records from the database.

Pay attention to the design tips offered here as part of the steps in creating your database.

- **Decide what tables you need and what each table should contain.** Decide which data items should be grouped together in their own tables and which should be separated into different tables. Data that seldom changes should be in tables separate from information that changes often. For example, in customer and order tables, each customer's name and address change only rarely. However, the list of orders associated with each customer may change very often. Therefore, you should separate the stable data (customer information) from the often-changing data (order information).

 Note: Even when you need to connect different pieces of information in your database, it's perfectly appropriate to have them in separate tables. For example, if you need to see which customers have placed orders, you can create a *link* between your Customers table and your Orders table. You'll learn how to do that in Chapter 4. For now, keep different kinds of information in separate tables.

- **Decide which information fields you need within each table.** For example, will you need to generate form letters that greet customers by their first names, as in "Dear Sally"? If so, you must separate first names and last names into different columns of the table.

Creating Tables with the Wizard

Just like the Access Database Wizard, Access provides a Table Wizard to help you construct tables. The Table Wizard includes 25 predefined tables for business uses and 20 for personal uses. Chances are, one of these tables matches exactly (or closely) what you need.

- **Business.** Tables that help you keep track of mailing lists, customers, employees, orders, invoices, reservations, billing time, and almost anything else you'd need to run your own firm, whether it be humble or globe-spanning.

- **Personal.** Tables that help you keep track of fun stuff, such as books, wine lists, photographs, addresses, and exercise and diet logs (well, it can't all be fun).

Also like the Access Database Wizard, you can easily start with a predefined table similar to what you want, and then modify it. In the personal tables, for example, Microsoft forgot to include a predefined table for your monster-truck magazines. The easiest solution is to start with a similar predefined table, such as Books, create it with the wizard, and then modify the wizard's design.

Phase 1: Starting the Table Wizard

Your first step is to start the Table Wizard. From there, you can choose and rename the fields to include in your new table, set a *primary key* (information unique to each individual record, such as a Social Security number or an account number) to identify each record, name your table, and even enter data in a datasheet or form. A primary key isn't anything too scary: It's just a table field with a value that uniquely identifies each record, such as a Customer ID number.

To see the Table Wizard in action, you'll create a table that holds contact information. There's a sample Access file all set for you to work in. Download CreatingTables.mdb from the "Missing CD" page (page 10).

1. **Open the CreatingTables.mdb database.**

   For example, choose File → Open, or double-click the file's icon. A window called CreatingTables: Database opens.

2. **In the Database window, click Tables in the Objects bar, and then click New.**

   You see the dialog box shown in Figure 2-1.

3. **In the New Table dialog box, click Table Wizard, and then click OK.**

   Access displays the first Table Wizard screen (see Figure 2-2).

4. **Make sure the Business radio button is turned on, and then in the Sample Tables list, click Customers.**

   The Sample Fields list shows the fields you can use from the table you clicked.

Figure 2-1. The New Table dialog box gives you five ways to create tables. This chapter explains two of them (the Table Wizard and Design View). The other one (Datasheet View) is a bad choice for designing any but the very simplest tables, as discussed in the box on page 60.

Phase 2: Choosing Fields for Your Table

Your next step is to choose fields from the Table Wizard's sample tables. Each sample table includes all the fields you'd normally need in that type of table. For example, the Mailing List sample table includes fields for name and address information, while the Products sample table includes fields for product ID, serial number, and unit price. (Not very catchy field names, but you can always rename them.)

To choose, remove, or rename fields:

1. **In the Sample Fields list, click CustomerID, and then click the right-arrow button.**

    The CustomerID field is designed to automatically assign a unique identifying number to each new customer record. As you'll see in the next section, this type of field helps you avoid duplicate records and, when you get a little

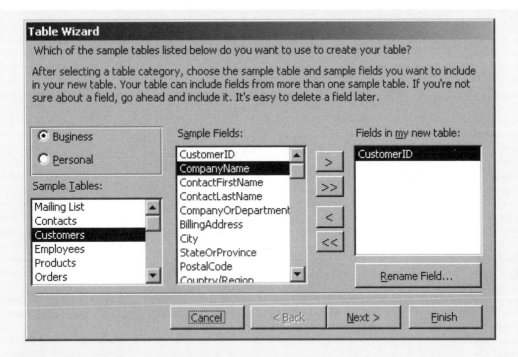

Figure 2-2. The first Table Wizard screen gives you 45 sample tables on which to base your table design. Normally, you use the fields from only one sample table, but you can also choose fields from other sample tables. Just click any other table in the Sample Tables list and choose from its assortment of fields.

more advanced, lets you link related tables together. So even if you don't think you need unique customer ID numbers now, include this field in the name of good planning.

2. **Repeat step 1 to add ContactFirstName, ContactLastName, BillingAddress, City, StateOrProvince, PostalCode, PhoneNumber, FaxNumber, and EmailAddress to your new table.**

The "Fields in my new table" list shows the fields you've chosen. However, you've decided not to include a fax number field, so you need to remove it.

Those Other New Table Options

The New Table dialog box (see Figure 2-1) gives you five different ways to create tables. This chapter shows you how to use two of them: the Table Wizard and Design View. The other methods for creating a new table—and when you may encounter them—are as follows.

* **Datasheet View.** This method lets you create tables by typing field names at the top of a row-and-column datasheet. When you first put information in the table, Access automatically assigns each column a *data type* depending on what kind of data it contains (text, numbers, and see page 74. Datasheet View is *not* a good way to design any but the very simplest databases—those containing only simple text and number fields. If your database is *that* simple, you'd be better off keeping it in a Microsoft Word document instead of an Access database.

* **Import Table.** This method lets you import data from other programs into Access tables. For example, you may have inventory data in an Excel worksheet, a Web page table, or an XML document. With the Import Table option, you actually copy the data into a table in your Access database, leaving the data source undisturbed. (See Appendix B for some of the basics on importing.)

* **Link Table.** This method lets you create a link between your Access database and an external data file but doesn't actually copy the data into your database. Its main advantage is that if the external data file is very large, you can save time and disk space by linking to it instead of importing the data.

Tip: When you're copying fields from the Sample Fields list, copy the fields in the same order as their columns should appear in your table's datasheet. You can change the order later on (see the box on page 74), but it's a pain.

3. **In the "Fields in my new table" list, click FaxNumber, and then click the left-arrow button.**

   Access removes the field from the design of your new table.

4. **In the "Fields in my new table" list, click Billing Address. Next, click Rename Field, type *Address* in the text box, and then click OK.**

   Access renames the field. The Fields list shows the new name.

    Tip: Once you create forms, reports, or queries that depend on this table, if you then rename any fields, you'll have to rename them everywhere else, too. Plan to stick with the field names you pick as you design your database.

You can stay in this wizard screen as long as you need to make changes in your table's fields. Here's a summary of how to choose, remove, and rename fields:

▶ In the Sample Fields list, click one field, click its name, and then click the right-arrow button.

▶ If you want to select *all* the fields, click the double-right-arrow button.

▶ In the "Fields in my new table" list, click the name, and then click the left-arrow button to remove a designated field.

▶ To remove all the fields you've chosen, click the double-left-arrow button.

When you've finished choosing and renaming fields, click Next. Access displays the second Table Wizard screen (see Figure 2-3). You'll tackle this material in the next section.

Phase 3: Naming Your Table and Setting a Primary Key

In the previous section, you added a field called CustomerID to your table. It's one of Access's built-in choices for any good Customers table. Like most fields that come with "ID" in their name, CustomerID is a *primary key* field—that is, it assigns each customer a unique identifying number. Among other useful things, primary keys help you avoid duplicate records and let you link related tables together. (See the box on page 64 for more detail.)

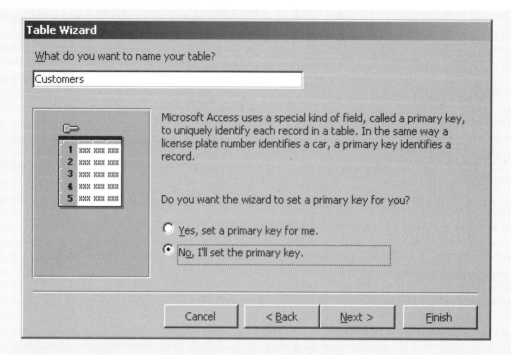

Figure 2-3. On the second Table Wizard screen, you can either accept the table name Access suggests or type a new name in the "What do you want to name your table?" text box. Here you also tell Access which field to use as the primary key.

In the second Table Wizard screen, you can either set the primary key yourself or let Access do it. If Access sets the primary key, it always uses a field such as CustomerID that's sure to be unique for each record in your table. In the Customers table, the CustomerID field is an *Autonumber* field: Each time you add a new record, Access automatically assigns a new number to the CustomerID field. (See page 77 for full detail on Autonumber fields.)

 Note: The principal advantage of setting the primary key yourself is when you're linking tables, as you'll learn in Chapter 4. A table may have more than one field that *could* be the primary key, but you need to tell Access which one.

Your next task on this screen is to name your table. You can make a table name up to 64 characters long, but you can't include periods, exclamation marks, brackets, or accents. You may've noticed that Access uses plain letters and digits, with no spaces or other characters for table and field names: That's not required, but it's a good rule of thumb, since even modern programs like Access can choke on space characters, as you'll see later in this book.

To set the primary key for your new table:

1. **In the second Table Wizard screen (see Figure 2-3), click the radio button labeled "No, I'll set the primary key."**

   You've just told Access that you already know what field you want to use for the primary key, as discussed on page 64.

2. **Click Next.**

   Access displays the Table Wizard's Primary Key screen. See Figure 2-4.

3. **In the Table Wizard's Primary Key screen, accept Access's suggestions for the primary key field: CustomerID and Autonumbering.**

   The Table Wizard's Primary Key screen lets you choose from three methods of adding values to your primary key field:

   To have Access automatically assign a different number to each record in its primary key field, leave the first radio button selected: "Consecutive numbers Microsoft Access assigns automatically to new records." This choice is by far the wisest to make because it completely eliminates the possibility that you (or a data-entry clerk) will enter duplicate numbers by mistake.

   To make the field a Number field in which you enter numbers, turn on "Numbers I enter when I add new records." This approach means more work for you than using an Autonumber field. However, if you want to custom-design your own field format, this approach gives you the flexibility to do it.

Primary Key Primer

Identification numbers are the bane of modern life. Whether you want to get a job, open a bank account, buy a car, rent an apartment, or even apply for a marriage license, you'll have to cough up your tax identification number. Your name just won't do it anymore, even if in an ideal world, it should.

For example, a Customers table may share a CustomerID field with an Orders table. Later (in Chapter 4), when you create the Orders table, you'll put the CustomerID field in that table, too.

There's a reason for the hassle about ID numbers: In any large population, hundreds or thousands of people have exactly the same names. Some even have the same addresses. You need ID numbers of some kind to uniquely identify each person so that you can know for certain with whom you're dealing.

You face the same problem when you work with any reasonably large database: Some records are inevitably very similar. If your sales order table has a charge attributed to John Smith, you'd better make darned sure it's the *right* John Smith before you send the bill. When you have 577 customers all named "John Smith," that's not a trivial exercise.

Primary keys solve that problem for you. Every table needs a *primary key*: one field that uniquely identifies each record. In a Customer table, the primary key may be the CustomerID field; in an Inventory table, it may be the Part Number field. No customer can have the same value in the CustomerID field as any other customer; no inventory item can have the same part number as any other.

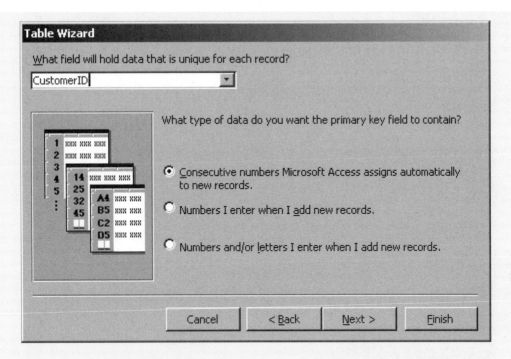

Figure 2-4. The Table Wizard's Primary Key screen lets you choose the field to use as your table's primary key and the method for adding key values to the field.

To make the field a Text field in which you enter text and/or numbers, click the third radio button "Numbers and/or letters I enter when I add new records." This approach means more work for you than using an Autonumber field, and you risk having two or more records with the same primary key value.

For the current example, you're going with the first option, so you don't need to change anything in the screen.

4. **Click Next.**

   Access displays the fourth Table Wizard screen, as shown in Figure 2-5. Because the example file contains more than one table, Access is offering you a chance to link them so they can share information. You'll see exactly how table relationships work in Chapter 4 (or consult the sidebar on page 68).

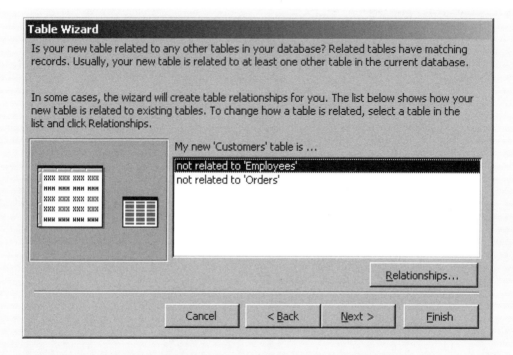

Figure 2-5. In the fourth Table Wizard screen, you can link your new table to other tables in your database that share at least one field with the new table. If you haven't yet created any other tables in your database, Access skips this screen.

5. **Click OK, and then click Next.**

   Access displays the last Table Wizard screen.

   Unless you want to go back and change anything (see Figure 2-6), your table is complete!

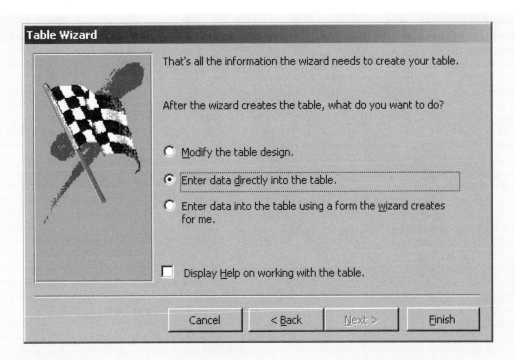

Figure 2-6. You're on the last Table Wizard screen. At this point, you can still go back and change any of the choices you made in previous dialog boxes. Clicking Finish creates your new table.

Phase 5: Creating Your Table

The last Table Wizard screen gives you three choices for what to do after Access creates your new table. The first radio button opens the table in the Design window where you can review or change the table design. The second radio button lets you go directly to entering information in the table. (Access has selected this button automatically for you.) The third radio button makes Access create a simple data-entry form for the table. You can then use the form to enter data into the table.

Relating with the Wizard

If you've been through the Table Wizard once, and now you're going back to add another table, Access displays the fourth Table Wizard screen (Figure 2-5).

Chapter 4 covers linked tables in great detail. But once you know how they work, you can save time by linking them right in the Table Wizard. To link your table to an already existing table:

1. In the "My new table is" list, click the line that says "related to 'Orders'."

2. Click Relationships. Access displays the Relationships screen (shown here).

The bottom third of the screen shows a graphical preview of the kind of link you get as you click the different radio buttons.

In this case, you want Access to connect one record in the Customers table to many records in the Orders table—a *one to many* link. Click the second radio button, the one labeled "One record in the (new) table will match many records in the (already existing) table." (See page 130 for more detail.)

To set up no link, select "The tables aren't related." This option has the same effect as if you'd simply clicked Next in the previous screen.

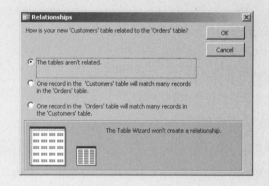

To create your new table:

1. **In the last Table Wizard screen, click the radio button labeled "Modify the table design."**

Access displays the table in the Design window. See Figure 2-7.

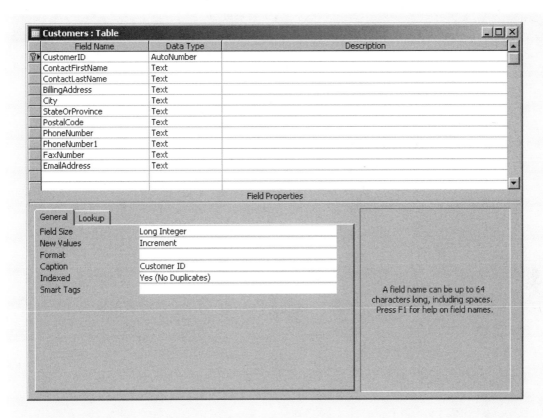

Figure 2-7. In the Table Design window, you can design new tables or modify exist-ing tables. Field descriptions are optional but helpful. In the lower-right corner of the Design window, Access displays a brief explanation of the selected item, such as a field name or data type.

2. **At the top-right corner of the Design window, click the Close button.**

Access closes the Design window. The Database window now lists your new table.

For this example, at the top-right corner of the Database window, click the Close button. Access closes the CreatingTables database.

A Field of (Database) Dreams

You're going to hear the word *field* used frequently with databases, and since it's something not familiar to everyone, you must understand what it is. A field refers to the area in which bits of data (a last name or an account number) are recorded and stored. If you've ever done data-entry work in which you fill out a form (like for a customer order), you know that hitting the Tab key moves you between spaces—or fields—on the form (called form fields) to enter individual bits of information.

As you create databases in Access, you'll discover that you can customize these fields in a number of ways.

For example, you may need more space for a street address than for a last name or a phone number entry, so you can change a field's properties to make it fit your situation.

To reduce the chance of mistakes or missing information in a record, you can also set conditions for the type of information that should be entered in a particular field. You can specify that a particular field can't be left blank, for example, or that any data entered conforms to certain formatting. Called *field validation*, it's the way Access makes sure that anything typed into a field fits the conditions you've set. See page 329 for more detail.

Creating Tables in the Design Window

When you plan your database tables as discussed at the beginning of this chapter, you may discover that the Table Wizard, which allows for quick setup of standard table types, simply doesn't have a table type that is a good match for your specific needs.

Next you have two options: You can choose a type from the wizard and then modify its design using the Design window, as you learned earlier in this chapter, or you can create a highly customized table from scratch using the Design window (as shown in Figure 2-7). Use the Design window to create a table on those rare occasions when you're doing something so unusual it would take less time to build a custom table than to adapt one of the standard tables.

Note: When you're working in the Design window, you're looking at Access's Design View. "Design view" and "the Design window" mean the same thing.

The Design window has two main sections:

▶ **The field entry area.** Here in the top half of the window, you add fields, choose their data types, and write descriptions of fields.

▶ **The field properties area.** In the bottom half of the window, you set the *properties* of each field (see Setting Field Properties on page 80), such as size, format, and default values. This area displays different properties depending on the data type of the field you've selected in the field entry area.

You can switch from one section to the other by pressing the F6 function key or by clicking the other section.

Adding Fields

The first step in creating a table in the Design window is to add a field. As you add each field, you set its properties before you add another field. If you change your mind about a field's properties, it's easy to go back and change them.

To start a table design and add fields:

1. **Choose File → New → Blank Database. In the dialog box, name the database *TableDesign* and click Create.**

   You can save it to, for example, your My Documents → Practice Databases folder (page 28).

2. **In the Database window, click Tables in the Objects button, and then click New. In the New Table dialog box, click Design view, and then click OK.**

   Access displays the Table Design window. Notice that the cursor is in the Field Name column of the first row in the field entry area. Notice also that the window's title bar shows the current name (Table1) of the table you're designing.

3. **To add the first field name and data type, type** *CustomerID* **as the field name. From the Data Type list box (Figure 2-8), select the Autonumber data type, and then type** *Customer's account number* **as the description.**

   Press F6 when you're done. Access moves the cursor down into the field properties area. You can now set properties for the field that's selected in the field entry area.

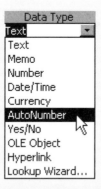

Figure 2-8. Each data type has its own properties and special uses. For best results, select the data type that best fits the type of data you include there. See page 74 for more detail.

4. **Click in the Indexed row, then click the down-arrow button at the right end of the row to open the list box, and then click Yes (no duplicates).**

   To set a field property, click in the row for the property, and then type the property value or choose it from a list box. Figure 2-9 shows the result.

5. **Press the F6 function key or click in the field entry area.**

   Access saves the field definition, including the field name, data type, description, and properties. As soon as you move the cursor out of a row by pressing Tab, F6, or clicking, Access saves the contents of that row.

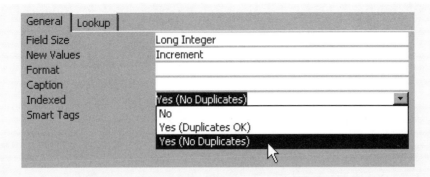

Figure 2-9. This field property list box is for an Autonumber field. Setting the Customer-ID field's Indexed property to Yes (no duplicates) means that no two records in the table can have the same value in the field—a requirement for using a field as a table's primary key.

6. **Repeat steps 4 to 7 to add the rest of the fields:**

FIELD NAME	DATA TYPE	PROPERTIES
FirstName	Text	No change
LastName	Text	No change
CustomerSince	Date	Format: Long Date
Balance	Currency	No change
SpecialOffers	Yes/No	

7. **To set the table's primary key, click the gray rectangle at the left end of the row for the CustomerID field, and then in the Access toolbar, click the Primary Key button; it has an image of a key.**

You're done. Saving and naming the table is the last step.

8. **To save the table design, choose File → Save. In the Table Name text box, type** *DesignWindowTable*, **and then click OK.**

At the top-right corner of the Design window, close the table by clicking the Close button at the top right corner of the Design window. If you're done working for now, close the TableDesign database.

Choosing Data Types

When you use the Design window to add fields to your table, it's vital to choose the correct *data type* for each field. A field's data type determines not only what kind of data it stores, but also what you can and can't do with the field. In addition, a field's data type determines what properties you can use in the field. Properties determine how the field displays data, what kind of formatting and error-checking you can build into the field, and how much disk space the field data takes. "Setting Field Properties" on page 80 has the full story.

Data Type Decisions

The Access Table Wizard has already chosen data types for your selected fields. For example, it made the CustomerID field an Autonumber field: That guarantees each record has a unique value in the field.

The other fields are all Text fields, including PostalCode and PhoneNumber—fields that you may expect to be Number fields. That's right: Just because a field holds numerals doesn't mean its data type is Number. For one thing, Text fields let you use formatting, such as (213) 555-0022. If you put that phone number in a number field, Access thinks you're trying

to subtract 22 from 555 and multiply the result by 213. Furthermore, if your field of numbers has leading zeros, making it text preserves those leading zeros. For example, in order for your mail to get delivered to the right place, you have to make sure Access doesn't change the Zip code 00345 into the number 345.

Unless you plan to use a number to do arithmetic in your database, you should store it in a Text type field to make sure that Access leaves it intact, like any string of text.

Text

Text is the American cheese of data types: bland, inoffensive, lacking the special features of other data types, but good for just about any string of printable characters. If you need to do arithmetic, use a Number type; if you need to play with dates or times, use a Date/Time data type. But if you just need a place to shove some data, Text is a good choice. Some points to remember about using the Text data type are:

▶ Text fields can hold up to 255 printable characters: letters, digits, and punctuation.

▶ All Text fields start out at 50 characters, but in the field properties area, you can change the size. Make the field size as small as possible but large enough to hold the largest data likely to go into the field. For example, a StateProvince field would need only two characters for U.S. state abbreviations but needs *three* characters if it also stores Canadian province abbreviations.

▶ You can use a Text field's Input Mask property to format the data in the field. For example, you could add the input mask (999)999-9999 to a PhoneNumber field to format phone numbers with parentheses and dashes. For more information, see "Setting Field Properties" on page 80.

Memo

Memo fields let you store more text data than you can fit into a Text field. Instead of holding only 255 characters, Memo fields can store up to 65,535 characters. But don't worry about filling up your hard drive; each Memo field uses only enough disk space to store the information it contains. If the Memo field of one record contains only 10 characters and that of another record contains 50,000, the first requires vastly less disk space than the second.

Because each Text field has a predefined size (such as 10 characters), Access can process Text fields more quickly than it can process Memo fields. Therefore, if you know in advance that all your records will have about the same size text in a certain field, it's better to use a Text field rather than a Memo field.

Number

Number fields give you a multitude of choices when you're going to do calculations with numbers. The Number data type has several subtypes, formats, and options. Some points to remember about using the Number data type are:

▶ Use Number fields only for numbers with which you'll do calculations. For other numbers, such as phone numbers or CustomerID numbers, use Text fields.

▶ The automatic size of a Number field is Long Integer, which stores numbers ranging from -2.15 billion to +2.15 billion. If the field won't store numbers that big, you can save some disk space by changing the Field Size property to a smaller type (Byte for 0-255, Integer for -32,768 to +32,767). If you need even bigger numbers, you can change the size to one of the astronomically large types (Double, Single, or Decimal).

▶ The Format property of Number fields lets you format numbers as general decimal numbers, dollars, euros, fixed decimal numbers, standard decimal numbers, and percents, as well as in scientific notation. However, if you want the field to hold money amounts, use the Currency data type instead, as Figure 2-10 explains.

Date/Time

Date/Time fields, as their name implies, let you store dates and times—nothing else. Keep these points in mind about Date/Time fields:

▶ You can use the Format property of Date/Time fields to control how Access displays dates onscreen and in printed reports. You can include just the date (12/12/05), the month name and day of the week (Monday, December 12, 2005), the time (12/12/05, 7:45 AM), or just the time (7:45 AM).

Currency

If you're storing money amounts, the Currency data type usually works better than a plain old Number field because it lets you format money amounts as dollars or euros, as well as in some other formats (see Figure 2-10). The Currency type differs from Text and Number types in that it has no Field Size property you can set: Access controls the size automatically.

Autonumber

Autonumber is a feature that lets you make Access do the dirty work of automatically numbering new records in sequence as you add them—and keeping track of what number it's supposed to be on. You can't enter information directly into an Autonumber field, which makes it ideal for primary key fields (the box on page 64).

General	Lookup		
Format	Currency		▼
Decimal Places	General Number	3456.789	
Input Mask	Currency	$3,456.79	
Caption	Euro	€3,456.79	
Default Value	Fixed	3456.79	
Validation Rule	Standard	3,456.79	
Validation Text	Percent	123.00%	
Required	Scientific	3.46E+03	
Indexed	No		
Smart Tags			

Figure 2-10. These formats are available for the Currency data type. The advantage of using the Currency data type is that it's simpler than the Number type and is designed specifically for storing money amounts.

Autonumber fields store integers (whole numbers), not decimal numbers or fractions. Each time you add a new record to your table, Access automatically adds one to the Autonumber field in the previous record and stores the sum in the new record's Autonumber field. (Database geeks call this *incrementing* the value.)

Warning: Autonumber may try to insert itself where it's not wanted, treating your manually assigned numbers as something to be autonumbered. Also, it can create a mess when importing data into your database (page 314).

Yes/No

Yes/No fields let you store the answers to Yes/No questions, such as "Does this customer get special offers?" Using the Format property, you can set a Yes/No field to display as Yes/No, True/False, or On/Off.

OLE Object

OLE (Object Linking and Embedding) fields let you link to data contained in Word or Excel files, image files, video files, and sound files. OLE is an important issue if you work with data created in other Microsoft programs like Excel. However, OLE is gradually becoming obsolete. For more information about OLE-related issues, see *Excel: The Missing Manual* by Matthew MacDonald.

Hyperlink

Hyperlink fields hold links to files on the Internet or on your company's internal network (intranet). By clicking a link in this field, you can open the file to which it points. (Some database management systems don't allow hyperlinks in fields. If you're planning to exchange information with other database software, avoid Hyperlink fields or change them to plain text.)

Lookup Wizard

Lookup Wizard fields let you create list boxes to choose values from either a list or another table. When you choose this data type, Access starts the Lookup Wizard, which guides you through the process of selecting or creating the data source for the field. For more information about lookup fields and the Lookup Wizard, see page 333.

Setting Field Properties

Each data type has different field properties. The number of possible combinations of properties is staggering, but the most important properties are easy to master. The primary uses of field properties are:

▶ To set the maximum size of fields.

▶ To set the format in which a field stores data. For example, you can set a field format to store information as all upper-case letters so when you type *fred*, the table gets "FRED."

▶ To set *input masks* for data entry. An input mask formats data as you enter it in a field. For example, you can create an input mask so that when you enter 2135551111 in a field, it appears as (213)555-1111. See Figure 2-11 for more detail.

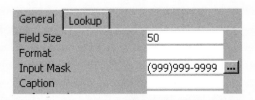

Figure 2-11. In this input mask, the 9s mean you can enter digits but not letters or other characters; Access adds the parentheses and dashes into the phone number display. Other input mask characters are the zero (0), which requires you to enter a digit; the "at" sign (@), which requires you to enter a text character or space; and the ampersand (&), which allows you to enter a character or space but doesn't require it.

▶ To set default values for fields. For example, you may set zero as the default value for an account balance field.

▶ To set up simple error-checking for fields. For example, you may set an order amount field to refuse any entry that's a negative number or greater than $100,000.

▶ To set a field as "required" so that data-entry clerks can't save a record if they haven't put a value in the field. What happens is that you'll see an error message disallowing the record unless you enter a value in a required field. For example, in an orders database, you may make the PartNumber field required to avoid having orders without the necessary product information.

 Note: You can find the full list of properties for each data type in Access's Help system (page 290). Search for *data type.*

To set field properties:

1. **Open the TableDesign database.**

   You can use the database you created earlier in this chapter (page 71).

2. **On the Database window's Objects bar, click Tables, then click the Design-WindowTable table, and then click the Design button.**

   Access opens the table in Design view.

3. **In the field entry area (the top part of the Design window), click the row for the Phone field. In the field properties area, click the Input Mask property and enter *(999)999-9999.***

   As discussed in Figure 2-11, this mask forces Access to always format the field's contents as a phone number.

4. **Click anywhere in the field entry area.**

   Access saves your change in the field property.

5. **Repeat steps 3 and 4 to set these other field properties:**

FIELD NAME	DATA TYPE	PROPERTIES
CustomerSince	Date/Time	Medium Date
PostalCode	Text	Field Size: 10
Balance	Number	Default Value: 0

Your table, with all its properly formatted fields, is complete. Close the window, or proceed to the next section where you'll learn how to make your table look even better. When you're finished, close the Design window and close the Table-Design database. Access automatically saves your design changes.

Adding and Editing Table Data

After you've created a table, you can use a table's Datasheet view to add new data, change data you've previously entered, and view any data in the table. Using Datasheet view is as quick as typing into a spreadsheet, and quite easy if you're already very familiar with the information you're entering. However, if your table has many fields, the information is complicated, or there are lots of values to remember, you could use a form, as you'll learn in the next chapter, to provide onscreen help and error-checking.

Adding Records to a Datasheet

Adding new records to a table is a breeze since it's already so easy to move around in a datasheet (see the box on the next page). If you're starting with a new table that has no records, Access automatically puts the cursor in the first column of the first row in the datasheet. You simply add the first record to that row. When you add data to the last column and press Tab, Access moves the cursor down to the next line, where you can enter another record.

Mousing Around a Datasheet

Any time you open a database, you can move around in a datasheet to view records or different columns of records either by using the keyboard or your mouse. If you can see the location in the datasheet on your screen, you can move there directly by clicking it with the mouse.

A group of buttons (shown here) appears at the lower-left corner of the Datasheet window. You can use them to move from record to record. From left to right:

✳ The first button, with an arrow pointing left to a vertical line, moves the cursor directly to the first record in the table.

✳ The second button, with an arrow pointing left, moves the cursor to the previous record.

✳ The box between the second and third buttons shows the current record number where the

cursor is located. By pressing the F5 key, you can type a record number into this box, and then press Enter to go directly to that record.

✳ The third button, with an arrow pointing right, moves the cursor to the next record.

✳ The fourth button, with an arrow pointing right to a vertical line, moves the cursor to the last record in the table.

✳ The fifth button, with an arrow pointing right to an asterisk (*), moves the cursor to a new blank line after the last record in the table. You can then add a new record on that line.

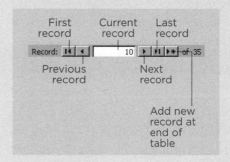

If you're adding records to a table that already contains records, you need to go to a blank row after the last record in the table. You can do that two ways:

▶ Clicking Add New Record at the bottom-left corner of the Datasheet window.

▶ Using your keyboard to move the cursor to the first blank row after the last record in the table.

To practice adding new records to a table, you can use the TableDisplay sample database. Download instructions are on page 10.

1. **In the TableDisplay database, open the DisplayData table, and then click Add New Record.**

   Access moves the cursor to the first column of the first row after the last record in the table. The first column contains an Autonumber field that Access fills in automatically.

2. **Press Tab to go to the next column. Type *Jack*, and then press Tab.**

   Access moves the cursor to the second column in the line.

3. **Add this data to the remaining columns, pressing Tab after each:**

FIELD NAME	DATA
LastName	Frost
Company	Frost's Flakes
Address	555 Northpole Circle
City	Froid
State	IL
PostalCode	60201
Phone	8475551234
CustomerSince	11-5
Balance	75.00

For the SpecialOffers column, just press the Space bar to leave it blank. (Sorry, Jack.) You've just entered an entire record.

 Tip: When you add a date to a Date/Time field, you only need to type the year if it's not the current year. If you're adding a date in the current year, just type the day and the month, and then press Tab. Access automatically fills in the current year.

4. **Click the First Record button to go back to the first record in the table.**

   Next, you'll learn how to go back and edit previously entered records.

Editing Records in a Datasheet

Once you've added records to a table, you can make changes simply by moving to the row and column you want, deleting incorrect or outdated information, and typing new information. You can also delete entire records.

In this example, you'll change some of the information, and delete a record entirely, in the TableDisplay database you opened in the previous section.

1. **Click in the Company column of record 11, which currently says George's Glitter. Next, delete the word *Glitter* and type *Geese*.**

   At the left end of the row, Access displays a pencil icon. The pencil icon means that you're currently editing a record and haven't saved your changes yet.

2. **Click or use the arrow keys to move the cursor to another row in the datasheet.**

   Access saves your change in the record. Notice that the pencil icon disappears from the left end of the row. To delete a record, you have to select the record, so make sure you've clicked to save your changes, and then go on to the next step.

3. **At the left end of the row for record 2 (Sally Case), click the Row Selector button.**

   Figure 2-12 illustrates the process.

4. **Choose Edit → Delete Record, and then click Yes.**

   Access deletes the record.

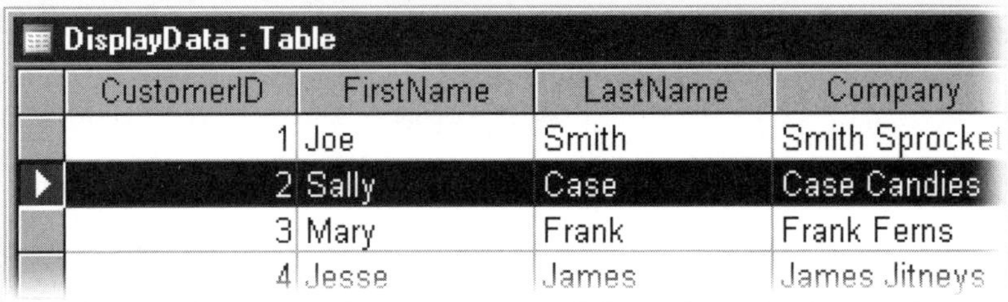

CustomerID	FirstName	LastName	Company
1	Joe	Smith	Smith Sprocke
2	Sally	Case	Case Candies
3	Mary	Frank	Frank Ferns
4	Jesse	James	James Jitneys

DisplayData : Table

Figure 2-12. Row Selector buttons are at the left side of the Datasheet window. When you click a row's button, it selects the entire row. To select multiple rows, just drag the mouse up or down. The highlight shows the rows you've selected.

Note: Alternatively, you can press the Delete key on your keyboard instead of choosing Edit → Delete Record. Be sure to first select the *entire* record.

Changing How a Table Displays Data

If you've followed along in this chapter and created a table or two, you have every reason to feel proud. But once you start adding information as described in the previous section, you may find that you can't see some information clearly or move around efficiently. Don't worry: Going back and making adjustments is what database design is all about. Datasheets are great for entering records and getting an overview of your information, and are very easy to modify. For example:

- Columns in the datasheet are often too narrow to display all the information they contain. You can make them wider.

- Access displays field columns in the same order as the fields appear in the table design. You can move columns left or right in the datasheet, so that it's easy to populate them in order.

- You can freeze columns so that as you scroll horizontally, the frozen columns stay on the screen. That way, you can always see the first column as a point of reference.

 Tip: For more options, choose View → Toolbars → Formatting (Datasheet) to display the Datasheet Formatting toolbar. This toolbar has buttons that let you change the datasheet's type fonts, colors, borders, and other display properties.

To try your hand at tweaking the Datasheet view, you can make some changes to a sample table whose columns need help with both size and positioning.

1. **Open the TableDisplay database, and then open the DisplayData table.**

   It's the same example file used in the previous section (page 84). If you have an Access table of your own that could stand improvement, you can use that instead.

2. **In the DisplayData table, start by widening the Address column. Drag the column border to the right until it shows all the address data.**

   To adjust the width of any column, simply move the mouse pointer in the heading row over the border between the heading of the column to resize and the next column to the right. You can see the resize pointer in Figure 2-13.

   Another way to resize a column is to double-click the column's right border in the heading row. When you do, Access "snaps" the column size to fit the data it contains.

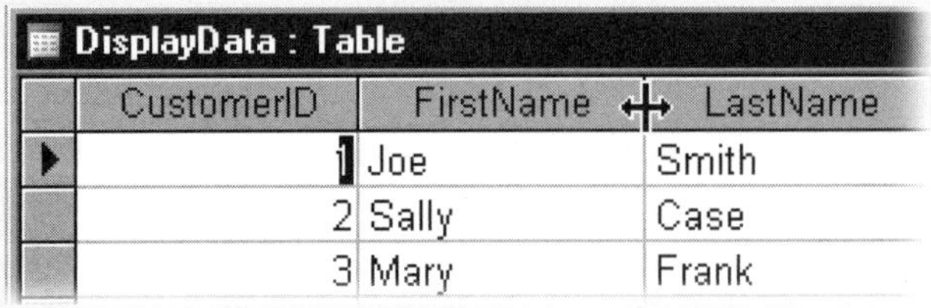

DisplayData : Table

	CustomerID	FirstName ↔	LastName
▶	1	Joe	Smith
	2	Sally	Case
	3	Mary	Frank

Figure 2-13. When dragging a column border to resize a column, notice that when the mouse pointer is in position to resize the column, the pointer changes into a double horizontal arrow.

3. **Move the LastName column so that it comes after FirstName. Click the LastName column heading, and then drag it to the left of the FirstName column.**

   As you drag, a vertical line shows where the column would go if you stopped dragging. When you release the mouse button, the column moves accordingly.

4. **To freeze the LastName column so that it remains visible as you scroll horizontally, click its heading in the Heading row, and then choose Format → Freeze Columns.**

   Access freezes the column. (If you change your mind and want to unfreeze the column, choose Format → Unfreeze All Columns.)

To finish this exercise, close the DisplayData table. You don't have to save any of these changes.

> **Tip:** You can print data directly from a datasheet, but it's not a good idea if your table has more than three or four columns. Access prints groups of columns on each page. You have to match up the rows on the sheets of paper to see all the columns for each record.
>
> A better alternative is to create a simple report for printing. To learn about creating reports, see Chapter 8.

CHAPTER 3:
CREATING FORMS TO ADD
AND DISPLAY DATA

▶ Form Basics

▶ Creating Autoforms

▶ Creating Forms with the Form Wizard

▶ Modifying the Form Design

▶ Creating Forms in Design View

THERE'S A REASON ALL DOCTOR'S OFFICES, schools, businesses, and governments use forms to collect information from you: Forms work. They ensure all the important information is obtained. And though you may resent having to fill them out, forms do make life easier.

In Access, forms don't just handle data collection. Onscreen forms can also provide help so people know what to type even if they're not familiar with your database. In addition, forms can error-check information as it's entered, preventing incorrect information from getting into the database. Furthermore, you can use Access forms to display information onscreen.

 Tip: You can use forms to print data, too, but it's not always easy to make an onscreen form look good on paper. Reports (Chapter 8) are usually better used for printing.

Access gives you three ways to create forms:

▶ **Autoforms** are the fastest and easiest way to create a form but give you very few design choices. You get what you get, though very often what you get is enough.

▶ **The Form Wizard** takes you through a series of screens that ask you questions about your form design. At the end, the wizard creates a form based on your answers. The Form Wizard gives you more choices than the Autoforms method and is much easier to use than creating a form from scratch in the Design window.

▶ **The Design window** requires the most work on your part but gives you the most control of all three methods. In the Design window, you manually lay out your form on a screen grid. You position the form's blanks, labels, buttons, and other features. The Design window method is fine if you need an unusual form layout (or you're just a die-hard do-it-yourselfer).

Tip: If you're not sure where to start, start with the Form Wizard, and then use the Design window to touch up your design. You'll get the best of both worlds!

Form Basics

No matter which of the three methods you use to create your forms, all forms have some features in common. These common features are:

▶ **Layout.** The basic arrangement of information on the form.

▶ **Controls.** The labels, text boxes, list boxes, buttons, and other items you put on the form.

▶ **Properties.** The aspects of the form itself and of the controls on the form. Common properties include height, color, type font, size, and data source (such as a table).

If you understand these common features, you'll know how to apply them to any form you create. You'll be able to rearrange the organization of your forms, change how they work, and change how they look.

Form Layouts

A form layout determines where fields, labels, and other items appear on the form. It also determines the general look of the form. No matter which layout you choose, your form will *work* the same way. The layout affects only how your form looks on the screen. (You'll find the following types of forms in the Form Wizard, but you can create most of them, or get the same effect, using the Auto-form or Design view, too.)

Access, through the wizard, includes these predefined layouts:

▶ **Columnar** forms place the table's fields in columns. To the left of each field, a text label shows the field name. Of all the types of forms, columnar forms most resemble paper forms. Use columnar forms for situations where it works well to show only one record on the screen at a time.

- **Tabular** forms make each table record into one horizontal row of fields, the same as in a datasheet. At the top of each column, a text label gives the field name. Tabular forms are laid out a lot like datasheet forms, except that you only see one record at a time, each record can have multiple rows, and the fields look like blanks on a form instead of table cells (see Figure 3-1). Use a tabular form when what you'll enter requires relatively narrow fields and you want to be able to eyeball more than one record on the screen at once.

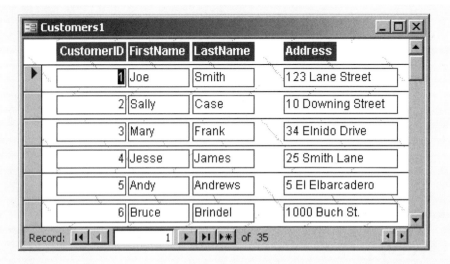

Figure 3-1. A tabular form combines the row-and-column layout of a datasheet with the general layout of a columnar form. Notice that, like all form windows, the tabular form has navigation buttons at the bottom so you can move from record to record in your table.

- **Datasheet** forms look just like table datasheets. There's not much reason to use datasheet forms, unless you really want your database to look and act like a spreadsheet. If you simply want to enter data into a table's datasheet, you can always use Datasheet view, so there's little need to create a Datasheet *form*.

- **Justified** forms look like a cross between a columnar form and a datasheet form.

- **PivotTable** forms lay out your data in a crosstab table format. PivotTables summarize your data by grouping it together. For example, an office equipment store could set up a pivot table to see how many typewriters each customer bought in each quarter of the year.

- **PivotChart** forms summarize your data, like PivotTable forms, but they do it by creating a graph.

JUMP START

Good Form

It's so easy to get wrapped up in the technical details of setting up a form, you may lose sight of why you're doing it in the first place. The goal of a form is to make viewing and entering information easy and efficient. If a form layout is cluttered, disorganized, or distracting, then the form isn't doing its job.

The basic principle is that the form layout itself should be "invisible," like good acting in a movie. You don't think, "That's Jamie Foxx playing the part of Ray Charles"; instead, you think, "That's Ray Charles." Likewise, a good form layout doesn't draw attention to itself. It disappears into its purpose, presenting blanks, labels, and buttons in a way that's easy to follow, so that whoever's using the database can think about the information, not the form. A good form layout should be:

* **Symmetrical.** Labels, blanks, buttons, and other controls should line up horizontally and vertically. You should also space them evenly around different areas of the form, so you don't have all your controls crammed into one small area while the rest of the form is empty.

* **Uniform.** Different visual elements of the form should match. Labels should be in the same type font or, at most, two different fonts. Buttons should be the same size, shape, and color, except when you use a different button look to indicate a different kind of button.

* **Uncluttered.** You should put plenty of space between different groups of controls on your form so they don't all run together. For example, you may use one area of your form for labels and blanks that contain customer name and address information and use another area for labels, blanks, and checkboxes that contain the customer's buying preferences.

Tip: For more information on PivotTables and PivotCharts, see *Excel: The Missing Manual* by Matthew MacDonald.

Controls

Controls make it easy to enter data into your form. Examples of controls include a label explaining the form, a box in which you type text, or a button you click to do something. Autoforms come with suitable controls built right in. You can add controls in the Form Wizard or Design window when you first create a form, and you can go back and add, edit, or delete them any time. Controls fall into the following three categories.

▶ A **bound control** is connected to a field in your data source. Any data you put into the control goes to the field. For example, if your form has a text box that's bound to the LastName field of a Customers table, then when you type a name in the text box, Access puts it into that field of a record in the table.

▶ An **unbound control** shows or does something on your form but isn't connected to any data source—for example, a label at the top of a form that simply identifies the form. Another example of an unbound control is an image of the company logo.

▶ A **calculated control** gets data from fields in your data source, does a calculation like a total, and then displays the result on your form (or report). However, the result of the calculation doesn't usually go back into your table: It's just for display on the form or report.

You can use more than a dozen different controls on forms. In this chapter, you'll learn about the ones you'll use most often. Some controls, like the following, appear in almost all computerized databases. (If they sound familiar, it's because they're distant cousins to the ones you see on Web page forms.)

▶ **Labels** simply display text on a form. That's usually all they do. You can use labels for any kind of explanatory text and can format them in any type font that you have available on your computer. At the top of a form you may put a label that says "Customer Record," while next to an account category field you may put a label that briefly lists the different categories of accounts. (If you're a programming wiz, you can even make labels do actions when you click them, but that's another book.)

▶ **Text boxes** take data and copy it to your table or other data source. They almost always have a label next to them that explains what they are. In fact, when you create a form to enter data into a table, Access automatically creates a field-name label for each field's text box on the form.

▶ **List boxes and Combo boxes** let you (actually, they force you) to choose from a list of values. You can use list boxes when you know in advance that you want a field to get one item from a short list of values. For example, if a type-writer store had three categories of customers (Regular, Preferred, and Gold Club), you could put a list box with those choices on your data-entry form for the Customers table. Not only do list boxes make it easier to enter information into the table, but they also prevent typing errors, since you must choose from the list box instead of keying the data into the field. Combo boxes are very similar to list boxes, but are often used more in data-entry forms, while list boxes frequently work best on forms where people need to be able to make multiple choices to run a query, report, or search.

▶ **Checkboxes** let you easily enter data into Yes/No fields (see Chapter 2). A Yes/No field, as its name implies, has only two possible values. If a checkbox is turned on, the corresponding Yes/No field gets a Yes; if the checkbox is turned off, the field gets a No.

▶ **Images** let you put graphics like photographs or logos on your forms.

Properties and the Property Sheet

Just like real-world objects, Access forms and controls have properties, as explained in the box on page 17. By changing the properties of those database objects, you can change how they look or what they do. You can view or change the properties of a form or control by displaying its *property sheet*, like the one in Figure 3-2.

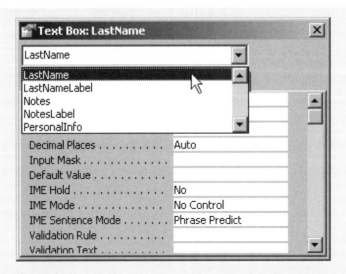

Figure 3-2. An object's property sheet has five tabs that display different groups of properties. Notice also the scroll bar at the right side, which lets you scroll to see other properties that aren't visible at the moment. The list box at the top of the property sheet lets you choose which object's properties it shows—a text box, in this case.

You can always open the property sheet for any Access item by choosing from the File menu, but there's a quicker way: Just right-click anywhere on the form and choose Properties from the pop-up menu. To view properties of a different object, either click it on the form or choose it from the list box at the top of the property sheet.

With the property sheet in front of you, all kinds of power is at your fingertips. You can resize, reposition, and reformat things, turn them on and off, and even make them invisible. If you design a form using any of the methods described in this chapter, and then later regret one of your choices, the property sheet is often the fastest (if a wee bit technical) way to undo or redo your work.

In Figure 3-2, for example, the Left property determines how far the text box's left edge is from the edge of the form; the Top property works the same way. By retyping the measurements for these properties, you can move the text box to a different location on the form. In fact, when you drag the text box with the mouse, the property sheet changes the Left and Top coordinates behind the scenes. The mouse is convenient and intuitive; the property sheet lets you be more precise and change lots of aspects of your form without leaving the keyboard. You can lead a long, happy Access life without ever opening the property sheet, but it'll always be there when you feel limited by the mouse.

Creating Autoforms

Easy is good. If easy does what you want, then there's no need to look any further. And Autoforms are easy. That's their main advantage.

Autoforms also have three disadvantages. First, they can only work with data from a single table, while forms you create with a wizard or in the Design window can work with data from multiple sources. Second, Autoforms typically include all the fields from your table or data source, while the wizard and Design window methods let you pick and choose the fields you want to include. Third, you can't use the justified layout with Autoforms, though you can use all the other layouts.

To get some practice, download the example file for this chapter from the "Missing CD" page (page 10). Open the CreatingForms database, and then follow the steps below to create an Autoform.

 Tip: The CreatingForms database is ideal for following the tutorials in this chapter, but it's unrealistic in one respect: The Customers table wouldn't normally have a Balance field showing each customer's account balance. In Chapter 4, you'll learn a better way to keep that kind of often-changing information in a separate (but linked) table.

1. **In the Objects bar, click Forms, and then click New at the top of the Data-base window.**

   Access displays the New Form dialog box (Figure 3-3). You can also open the New Form dialog box by choosing Insert → Form.

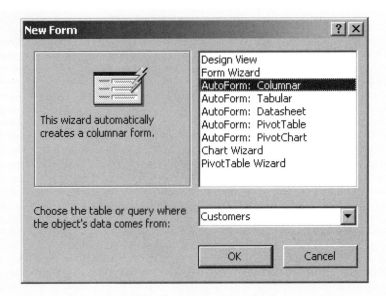

Figure 3-3. The New Form dialog box lets you create forms by any of the methods Access offers: Autoforms, the Form Wizard, and the Design window. You can also create charts and pivot tables, but you'll probably do that less often.

2. **In the list box, click Autoform: Columnar.**

   That unlabeled white box lists all the kinds of forms Access can create using either an Autoform or the wizard.

3. **From the "Choose the table or query" drop-down menu, choose Customers, and then click OK.**

   Access creates a form just like the one shown in Figure 3-4.

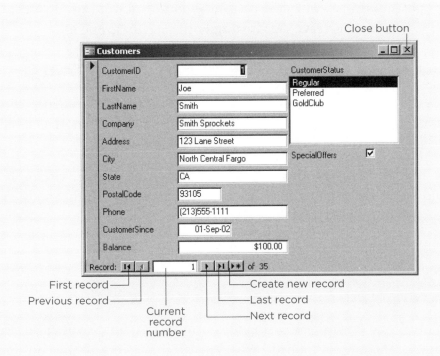

Close button

Figure 3-4. Notice that the CustomerStatus field contains a list of values with one value highlighted. That's because in the Customers table design, the CustomerStatus field is a list box from which you can choose from a lookup list of values, as described on page 333.

4. **Choose File → Save. In the Save As dialog box, type *frm_Customers*, and then click OK.**

Access offers to save the Autoform with the default name *Customers*. But you may want to take a naming tip from the pros: Save objects like tables and forms with a prefix that helps distinguish similarly named objects. For example, rather than just save a form as Customers, you can save it as *frm_Customers* to avoid confusion with the *table* named Customers. (In fact, you could even name the Customers table *tbl_Customers*.)

When you're done, you can close the Customers form window. If you're moving on to the next section, leave the CreatingForms database open.

Creating Forms with the Form Wizard

The Form Wizard is the happy medium of forms creation. Using it is almost as easy as creating an Autoform, but the wizard gives you a lot more flexibility. Unlike an Autoform, the wizard lets you do the following:

▶ Use multiple tables or other data sources with your form. For example, you could put all the fields from a Customers table on your form, and then add one field from an Orders table.

▶ Choose which fields you want to include on your form.

▶ Specify the order in which fields appear on your form.

▶ Select a visual style for your form.

There's really no downside to using the Form Wizard unless you need a form with unusual features or tabbed pages: The wizard can create any common type of form. Most of the time, you'll need to fine-tune the forms created by the wizard, but using it is still much quicker and much less work than doing all the form layout yourself. You go through five chief phases to design a form using the Form Wizard.

Phase 1: Choosing a Record Source

In phase 1 of the process, you start the Form Wizard and choose a record source. Your record source can be a table from any open Access database or a query.

Open the CreatingForms example database. It's the same one used in the preceding section. Next you'll do the following:

1. **In the Database window's Objects bar, click Forms, and then double-click "Create form by using wizard."**

   Access displays the first Form Wizard screen, as shown in Figure 3-5.

An alternative method: In the Objects bar, click Forms, and then click New. Click Form Wizard, choose a table from the pop-up menu, and then click OK.

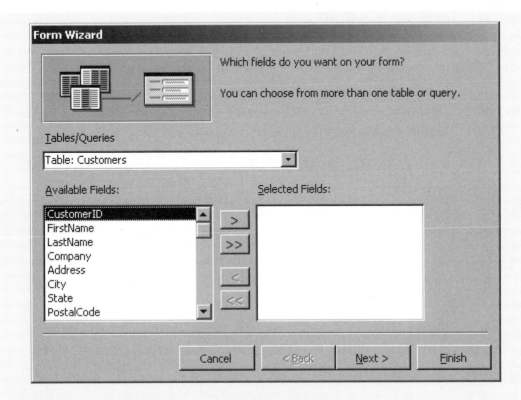

Figure 3-5. After you choose a table in the first Form Wizard screen, the fields from that table appear in the list box at the left. Move the fields you want to include on your form into the list on the right by using the arrow buttons. The whole routine is described on page 102.

2. **Click the Tables/Queries list box and observe that it lists all the tables in your database. Choose Table:Customers.**

The wizard selects the Customers table as the data source for your form and shows the table's fields in the Available Fields list.

The next phase is important: telling Access which fields you want to appear on the form, which may not be all of them. For example, if you're creating a simple form for quickly looking up phone numbers, you can leave off, say, PostalCode.

Phase 2: Choosing Fields

In this phase, you choose the fields that you want to appear on your form, providing the groundwork for your form's layout. Unlike an Autoform, the Form Wizard lets you choose not only which fields to include, but also the order in which they'll appear on the form. The wizard gives you four buttons to use to select and unselect fields from your form (see Figure 3-5):

- The > button moves the currently highlighted field from the Available Fields list to the Selected Fields list so that Access includes it on your form.

- The >> button moves all fields from the Available Fields list to the Selected Fields list so that Access includes all of them on your form.

- The < button removes the currently highlighted field from the Selected Fields list and puts it back in the Available fields list. The field doesn't appear on your form unless you move it back into the Selected Fields list.

- The << button removes all fields from the Selected Fields list and puts them back in the Available Fields list. It's a godsend when you realize you've chosen fields in totally the wrong order. Click this button if you need to start fresh.

In this example, suppose you want to use *all* your fields on the form but not in the same order as they appear in the table. Here's how to do it:

1. **In the Available Fields list, click CustomerID, and then click the > button.**

   The wizard moves the CustomerID field into the Selected Fields list.

2. **In the Available Fields list, click FirstName, click the > button, and then add the LastName field in the same way.**

   The wizard moves the FirstName and LastName fields into the Selected Fields list. On your form, the FirstName field appears before the LastName field.

3. **Oops—you've changed your mind about putting the FirstName field first, so click it to make sure it's highlighted, and then click the < button.**

   The wizard removes FirstName from the Selected Fields list.

   As you may have noticed in steps 1 and 2, when you click the > button to add a field, Access places it *below* whatever field's currently highlighted in the Selected Fields list. You want FirstName to come *after* LastName, so make sure LastName is highlighted in the Selected Fields list before going on to the next step.

4. **In the Available Fields list, click FirstName. Click the > button.**

   FirstName shows up below LastName in the Selected Fields list. (If you do something different and get confused, remember what the << button is for.)

5. **The remaining Available Fields list is already ordered correctly for the form, so click the >> button to move all of the fields at the same time.**

   The wizard moves all the fields to the Selected Fields list and adds them under the FirstName field. The fields appear on the form in the same order as the list.

6. **Click Next.**

   Access displays the second Form Wizard screen (Figure 3-6).

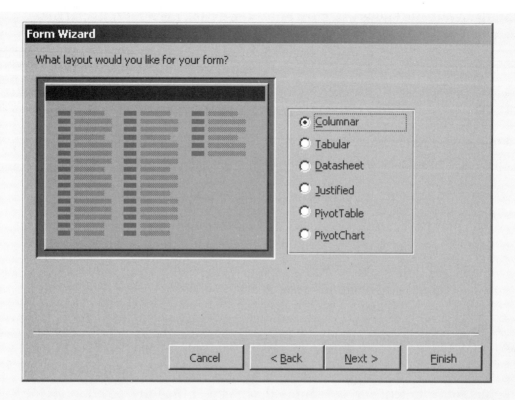

Figure 3-6. Notice that as you click the different radio buttons (Columnar, Tabular, and so forth), the left side of the screen shows a preview of how your form looks with that layout.

Phase 3: Choosing a Form Layout

In this phase, you choose how to arrange the controls on your form. The Form Wizard gives you almost exactly the same layout choices as you get with Auto-forms: Columnar, Tabular, Datasheet, Pivot Table, and Pivot Chart (page 93). The only additional layout you get is Justified, which arranges the fields in a neat series of boxes on the screen.

In this example, you'll get to see how a Justified layout looks, compared to the Columnar layout used for the Autoform earlier in this chapter. Here's how to choose the layout for your form:

1. **On the third wizard screen, the Columnar layout is already selected. Click the Justified radio button.**

   The screen shows a thumbnail preview of the justified form layout. (If you want, click the radio buttons for the other form layouts to see how they look.)

2. **Click Next.**

   Access applies the justified layout to the form and displays the third Form Wizard screen as shown in Figure 3-7.

Phase 4: Choosing a Form Style

In this phase, you choose a *form style*, a bunch of visual settings that determine how your form looks, including elements like your form's background color, type font, and whether or not field boxes have a 3-D look. Just like form layout, form styles are purely cosmetic and have no effect on how your forms work. Therefore, you can pick any style that pleases you.

 Tip: Access's predefined form styles make your work easier. Because each style is a collection of visual settings, you can get the same result by using a form's property sheet to choose each setting manually. If you get your form looking a way you especially like, you can even save that collection of settings as a new form style: See the box on page 122.

Access lets you pick from 10 different predefined styles for your forms. If you think they're exactly the same ones you chose from for your database as a whole in Chapter 1, you're right. When the third Form Wizard screen opens, it shows the style you picked the last time you created a form. If you haven't created any forms before, it shows the Standard style.

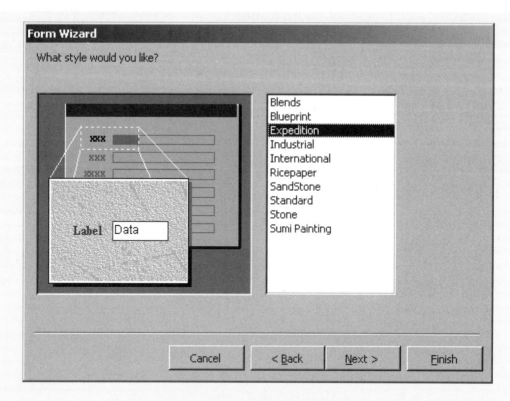

Figure 3-7. The third Form Wizard screen lets you choose a visual style for your form. You can sample the different styles by clicking the radio buttons.

To choose a form style:

1. **Click several styles in the list to see how they look.**

   As you click styles, the screen shows a preview of each, as shown in Figure 3-7.

2. **Click the Expedition style for a nice, earthy effect, and then click Next.**

   Access applies the Expedition style to the form and displays the final Form Wizard screen (see Figure 3-8).

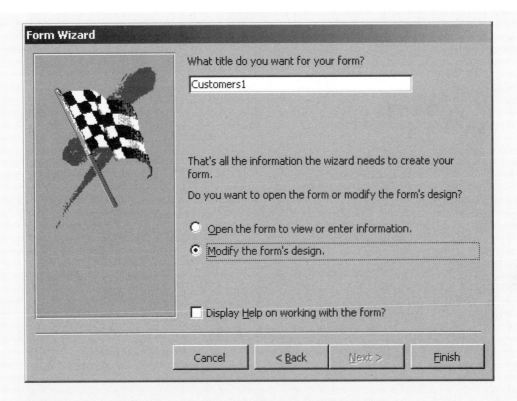

Figure 3-8. The final Form Wizard screen lets you choose a name for your form and either start entering data or modify the form design. If you need help working with the form, turn on the checkbox labeled "Display Help on working with the form."

Tip: If you want to change the style of a form you've already created, open the form in the Design window and choose Format → Autoformat. Click the style you want, and then click OK.

Phase 5: Naming and Saving the Form

The final phase lets you name and save your form. Yet the form name you choose here doesn't appear on the form itself as a form title: Access uses the form name to identify the form in your Database window. If you want to add a form title, you'll need to use the Design window and put the title in a label control.

To name your form:

1. **In the "What title do you want for your form?" box, delete the name that's already there and type** *frm_Customers_just*.

   Access lists the form in the Database window.

2. **Click Finish.**

   Access creates the form and opens it on your screen (see Figure 3-9).

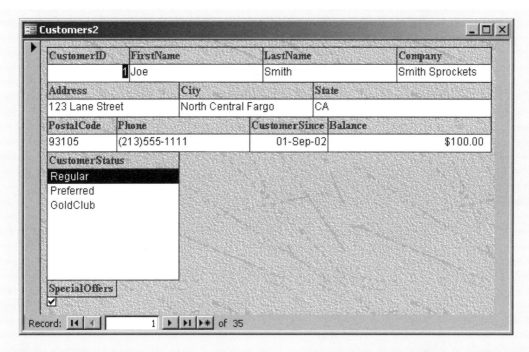

Figure 3-9. The frm_Customers_just form is a good example of a simple form. The label above each field is just the name of the field: CustomerID, FirstName, and so forth. You can change these labels to friendlier descriptions of the fields on the form.

Tip: If you ever want to go straight to the Design window to modify a form you just made, turn on the radio button labeled "Modify the form's design" before you click Finish.

Modifying the Form Design

After you've create a form using the Autoform or Form Wizard, you can open the form in Design view to tweak it a bit and make sure the results are exactly what you want. You may not get many design choices with an Autoform, and even the Form Wizard doesn't give you full control, but once you've saved a form you've made using either of those methods, you can open it up in Design view and modify it any way you like.

Open the frm_Customers form you created earlier in this chapter. If you don't have one, create a quick Autoform now, as described on page 97. Take a look at the Columnar layout that Access designed for you. It's got a few flaws:

▶ The field labels have no spaces in them.

▶ The form has no title at the top.

▶ The Special Offers checkbox is higher than its label. (Admit it: This is driving you crazy.)

To modify the form, choose View → Design View or click the Design button (with little pictures of a pencil and a triangle) at the left end of the Access toolbar. Access opens your form in the Design window (see Figure 3-10). Maximize the Design window.

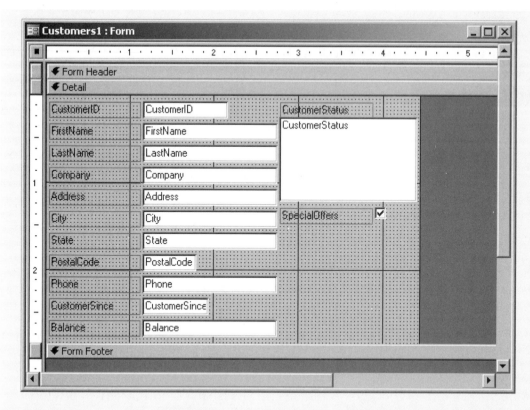

Figure 3-10. The Design window shows your controls against a grid that helps you position them on the form. You can turn the grid on or off by choosing View → Grid.

Editing the Labels

The first change you want to make is to put spaces into the field labels. If the form's property sheet isn't visible, choose View → Properties or press Alt+Enter to display it. Then proceed as follows:

Using the Toolbox

When you have a form open in Design view, Access displays the Toolbox, which contains controls you can put on your form. If the Toolbox isn't visible on your screen, choose View → Toolbox to make it appear. Choosing View → Toolbox again dismisses it, but such drastic measures are rarely necessary. If the Toolbox is blocking part of the form you're working on, simply drag it out of the way by its title bar.

The arrow button at the upper left is the tool you'll use most often—the selection tool. You click with the selection (arrow) tool to tell Access which design element in the window you want to work on. The other buttons let you add and edit labels, controls, and other elements of a form. If you're not sure what a tool does, just hold the mouse pointer over it and a tool tip explains its purpose (label, text box, and so forth).

1. **Click the CustomerID label to select it, and then click it once more between "Customer" and "ID."**

   Access positions the text cursor right after the "r" in "Customer." (If the Toolbox or property sheet's in your way, just drag them away from the Design window.)

2. **Press the Space bar, and then click a blank area of the form.**

   Access inserts a space between "Customer" and "ID."

3. **Click the FirstName label to select it, and then look at the property sheet.**

   The list box at the top of the property sheet says FirstName_Label: It means that if you make any changes in the property sheet, Access applies them to the FirstName label.

4. **In the property sheet, click the Format tab to make sure it's in front. Then in the Caption box, click right between "First" and "Name" in the word "FirstName." Press the Space bar, and then press Enter.**

   Access inserts a space in the label. It now says "First Name." If you want, use either method to insert spaces between words in other labels.

Adding a Title in the Form Header

Next, say you want to add a title at the top of the form. To do that, you'll use the Form Header section of your form: That's where you put titles, logos, and other material that you want at the top of the form. Forms also have a Form Footer section where you can put material that you want at the bottom of the form. To add a title to the Form Header section:

1. **Open the list box at the top of the property sheet, and then choose Form Header.**

   Access selects the Form Header section. If you make any changes in the property sheet, Access applies them to that section of the form.

2. **Click the Format tab to make sure it's in front, click in the Height box, and then delete its contents. Type *1.5*, and then press Enter.**

   Oops! That's a bigger form header than you wanted.

3. **Hold the mouse pointer over the top border of the horizontal gray bar at the bottom of the Form Header section until the pointer turns into a double arrow; see Figure 3-11. Slowly drag the border up until it's even with the thin black grid line that marks a one-inch height for the section.**

Access changes the section height to one inch. Notice that the Height box in the property sheet now indicates the same thing: one inch.

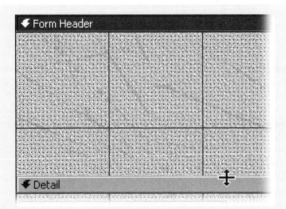

Figure 3-11. Whenever you hold the mouse pointer over a border you can drag, the pointer turns into a double arrow. That applies to sections, fields, labels, and pretty much everything else in Access. As soon as you see that double arrow, you know it's positioned over something you can drag.

4. **In the Toolbox, click the Label tool. That's the tool marked with the letters *Aa*. Click near the top-left corner of the Form Header section. (For more information about the Toolbox, see the box on page 111.)**

A small text box appears where you can type a label.

5. **Type *Cambridge Typewriters Customer*, and then press Enter.**

   Access adds the label to your form. The label is still selected.

6. **In the property sheet, scroll down in the Format tab, and then click in the Font Size box. An arrow button appears, indicating that the box has a drop-down list. Click it, and then choose 18.**

   Now that you've resized the text, you need to make room for it, which you'll do next.

7. **Position the mouse pointer over the bottom-right corner of the label until the pointer turns into a double arrow. Drag the corner down and to the right to make the label big enough to show the enlarged text.**

Dragging a Control

Next, you'll drag the Special Offers checkbox down a bit so it isn't higher than its label. Dragging a field is a little trickier than you may imagine. When Access puts a field on a form, it groups the field together with its label. If you try to drag the field, you end up dragging the label at the same time.

The solution is to look at the mouse pointer. When you click a field to select it, you automatically select its label at the same time. If you then hold the mouse pointer over the field, the pointer changes into one of two shapes:

▶ **A hand with all five fingers extended.** Dragging with this pointer drags both the field and its label.

▶ **A hand with only one finger extended.** (No, it's not *that* finger.) This pointer lets you drag *only* the label or the field—whichever one the pointer is over.

To drag the checkbox, scroll down in the Design window, if necessary, so you can see the Special Offers label and checkbox. Next:

1. **Click the checkbox to select it. Move the mouse slightly over the checkbox and the label and observe what happens to the pointer.**

   Sometimes the pointer has its normal appearance (an arrow), sometimes it's the five-finger hand, and sometimes it's the one-finger hand.

2. **When the mouse pointer turns into a one-finger hand over the checkbox, drag the checkbox down a tad.**

   The checkbox is now even with the label.

3. **Choose File → Save to save the design changes, and then choose View → Form View to see the results of your hard work.**

   Because you added a form header, you may need to make the Form window bigger to see the entire form. You can drag the bottom border of the Form window (with the double-arrow pointer) in the same way as anything else in Access.

Close the form when you're done.

Creating Forms in Design View

Normally, it's most efficient to create your forms with the Form Wizard and then use the Design window to modify them. However, there are times when you should start in the Design window, especially if you're brimming with creative ideas or have a very complex form in mind. For example, for a form with multiple tabbed pages, the Design window is often easier because you create the tabbed pages at the outset. If you'd started with the Form Wizard, you'd spend lots of extra time trying to rearrange the fields from the original nontabbed design.

In this section, you'll learn the basics of creating a form in the Design window. Along the way, you'll learn to use the Image control in the Toolbox.

Phase 1: Starting Your Design

For your first form, you'll start with a fairly simple one. Because it's already got some good tables to work with, open the CreatingForms database. If you haven't downloaded the example files for this chapter, do so now (page 10), because there's an image file in there you'll need for this tutorial. Then follow these steps:

1. **In the Database window, click Forms in the Objects bar, and then double-click "Create form in Design view."**

   Access displays the Design window as shown in Figure 3-12. To set up your workspace, double-click the Design window's title bar (it says Form1:Form) to maximize the window. If the property sheet doesn't appear, choose View → Properties to display it. In the next step, you'll define the boundaries of the form itself.

2. **Drag the bottom border of the work area down to three inches on the vertical ruler. Then drag the right border of the work area out to six inches on the horizontal ruler.**

   To this blank canvas, you need to add the individual parts that make up a form. In this example, you'll add a header and footer.

3. **Choose View → Form Header/Footer to add header and footer sections to the form.**

   Notice that your form now has three sections: Form Header, Detail, and Form Footer. The Detail section is where you put most of the form content, like fields and labels. Use the Form Header section for logos, form titles, and other material you want at the top of your form. Use the Form Footer section for material you want at the bottom of your form.

4. **Drag the bottom border of the Form Header section down to the one-inch mark on the vertical ruler.**

   You've just created a one-inch-deep header for your form.

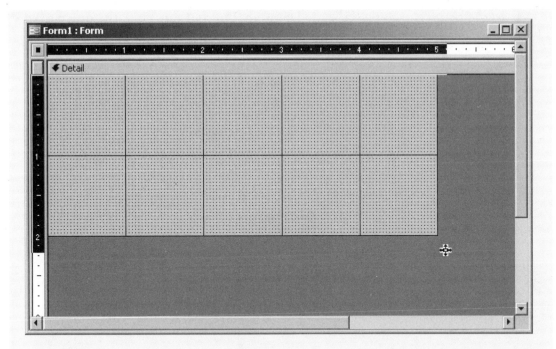

Figure 3-12. The Design window includes a work area with grid lines where you can put form controls, as well as vertical and horizontal rulers to help you position the controls. When you start a form design, the work area is only five inches wide by two inches high, so you usually need to drag its borders to make it big enough for your form.

Phase 2: Choosing a Data Source

Next, you need to choose a data source for your form. Not all forms use a data source, but for data entry and display, you have to associate your form with at least one data source:

1. **In the property sheet, make sure that the list box at the top of the sheet shows that you've got the form selected. If it doesn't, open the list box and select Form.**

    Another way to select the form is to choose Edit → Select Form. A third way is to press Ctrl+R.

2. **In the property sheet, click the Data tab. On that tab, click the down arrow to open the Record Source list.**

   The list contains all the tables in the database.

3. **Click Customers.**

   Access selects the Customers table as the data source for your form. As soon as you choose a data source, Access displays list of fields from the data source you chose (see Figure 3-13).

Figure 3-13. The field list includes all the table fields that you can put on the form. If it disappears for any reason, you can bring it back by choosing View → Field List.

  Tip: If you start your form design by clicking New in the Database window, Access displays the New dialog box, and you choose your data source by opening the list box in the dialog box.

Phase 3: Adding Fields to the Form

Your next step is to add fields from the field list to the form. You'll also align the fields and their labels so that the form looks nice and symmetrical.

1. **In the field list, click FirstName and drag it onto the Detail section about a half inch below the top and one inch from the left margin.**

   If you drag a field too close to the left margin of the form, the field box sometimes overlaps with its label because the label has bumped up against the left margin. You can use the one-finger mouse pointer to drag the field box away from the label, but it's usually easier just to delete the field from the form and drag it onto the form again.

2. **In the field list, click LastName and drag it onto the Detail section about one inch from the top margin and three and a half inches from the left margin.**

   Access puts the field on the form. The form looks awful because the First-Name field isn't even with the LastName field. You can see that the LastName field is selected because it has the border with the drag handles.

3. **Position the mouse pointer above and to the left of the FirstName field, and then drag down and to the right until the pointer is below and to the right of the LastName field.**

   You've selected both the FirstName and LastName fields, as well as their labels.

4. **Choose Format → Align → Top.**

   Access aligns the fields vertically. You can use the same trick (Format → Align) to align selected controls horizontally.

Phase 4: Adding Images to the Form

Since the whole point of designing your own form is to exercise some creativity, you'll add an image to the Form Header section. This image isn't connected to any field; it's just to make the form look nicer. Even if you're aesthetically challenged, give it a shot:

1. **In the Toolbox, click the Image control.**

   The Image control has a picture of a mountain with no cactus. If you're not sure which is the Image control, hold the mouse pointer over the controls in the Toolbox. Tool tips pop up to identify each tool for you.

2. **Click the top-left corner of the Form Header section.**

   Access displays the Insert Picture dialog box.

3. **Browse to and select RoyalQuietDeluxe.jpg, and then click OK.**

   Access inserts the image at the top-left corner of the Form Header section. If it's not exactly where you want, you can drag it just like any other control.

Phase 5: Adding a Form Style

Even when you start in Design view, you can add one of Access's canned styles to a form just as you do when you use the Form Wizard. The process is a little odd, but here it is:

1. **Choose Edit → Select Form to select the entire form.**

   You'll know you've done it right if little boxes and selection handles appear all over your form in the Design window.

2. **Choose Format → AutoFormat to open the AutoFormat dialog box (Figure 3-14). In the Form AutoFormats list, click the Blends style, and then click OK twice.**

   Access applies the style to the form.

Phase 6: Naming and Saving the Form

Your final step is to name and save your form design. By now, these steps should be familiar:

1. **Choose File → Save.**

   Access displays the Save As dialog box.

2. **In the Form Name text box, type *frm_Customers_design* and click OK.**

   Access saves your form.

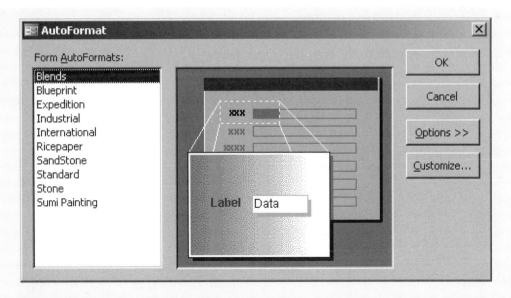

Figure 3-14. In the AutoFormat dialog box, you can choose a style for your form. You can also click the Options button at the right side of the dialog box to apply the style only to the type fonts, color, or border of the form.

3. **Choose View → Form View to display your form for data entry.**

   Notice that the form has the same navigation buttons at the bottom of the window as you've seen before: First Record, Previous Record, Next Record, Last Record, and New Record. You can enter records exactly as described on page 46.

When you're done admiring your work, click Close at the top-right corner of the Design window.

In the next chapter, you'll learn how to crank up your databases with table-to-table links. A whole new level of possibility awaits: When you use related information from multiple tables in a database, you can make your forms, reports, and other database tools work even harder for you.

Create Your Own Form Styles

Once you've got a form looking just the way you want, you can save its visual attributes as a new style so you can reuse it later. You can start with any of Access's styles, improve upon it, and then immortalize it.

Make sure that the form is open in Design view, and then choose Format → AutoFormat to display the Autoformat dialog box. Next, do the following:

1. Click Customize, and then select "Create a new Autoformat based on the form." Click OK.

2. In the Style Name box, type a name for your new form style.

3. Click OK again. Access creates your new style and adds it to the style list.

4. Click Close to close the AutoFormat dialog box.

Simple as that. The key is to get the style just the way you want it, and then choose AutoFormat.

You can then apply this style of your own to any Access form by choosing Format → AutoFormat and selecting it from the list.

CHAPTER 4:
LINKING TABLES TO
COMBINE DATA

▶ Why Relate?

▶ A Relational Database Tour

▶ Linking Tables in the Relationships
  Window

▶ Using Subdatasheets to View Related
  Items

▶ Creating Subforms

IT'S TIME TO LEARN THE MOST POWERFUL technology of all: the very heart of Access and most other modern database managers. So far, this book has dealt only with *flat* databases—those with only one table, or with several tables that aren't linked in any way. Each record in a flat database can hold bits of information (fields) about an individual item, and your forms, searches, and sorts are limited to shifting that information around in various ways. Flat databases are perfectly good for some purposes, as explained in the box on page 126.

Ultimately, however, flat databases have a severe limitation: They can't understand how different masses of information are somehow related to each other the way you can. For example, a Customer database, if it has just that one table, can store information on thousands and thousands of customers and perform sorts and reports on it in seconds. Same thing with tables for Orders and Products. But say you have a nationwide business where you want to increase your sales by targeted marketing for each region of the country. You need the answer to a broader question like, "What do my customers on the West Coast purchase differently from my customers on the East Coast?" *You* can see the connection between your Customers' state of residence, the products they buy, and the total amounts ordered in each state, but you need your *database* to go through all those records and come up with the answer for you.

The problem is, you know the information is in there somewhere, but you have no idea how to tell your database to total up the orders (from the Orders table) for each product (in the Products table) and sort them by state (from the Customers table). Well, that's exactly what you'll learn how to do in this chapter. In Access, it's not hard at all to create the connections—known as *relationships*—between the tables in a database.

In this chapter, you'll learn how to design and create linked-table, that is, *relational* databases. You'll learn:

▶ Why relational databases are faster and more efficient.

▶ What *kinds* of links you can create.

What Relational Means to Me

These days, the word *relational* refers to any database program that lets you link tables together. Access encourages this view by calling its table-to-table links *relationships*.

Although the ability to link tables is one of the most important features of relational databases, the term "relational" originally referred to something much more specific. It meant that the database followed the *relational data model,* which is a set of

rules devised in the 1970s by E.F. Codd, a database scientist at IBM Corporation.

No modern database manager, including Access, follows the relational data model completely. For example, although the relational data model forbids record numbers, Access uses record numbers in tables and works just fine. Still, Access and its contemporaries owe a debt of allegiance to Codd's work.

▶ How linked tables let you view one table's datasheet inside another table's datasheet.

▶ How to create forms that include subforms, which display information from a linked table.

Why Relate?

Relational databases have all the advantages of nonlinked databases and none of their disadvantages. Just as in a flat database, you can keep all your information in one file. But unlike a flat database, you can add more records without changing your table designs, you don't risk errors or inconsistencies, and you don't waste disk space with lots of empty columns.

In relational databases, you split up different kinds of information into separate tables. Next, you relate the tables, two at a time, by telling Access about a field that's the same in both tables. The shared field lets Access pick out which records

When Flat Is Fine

As long as your information is simple (for example, consisting only of customer records) and you don't have huge numbers of records, a nonlinked table is fine. Linking up tables in Access is easy, but don't do it if you don't really need to. You can use nonlinked tables when:

* **You need to store only one kind of data.** For example, if you want to keep only names and addresses, the titles of movies you have on DVD, a list of your family members' birthdays, or the dog's feeding schedule.

* **Your information doesn't change much, or it changes at the same time.** If Sally gets a new phone number or (in a momentary lapse of good taste) you buy a DVD of the movie *Glitter*, you can easily go into your table and make the change. In a flat database, nothing else depends on the data you change, so there's no danger that you'll make your data inconsistent.

* **You don't need to combine different kinds of information.** You'll never need a report that combines your family members' birthdays with the names of DVD movies you own and the dog's feeding schedule. Therefore, you can use nonlinked tables for all that data.

in one table go with which records in the other table. For example, the CustomerID field you've seen in the Customers table (page 61) serves as a link between each customer and the orders he or she places. Since they're unique and unchanging, primary key fields are often also shared fields.

At the beginning of this chapter, you saw an example of a database that calls for linking tables of Customers, Orders, and Products. Even a seemingly simple database, like the Contact Management template that comes with Access, relies on relationships between people and call records. Open it up in the Database window and choose Window → Relationships to see for yourself. How can you tell if your own information needs the relational treatment? Basically, if you're creating a database for a home-based business or volunteer project, you probably need to link your tables together.

Dig out those notes you took when you were planning your tables in Chapter 2 (page 54), and see if any of the following points apply:

▶ **You need to store several kinds of data.** If you're running a small business and need to keep information about customers, orders, and inventory, non-linked tables will make you do a lot of extra work. The worst thing you can do is shove all that information into a single table. Combining vastly different kinds of information in a single table is a prescription for disaster. If your table includes information about customers, orders, and inventory, you'll have a hard time finding anything. Think of a five-inch-thick file folder and multiply by 10.

▶ **Different kinds of information change at different times.** The names and addresses of individual customers change only occasionally, but the list of orders from each customer may change daily or even hourly. If you keep customer names and addresses in the same table as customer orders, then each customer record must have enough fields to hold the largest number of orders you'll get from any customer. If even one customer places more orders than that, then you have to change your table design to add more fields for the extra orders.

▶ **You need to combine different kinds of data.** You may often want to look at a report of orders from each customer. If your customer and order records are in the same table, you can produce such a report, but your table's a mess. If your customer and order records are in separate, nonlinked tables, then your tables are fine but you can't combine their information to show which orders came from each customer.

How to Spot a Bad Database

Even after reading the beginning of this chapter, perhaps you still can't see why you'd separate your information into tables that you'll have to link together anyway. Seeing is believing, so the example files for this chapter include an example of how *not* to create a database.

The SpiesAndStuff_bad database simply contains the names and ID numbers for the Acme Spy Agency, plus information about the equipment issued to each spy. Oh, and the dates each spy checked equipment in and out *all in one table*.

As shown here, the table illustrates all the disadvantages of nonlinked design. You have to enter the same data (like equipment description) over and over. If you make a typing error, the information in different records is inconsistent and you have no way to know which is correct. For example, James Brawn was issued a "Great Big Freudian Gun with

nightscope" (item #99), while Jacqueline Brower was issued a Great Big Freudian Gun—with no mention of a nightscope.

Meanwhile, veteran spies like James Brawn have been on so many missions that you run out of columns for more equipment. Newer spies like Matt Kelm and Mata Harriett have no information in their equipment columns—a waste of time and disk space. And what do forms or reports come out looking like? Try creating one at your own peril.

Unfortunately, there's no easy way to fix a database like this. You have to create the necessary separate tables: one for spies, one for equipment and its IDs and descriptions, and one for records of equipment issued and returned.

A Relational Database Tour

Download (page 10) and open the SpiesAndStuff_End database to walk through a preview of how a relational database works. By the end of this chapter, you'll know how to create all the features you see in this database. After you've opened the SpiesAndStuff_End database, choose Tools → Relationships to inspect how it links tables together (see Figure 4-1).

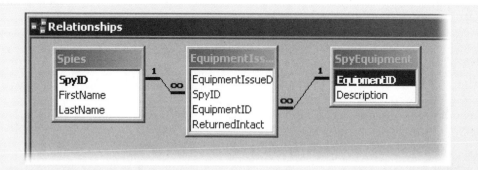

Figure 4-1. The Relationships window shows you not only which tables are linked, but how they're linked. The link lines have "1" at one end and an infinity sign (a sideways "8") at the other end. That means the link is a one-to-many relationship, as discussed in the box on page 130.

This database contains three tables:

▶ The **Spies** table lists each spy's secret ID number as well as his or her first and last names.

▶ The **EquipmentIssued** table lists the date you issued the equipment, the secret ID number of the spy to whom you issued it, the secret inventory ID number of the equipment, and whether or not the spy returned it intact.

▶ The **SpyEquipment** table lists the secret inventory ID number and the description of each piece of equipment.

The Relationships window shows that the Spies table is linked to the EquipmentIssued table in a one-to-many relationship, meaning that you can issue equipment to each spy as many times as needed. Likewise, the SpyEquipment table is linked to the EquipmentIssued table in a one-to-many relationship, meaning that you can issue each piece of equipment as many times as needed. For more information about the different types of relationship, see the box below.

LEARNING THE LINGO

Relationship Types

Records in two tables can relate to each other in three possible ways:

* **One-to-one.** Each record in one table (A) corresponds to exactly one record in the other table (B). In Access, one-to-one relationships work fine, but they're pretty rare. Just about the only reason to have a one-to-one relationship is to save disk space: You can have a separate table holding large image files, with a one-to-one relationship to the table that has the image's filename, description, and thumbnail. That way, you can take just the thumbnail table on your laptop, and leave the big image file at home.

* **One-to-many.** Each record in table A links to one *or more* records in table B. Each record in table B, however, can link to only *one* record in table A. In a customer order database, for example, each customer (in the "one" side table) may have placed any number of orders (in the "many" side table). However, one order *never* has more than one matching record in the Customers table.

* **Many-to-many.** Each record in table A can link to one *or more* records in table B *and* vise versa.

Although your human brain can handle many-to-many relationships (each spy can have possession of more than one piece of spy equipment, and each piece of equipment passes through the hands of any number of spies), computers have trouble with the concept.

To keep from getting confused, every database program handles the dilemma of many-to-many relationships differently. Access has a feature called *subdatasheets* that lets any number of records in one table link to any number of records in another table. See page 132 for the full story.

Common Fields

A *common field* is a field that lets you match records in one table with records in another table when you link the tables together. All the tables you link together must include the common field: Without it, Access has no way to match up records. For example, in your spy database, both the Spies table and the EquipmentIssued table have a SpyID field. When you issue equipment to a spy, the equipment-issue record has these fields:

▶ **EquipmentIssueDate.** The date you issued the equipment.

▶ **SpyID.** The secret ID of the spy who got the equipment. The same field also appears in the Spies table. When you link the Spies table to the EquipmentIssued table, this field lets Access determine which equipment-issue records go with which spy. If an equipment-issue record has a SpyID value of 1, then you know that the equipment was issued to spy #1, James Brawn.

▶ **EquipmentID.** The secret inventory ID of the equipment. The same field also appears in the SpyEquipment table. When you link the EquipmentIssued table to the SpyEquipment table, this field lets Access match up the equipment-issue data (date and spy ID) with descriptions of the equipment that you issued.

▶ **ReturnedIntact.** This Yes/No field shows if the spy returned the equipment in one piece, which almost never happens.

Therefore, you can see that the EquipmentIssued table has not one, but *two* common fields. The SpyID field lets you link the EquipmentIssued table to the Spies table, while the EquipmentID field lets you link it to the SpyEquipment table.

 Tip: You may wonder why equipment descriptions aren't included in the EquipmentIssued table and are in their own separate table instead. The reason is that separating the descriptions into their own table minimizes repetition of the information and makes for a more efficient database. Instead of repeating equipment descriptions, EquipmentIssued repeats only the equipment inventory numbers.

Close the Relationships window. Next, you'll see what an individual table in a relational database looks like. In the Database window, double-click the Spies table. Access displays the Spies datasheet (see Figure 4-2), which looks like any datasheet in a flat database. The little + signs indicating links are the only giveaway.

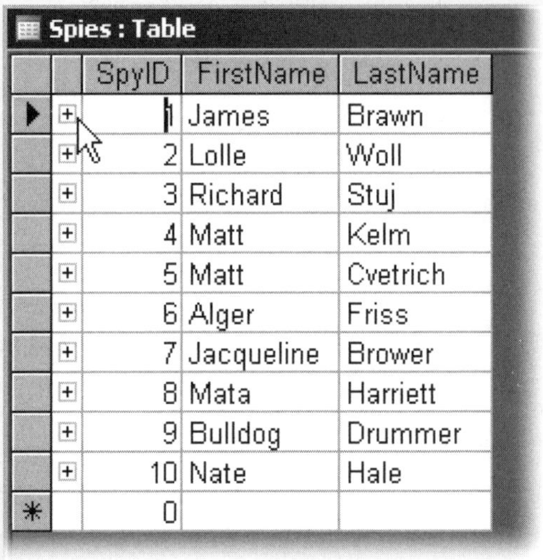

		SpyID	FirstName	LastName
▶	+	1	James	Brawn
	+	2	Lolle	Woll
	+	3	Richard	Stuj
	+	4	Matt	Kelm
	+	5	Matt	Cvetrich
	+	6	Alger	Friss
	+	7	Jacqueline	Brower
	+	8	Mata	Harriett
	+	9	Bulldog	Drummer
	+	10	Nate	Hale
✳		0		

Spies : Table

Figure 4-2. The Spies datasheet has a feature indicating that it's linked to another table. The + signs to the left of each record show that each spy's record is linked to one or more records in a different table.

Subdatasheets and Subforms

With the Spies datasheet open, at the left end of the row for James Brawn, click the + sign. Access opens a subdatasheet that shows records of all the equipment you've issued to James Brawn (see Figure 4-3). You'll learn about subdatasheets later in this chapter, in the section "Using Subdatasheets" on page 141.

Access's subdatasheets give you the flexibility to link many layers of information in one database. They also make it easy to create new forms for very specialized purposes. Close the Spies datasheet and, on the Database window's Objects bar, click Forms. Next, double-click the Spies form. For each record you display in the

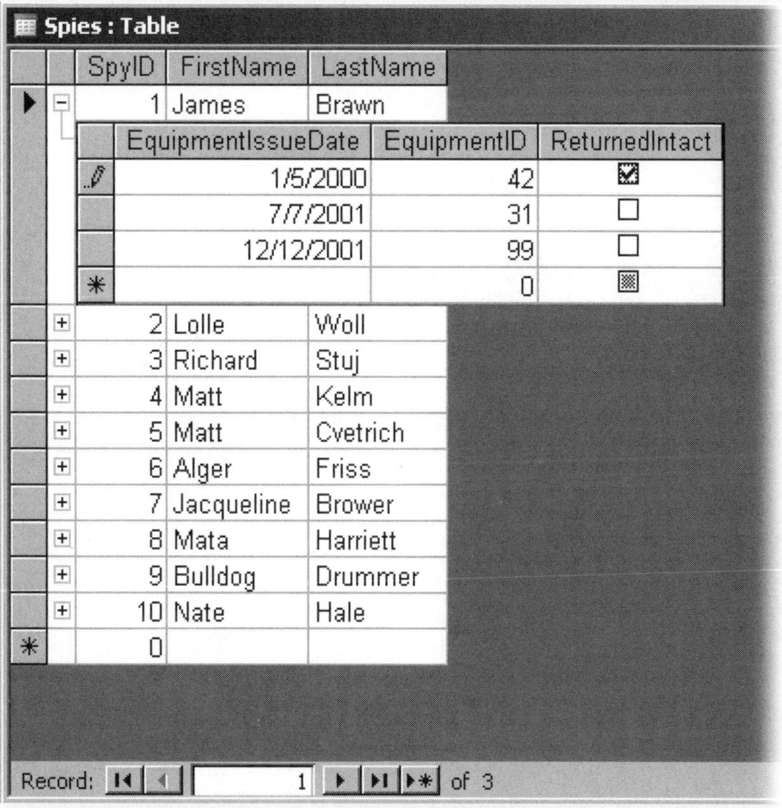

Figure 4-3. When two tables are linked, at the left end of a record you can click the + sign to see all its related records in a different table. To close the subdatasheet, sign at the left end of the record click the - symbol.

form, Access shows a subform with all the related records in the EquipmentIssued table (see Figure 4-4).

At the bottom of the Spies form, click Next Record (the right-arrow button) to look at the record of your next spy, Lolle Woll. The subform updates to show equipment you've issued to Fraulein Woll. Click Last Record (the right arrow pointing at a vertical line) to see the record of Nate Hale, your only spy who returns equipment intact.

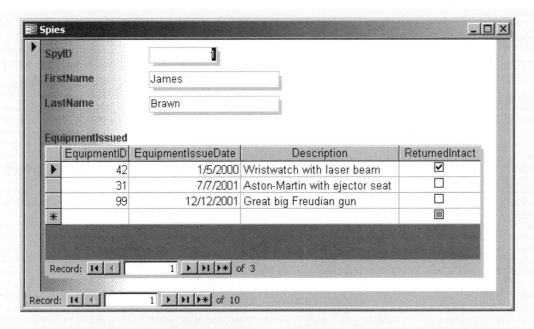

Figure 4-4. When two tables are linked, you can create forms with embedded subforms. For each record you display in the main form, the subform shows its related records in a different table.

When you've finished inspecting the subdatasheet and subform, close the SpiesAndStuff_End database.

Linking Tables in the Relationships Window

Your first step in creating a linked-table database is, unsurprisingly, to set up some links. Download (from the "Missing CD" page described on page 10) and open the SpiesAndStuff_Start database.

The tutorial on the following pages shows you how to create relationships between existing tables in this database. You can work with any database of your own as long as:

- Your database has more than one table, and you've thought through which records you wish to link and why. For example, you need to connect customers to orders *so that* you can show customer information on an order form. Review Chapter 2 for advice on organizing your tables.

- You've sketched out (on paper or onscreen) your one-to-many relationships. Review the box on page 130 if you're not sure which records to link.

- Each table that you want to link has a common field with the table to which you link it. The common field should be a unique value like SpyID or EquipmentID. (See page 64 for a refresher on primary keys.)

Adding Tables to the Relationships Window

After you've done your planning, your next step is to add the tables to the Relationships window where you can create the links. To add tables to the Relationships window:

1. **Choose Tools → Relationships to open the Relationships window. Then choose Relationships → Show Table.**

   Access displays the Show Table dialog box (see Figure 4-5).

2. **In the dialog box, click Spies, and then click the Add button.**

   Access adds the table to the Relationships window.

3. **Using the same method, add the EquipmentIssued and SpyEquipment tables to the Relationships window.**

 Tip: You can also add a table to the Relationships window by double-clicking the table name in the Show Table dialog box.

When you've finished, the Relationships window contains all three tables but doesn't yet show any links between them. You'll create the links next.

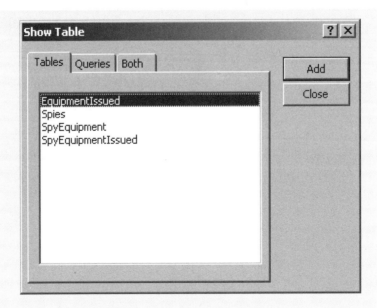

Figure 4-5. Use the Show Table dialog box to add tables to the Relationships window, so that you can then link them together. The Tables tab lists all the tables you've created in your database.

Adding Relationships Between Tables

You need to create relationships between tables before you can have Access combine information from the different tables in your forms, reports, and so on. Once you've added tables to the Relationships window, you're ready to create those relationships by linking the tables together. Here's how it's done:

1. **Drag the SpyID field from the Spies table onto the SpyID field in the EquipmentIssued table.**

   Access displays the Edit Relationships dialog box (Figure 4-6), showing the specifics of the relationship you just created.

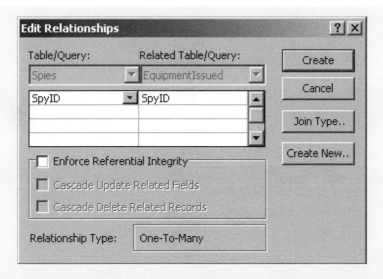

Figure 4-6. The Edit Relationships dialog box lets you view and change the features of a link. At the bottom of the dialog box, Access tells you what kind of link it'll create: Most of the time, your links will be one-to-many.

 Tip: Normally, the field you use to link tables has the same name in both tables, but it doesn't have to. You can use differently named fields to link two tables as long as they're the same data type and, if they're Number fields, their FieldSize is set to the same value. Regardless of their names, the two fields must contain the same information (like spy ID numbers); otherwise, there's no way for·the link to work.

2. **Click the checkbox labeled Enforce Referential Integrity to turn it on.**

   As discussed in the box on page 138, enforcing referential integrity prevents you from accidentally deleting linked records.

3. **Click Create.**

   Access creates the link between Spies and EquipmentIssued. See Figure 4-7 for the result.

This link includes only records from Spies and EquipmentIssued that have matching values in the SpyID field. This type of link is called an inner join, and it's what Access automatically creates unless you tell it otherwise. See the box on page 140 for the full story.

Integrity in Relationships

Integrity is just as important in database relationships as it is in real life. In the SpiesAndStuff database, the Enforce Referential Integrity checkbox for the link between the Spies table and the EquipmentIssued table is turned *on* (see Figures 4-6 and 4-7). In Access, the purpose of integrity is to avoid *orphaned* records— that is, a record whose primary key doesn't match anything in a related table. With this feature turned on, Access won't let you edit or delete primary key fields, no matter how hard you hit those keys.

If you choose *not* to enforce referential integrity, the database lets you, for example, delete a spy's record in the Spies table while the spy still has linked equipment records in the EquipmentIssued table. The orphaned equipment records refer to a spy record that no longer exists. You can turn off referential integrity if you're making rampant changes in your database and want to edit all the primary keys, but you'll have a lot of work reestablishing the relationships later.

4. **Drag the EquipmentID field from the SpyEquipment table onto the EquipmentID field of the EquipmentIssued table. In the dialog box, turn on Enforce Referential Integrity, and then click Create.**

   Access creates a one-to-many relationship (link) between the SpyEquipment table and the EquipmentIssued table.

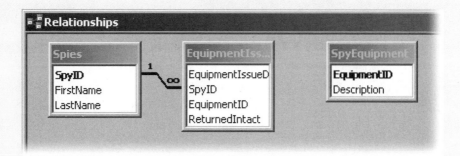

Figure 4-7. The Spies table has a one-to-many relationship (link) with the Equipment-Issued table. If you don't turn on referential integrity, the link line won't show the 1 and infinity symbols. However, the link is still one-to-many and works the same way.

You've just created all the relationships you need to make this database work. In the next section, you'll learn how to go back and remove or edit these links as your database grows and evolves.

Modifying or Deleting Relationships

You may need to change or delete a relationship if you made a mistake in setting its properties or simply created the wrong relationship. Fortunately, relationships in Access (just as in life, sadly enough) aren't set in stone. You can change them or delete them at any time:

▶ To change a relationship, in the Relationships window, double-click its link line. Access displays the Edit Relationships dialog box. Make any changes you want, and then click OK to close the dialog box.

▶ To delete a relationship, in the Relationships window, click its link line. Press the Delete key and then click Yes. Access deletes the relationship.

Tip: If the Show Table dialog box is visible, you must close it before Access will let you click anything in the Relationships window.

In addition to deleting relationships, you can remove an entire *table* from the Relationships window by deleting any links it has with other tables, and then clicking the table and pressing Delete.

Printing Relationships

If your database has lots of relationships, you may want to print a diagram of the relationships so you can study and analyze them when you're away from your computer. Seeing the big picture on paper can help you figure out where additional links should be made or how you should modify your database design.

Make sure that your printer is turned on and ready to print. With the Relationships window open, choose File → Print Relationships. Access displays a print preview of the relationships diagram.

Choose File → Print, and then click OK to make Access print the relationships diagram. Close the Print Preview window when you're done.

Using Subdatasheets to View Related Items

One of the reasons Access is so flexible is that it lets you create subdatasheets to link tables together in multiple ways. Subdatasheets are also what let you create forms within forms (see the box on page 143). Are you ready for the really good news about subdatasheets? Here's what you have to do to create them: Nothing. Nada. Nichts. Rien.

After you've set up a relationship between two tables, Access automatically adds a subdatasheet of the "many" table to the datasheet of the "one" table. A subdatasheet is simply a datasheet nested within a datasheet, which specifically shows information related or linked to the original datasheet. Just like Datasheet view in Chapter 3, a subdatasheet gets is own Subdatasheet view.

Here's how to see the subdatasheets that Access has created in the SpiesAndStuff_End database:

1. **On the Database window's Objects bar, click Tables, and then double-click the Spies table.**

   Access displays the datasheet for the Spies table. Notice that there's a + sign at the left end of each row in the datasheet.

2. **Click the + sign for spy #6, Alger Friss.**

   Access displays a subdatasheet that shows all the equipment issued to Mr. Friss. The + sign turns into a - sign.

3. **Click the + sign for spy #2, Lolle Woll.**

Access displays the subdatasheet for Fraulein Woll (see Figure 4-8). You can keep clicking + signs to open up any number of subdatasheets at once. (Your monitor may get a bit crowded, though.)

To close a subdatasheet, click its - sign.

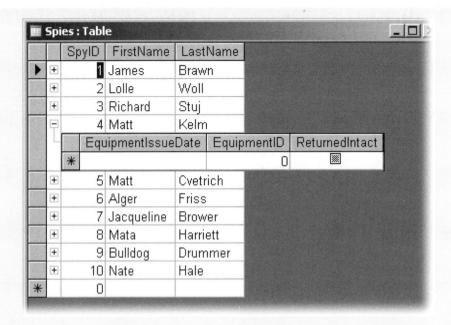

Figure 4-8. The subdatasheets show all the records from a linked table that have the same values in the link field as the selected records in the main table. If the linked table has no records that match a record in the main table, Access still displays the subdatasheet, but it's empty.

Close the datasheet window when you're done.

Forms Within Forms

Now that you know how to create the relationships that tie information located in different tables together, you can use those relationships to create forms way beyond anything a flat database ever dreamed of. The most common type of relationship between database tables is called one-to-many, which, as defined earlier, means that unique information from one table (the one) may relate to multiple records contained in another table (the many).

Suppose you have a customer database in which you have three tables. The first table holds the customer's name and address, the second lists details for each order number, and the third specifies the products available for ordering. And you've created a one-to-many link from the Customers table to the Orders table.

Rather than setting up two forms and moving back and forth between them to enter the customer information and the order details, you can create a *hierarchical* form that takes advantage of the links between the tables. It takes a little longer to set up, but data entry becomes much, much faster and easier. Less error-prone, too.

A hierarchical form is actually a composite: a main form combined with one or more subforms. The main form lets you type the customer's name and address laid out in a columnar format, and an embedded datasheet-style subform lets you key in the items for the customer's order.

Best of all, the Form Wizard (page 144) lets you set up the main form and the subform at the same time and decides for you which details go in each form. The wizard also adjusts the layout to make sure all these details fit together on a single data-entry screen. Finally, the wizard lets you select information from two different tables (or queries). All you have to do is run the wizard *after* you've set up all the appropriate tables and relationships.

Creating Subforms

You can create subforms when you want to view a record in a form with all its linked records in another table—and even add records to the linked table at the same time. Creating subforms isn't as effortless as creating subdatasheets, but it's still pretty easy. After you've linked tables, you can create forms that draw fields from both tables. If the tables have a one-to-many relationship, the form displays information from the "many" side of the relationship in a subform.

By way of example, you can create a form with an embedded subform in the SpiesAndStuff_Start database you've been using in this chapter. By combining fields from the Spies table (the "one" table) and the EquipmentIssued table (the "many" table), this hierarchical form lets you enter a new spy *and* issue the new recruit some equipment—all on one convenient screen. (See the box on page 143 for the inside scoop on hierarchical forms.)

1. **On the Database window's Objects bar, click Forms, and then double-click "Create form by using wizard."**

   Access displays the first Form Wizard screen (see Figure 4-9).

2. **From the Tables/Queries list box, choose Table: Spies, and then click the double right arrow button to move all the fields into the Selected Fields list.**

   You've just added all the fields in the Spies table to your new form. You also need a couple of fields from the EquipmentIssued table.

3. **From the Tables/Queries list box, choose Table: EquipmentIssued. In the Available Fields list, double-click EquipmentIssueDate and EquipmentID.**

   Access moves the fields into the Selected Fields list.

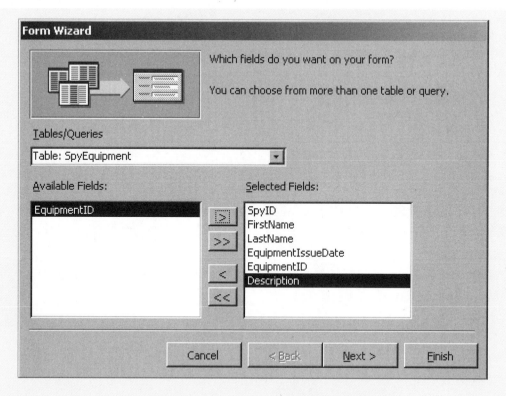

Figure 4-9. When your database includes linked tables, the first Form Wizard screen lets you choose fields from more than one of the linked tables to include on your form.

4. **From the Tables/Queries list box, choose Table: SpyEquipment. In the Available Fields list, double-click Description, and then click Next.**

Access moves the Description field into the Selected Fields list, and then displays the second Form Wizard screen (see Figure 4-10).

Tip: The second Form Wizard screen lets you choose whether you want linked-table data to appear in a subform or a linked form. A subform shows information in an area on the main form. If you choose a linked form, a button appears on the main form and, when clicked, opens the linked form in a separate small window.

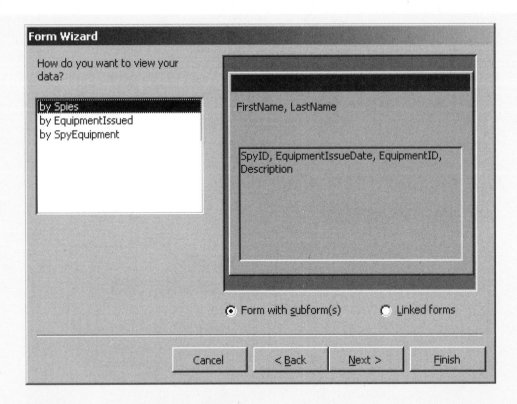

Figure 4-10. When you choose fields from more than one table, the second Form Wizard screen lets you choose which table's information to use for the main form and which table's information to put in the subform.

5. **Because you want Spies table data to appear on the main part of the form, leave "by Spies" selected under "How do you want to view your data?," and then click Next.**

Access displays the third Form Wizard screen (see Figure 4-11). It asks how you want the subform to display your data.

6. **Click the Datasheet radio button, and then click Next.**

Access displays the fourth Form Wizard screen, in which you select a form style.

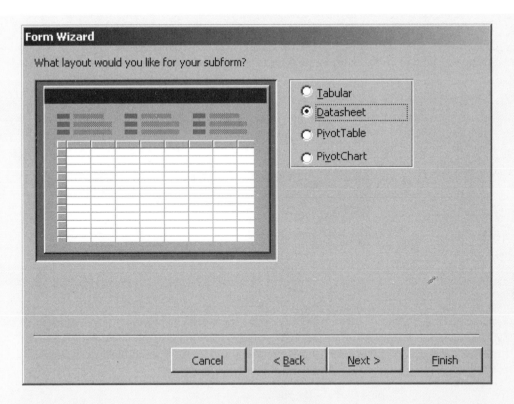

Figure 4-11. When your database includes linked tables, the third Form Wizard dialog box lets you choose how to display linked-table data in the subform. Datasheet is generally your best choice, because of its compact size. But you can click the others to see a preview.

7. **Click Blends, and then click Next.**

   Access displays the last Form Wizard dialog box. This dialog box lets you name both your form and its subform (or linked form). You can then view the form or open it in the Design window for modification.

8. **The form and subform names that Access suggests are fine, so click Finish.**

   Access displays your new form (see Figure 4-12). In the main form, it shows information for the first Spies table record, spy #1 James Brawn. In the subform, it shows all spy equipment issued to Mr. Brawn.

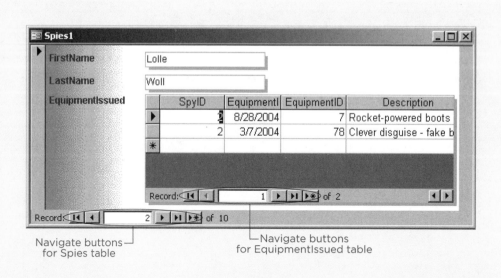

Navigate buttons for Spies table

Navigate buttons for EquipmentIssued table

Figure 4-12. Using the Form Wizard, you can create a form with an embedded subform. You can use the navigation buttons at the bottom of the main form window to move from record to record in the Spies table. You can use the navigation buttons at the bottom of the *subform* window to move from record to record in the EquipmentIssued table.

Adding Information in a Subform

Subforms are more than just a good way to look at linked-table data; they're also a good way to enter it. Suppose that as you're looking at the form for James Brawn, he comes in and asks for a clever disguise. You consider giving him a chiffon evening dress, but it's not *that* kind of spy agency, so you decide to give him item #87, a Santa costume. To add information to James Brawn's subform:

1. **At the bottom of the subform window, click New Record (the right arrow pointing at an asterisk).**

   Access moves the insertion point to the first column of a blank row at the bottom of the subform datasheet.

2. **In the EquipmentIssueDate field, type *3/21/2005*, and then press Tab.**

   Access moves the insertion point into the EquipmentID column of the subform's datasheet.

   Are you ready to see something cool?

3. **For the equipment ID, type *87*, and then press Tab.**

   Based on the equipment ID you entered, Access automatically looks up the equipment description in the SpyEquipment table and fills in the next column.

4. **At the bottom of the subform window, click First Record (the left arrow pointing at a vertical line).**

   Access saves your new record in the linked table and moves the insertion point back to the first equipment record for James Brawn.

Close the Form window when you're done. Notice that the Database window lists not only the main form you created, but also its subform.

PART TWO: ORGANIZING INFORMATION

CHAPTER 5:
SORTING AND FILTERING

▶ **Sorting Database Records**

▶ **Finding Data with Filters**

WHEN YOUR ACCESS DATABASE contains just a small number of records, it's a breeze to go in, look up information, and find what you need. Once that database swells to a few hundred or a few thousand records, you've got a different situation on your hands. For instance, you may need to put the records in order so you can scan them more easily, or quickly locate everyone who lives in Chicago and whose account balance is more than 30 days past due.

In this chapter, you'll see how you can use tools like sorting and filtering to view your records and the information they contain. You'll also learn how to use sorting when you want to put all your records in order, like alphabetical order, and use filtering, alone or in combination with sorting, to pull out only the records that meet a particular condition.

Sorting Database Records

In the days before computers, the word *sorting* implied drudgery like putting a huge pile of index cards in alphabetical order. Access can do such tasks much faster than you can by hand (and without spilling coffee on a single card), so you can save your organization skills for planning your database.

Before you do anything more than enter the first few records into the database, Access performs an automatic sort based on the primary key field. Look at any of the databases you've worked with so far, and you'll see that the records are automatically sorted so they're in ascending order based on whatever number or other information is in the designated primary key field (like an account number, for example).

Yet at any time you choose, like when you're going in to look for specific records, you can re-sort your records using a field that's different from the primary key, or even using multiple fields. In other words, you can sort your database by last name instead of by account number, or sort by city *and* by last name *within* each city.

Beyond choosing one or more different fields on which to sort, you can choose between two basic ways your sort can run. An *ascending* sort lists results lowest to highest, oldest to newest, beginning of alphabet to end, and so on. Access's automatic primary key field sort is ascending. A *descending* sort starts with the last number or letter and works backward.

To work through the sorting exercises in this chapter, download its folder from the "Missing CD" page (page 10). Open the OurClub database, and then open the Members table.

Ascending Sorts

Sorts performed in an ascending order are the most common. Typically, you see these sorts when you're listing names alphabetically, dates chronologically, or account numbers sequentially. The most basic example of ascending sorts is when you want to display customer or employee last names starting with A and working forward to the Xs, Ys, and Zs, or you want to list a group's members from youngest to oldest.

Say you've got the job of putting together a database for a club where you've started entering records. The result may look a lot like what you see in the Members table you've got open. You get a call from somebody in the club asking if there are any members in Colchester, Vermont. Since you aren't sure of the answer, it's time to look at your database. While your records are already sorted in Datasheet view by the primary key, the members' city of residence isn't your primary key.

You'll select the City field and do an ascending sort, since Colchester starts with a letter near the beginning of the alphabet. To do so, right-click the column labeled City. From the shortcut menu (Figure 5-1), choose Sort Ascending. Next, you can scroll down to look for any entries in Colchester, and then look in the State column to be sure the Colchester listed is indeed in Vermont (VT).

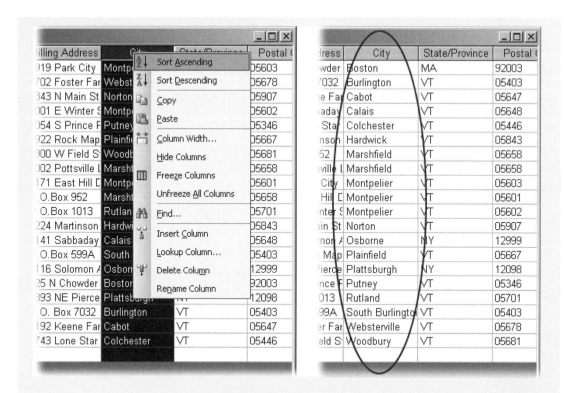

Figure 5-1. When you right-click a column in Datasheet view, you can choose a number of options, including Sort Ascending. You can also click the Sort Ascending toolbar button, or choose Records → Sort → Sort Ascending.

With your sort complete, you can tell your caller that, sure enough, you've got someone in Colchester, and then you can provide any desired details. Later in this chapter, as you begin to apply filters to your database records, you'll discover a way to narrow your search so that you see *only* the Colchester records. (Or specifically Colchester, Vermont, so you don't accidentally cause a *very* expensive long-distance phone call to the oldest town in Great Britain.)

Tip: You can also perform a sort from Form view. But you can sort only on one field at a time, unlike multiple fields in Datasheet view.

Descending Sorts

Descending sorts work almost identically to ascending ones, except the results are reversed. Suppose you've entered about 20 records, but now you're wondering whether you've already entered a certain name. The member's name, you remember, is Kit VanHorn. In this case, you want to re-sort your records based on last name, and since the last name falls near the end of the alphabet, a descending sort is the fastest way to check.

To do so, perform the same steps you did for ascending sorts, with a slight twist: In the Members table, right-click the MembersLastName column, and then click Sort Descending. (Again, you're free to click the Sort Descending toolbar button, or choose Records → Sort Descending.) Now scan down from the first record (for Wilkes) and you see that, yes, somebody did already enter the record for Ms. VanHorn.

Sorting on Multiple Fields

Since you've already sorted based on a single field, remember you're not limited to a one-field sort (unless you're using Form view, as previously mentioned). For example, when you sort your database by city, as in the Colchester example, there's always the chance that you'll have members located in cities of the same name in two or more different states. So you may want to sort by both the City and State fields to be sure all entries for Colchester, Vermont, are grouped together. When you scan your list, you can easily make sure you've got the right Colchester.

A sort by City and State fields is a common example for more reasons than that one. Access is a bit fussy about multiple field sorts. When you click to select columns for sorting, the program wants the two fields to be adjacent to each other.

Fortunately, the OurClub database, like most of its kind, has the City and State fields side-by-side.

To do this two-field sort, start by clicking the City column. Next, press the Shift key while simultaneously clicking the State/Province column. On the toolbar, with both columns highlighted, click Sort Ascending. As it turns out, there's just one Colchester listed, and it's indeed in Vermont (Figure 5-2).

Middle Initial	MemberLastNar	Billing Address	City	State/Province	Postal Code	Cou
	Wilkes	1919 Park City	Montpelier	VT	05603	US
E	Barnes	4702 Foster Far	Websterville	VT	05678	US
	Jurkowitz	2343 N Main St	Norton	VT	05907	US
A.	Early	3001 E Winter §	Montpelier	VT	05602	US
	Oshawara	7054 S Prince F	Putney	VT	05346	US
M	Polow	8922 Rock Map	Plainfield	VT	05667	US
R	Rabinoquin	4900 W Field S	Woodbury	VT	05681	US
G	Bailey	5002 Pottsville L	Marshfield	VT	05658	US
	Signorelli	6171 East Hill [	Montpelier	VT	05601	US
A	Donal	P.O.Box 952	Marshfield	VT	05658	US
H	Gomez	P.O.Box 1013	Rutland	VT	05701	US
F	Kalsebbe	5224 Martinson	Hardwick	VT	05843	US
K	Beyersdorf	2141 Sabbaday	Calais	VT	05648	US
	Roblik	P.O.Box 599A	South Burlingtoı	VT	05403	US
W	Disraelis	1116 Solomon /	Osborne	NY	12999	US
D	Kingsley	625 N Chowder	Boston	MA	92003	US
C	Sayers	5893 NE Pierce	Plattsburgh	NY	12098	US
	Meyers-Abdul	P.O. Box 7032	Burlington	VT	05403	US
	VanHorn	9192 Keene Fai	Cabot	VT	05647	US

Figure 5-2. While you can select two or more columns side by side, notice that you can't click a column that isn't adjacent. Unlike, say, Microsoft Excel, Access doesn't let you choose nonconsecutive rows or columns by Ctrl-clicking.

Tip: When you sort on multiple fields as described in this section, Access sorts all the values in the fields in the same order, either ascending or descending. If you need to mix it up and sort by ascending for one field but by descending for another, that's a job for Advanced Filter/Sort (page 178).

Moving fields for multiple choice sorts

You're not limited to sorting on just two fields; you can pick three or four if the situation (or a gigantic database) demands it. In fact, you're not even limited to fields located in adjacent columns. In this section, you'll learn how to do a switcheroo, moving columns around—albeit temporarily.

The trick is to move the fields you want to sort so that they *do* sit side-by-side, and then sort. Don't worry—you haven't changed anything permanently. When you go to close the table or the entire database, Access asks if you want to save the change you made to the field order (see Figure 5-3). All you have to do is click No, and Access saves the table and its fields using the original order, discarding your temporary swap, along with your sort, in the virtual bit stream.

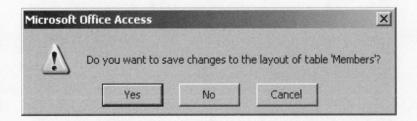

Figure 5-3. Changes you make through sorting or field swapping are as permanent or temporary as you like. Click Yes to accept the changes you've made, and Access writes your modifications into the design. Click No to make Access forget the whole thing.

To get a feel for how to rearrange your fields, look at the Members table in the OurClub database. Assume you want to group your records by the City field as well as by Area Code and Phone Number, since you want to call your fellow club members in Montpelier to let them know of an emergency meeting. While the Area Code and Phone Number are right next to one another in the table, the City field isn't adjacent. Here's how to temporarily shift the City field so it sits next to the other two:

1. **At the top of the City column, click *and hold* the mouse button on the field selector.**

   Keep holding all the way through the next step.

2. **Drag the column across to just before the Area Code field column. Release the mouse button.**

   The column drops into place—*automagically!* Now that all three desired fields are side-by-side, you want to arrange them in the order by which you want Access to sort.

3. **Click the City column, and then press Shift while you click the Area Code and Phone Number fields.**

   If you did it right, all three columns together are highlighted.

4. **From the toolbar, click Sort Ascending.**

   You can also choose Records → Sort Ascending, or right-click any one of the highlighted columns, and then choose Sort Ascending from the shortcut menu.

   Access sorts the records first by city, then by area code within each city, and finally by phone number, nice and neat, as shown in Figure 5-4.

Now you can look for those records listed for Montpelier, and you've got the phone numbers right there to begin dialing.

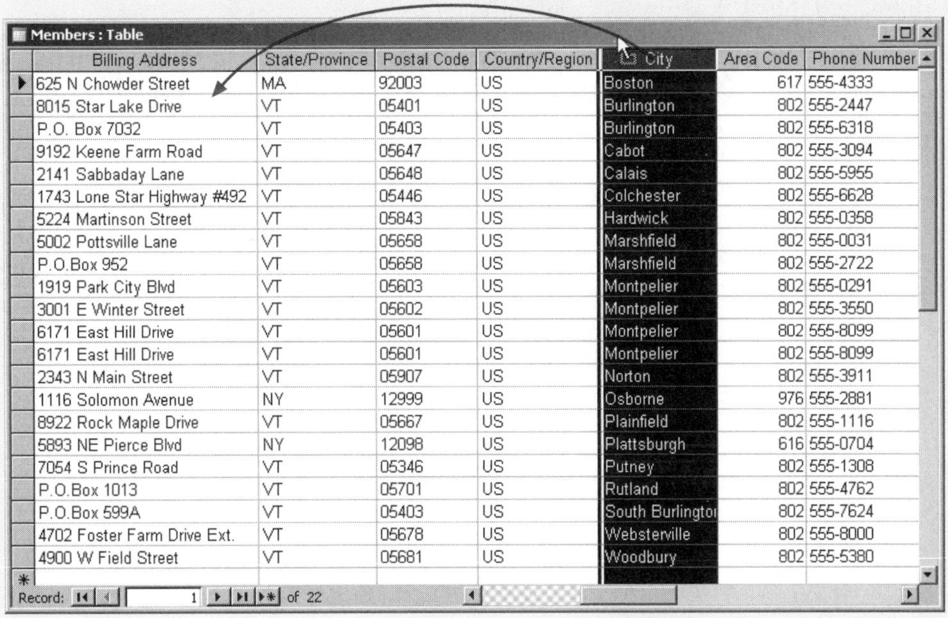

Billing Address	State/Province	Postal Code	Country/Region	City	Area Code	Phone Number
625 N Chowder Street	MA	92003	US	Boston	617	555-4333
8015 Star Lake Drive	VT	05401	US	Burlington	802	555-2447
P.O. Box 7032	VT	05403	US	Burlington	802	555-6318
9192 Keene Farm Road	VT	05647	US	Cabot	802	555-3094
2141 Sabbaday Lane	VT	05648	US	Calais	802	555-5955
1743 Lone Star Highway #492	VT	05446	US	Colchester	802	555-6628
5224 Martinson Street	VT	05843	US	Hardwick	802	555-0358
5002 Pottsville Lane	VT	05658	US	Marshfield	802	555-0031
P.O.Box 952	VT	05658	US	Marshfield	802	555-2722
1919 Park City Blvd	VT	05603	US	Montpelier	802	555-0291
3001 E Winter Street	VT	05602	US	Montpelier	802	555-3550
6171 East Hill Drive	VT	05601	US	Montpelier	802	555-8099
6171 East Hill Drive	VT	05601	US	Montpelier	802	555-8099
2343 N Main Street	VT	05907	US	Norton	802	555-3911
1116 Solomon Avenue	NY	12999	US	Osborne	976	555-2881
8922 Rock Maple Drive	VT	05667	US	Plainfield	802	555-1116
5893 NE Pierce Blvd	NY	12098	US	Plattsburgh	616	555-0704
7054 S Prince Road	VT	05346	US	Putney	802	555-1308
P.O.Box 1013	VT	05701	US	Rutland	802	555-4762
P.O.Box 599A	VT	05403	US	South Burlington	802	555-7624
4702 Foster Farm Drive Ext.	VT	05678	US	Websterville	802	555-8000
4900 W Field Street	VT	05681	US	Woodbury	802	555-5380

Record: 1 of 22

Figure 5-4. After you've dragged the field into place and performed your sort, you can either abandon the changes, as mentioned earlier in this section, or simply drag the entire column back to its original position, repeating steps 1 and 2 on the previous page, but returning the City field back just before State/Province.

Saving Your Sorting Choice

Don't close that OurClub database! At least, don't do so before you understand how Access automatically saves your work. Otherwise, you may make your changes permanent when you don't want them to be.

Now, Access is kind. As you start to close the table or database, Access asks you if you want to save the changes you've made to layout or design. You saw this kindness in action back in Figure 5-3. Normally, when you perform a sort (or apply the filters you'll work with in the next section), you won't want those changes to stick around. So click No when Access asks. If you do want to preserve the arrangement, simply click Yes instead.

To be doubly sure to return everything in the database to its original order after a sort or filter, choose Records → Remove Filter/Sort (Figure 5-5), or right-click the datasheet, and then, from the shortcut menu, select Remove Filter/Sort. You can use this command any time before you close a table or perform any other work.

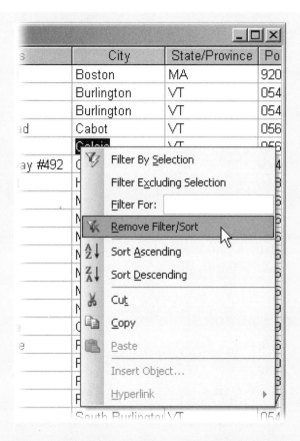

Figure 5-5. To undo a sort, right-click any field in a sorted column and click Remove Filter/Sort. Even if you don't take this step, you can always back out by choosing No when Access prompts you to save your changes when you close the window.

Finding Data with Filters

Filters are nothing unique to databases. For example, sunglass lenses selectively filter out UV rays while letting in enough light for your eyes to see. In a better analogy, your brain is constantly filtering out irrelevant details so you can focus on the more important things.

Filters in a database do the same critical job: They let you sweep aside (or temporarily hide) everything that isn't exactly what you're looking for at that particular moment. Like sorting, you use filters to look up information quickly, typically without keeping those filters in place any longer than it takes to find what you need.

When you sort as described in the previous section, you can still *see* all records; you've just grouped them by field so you can look through them in a more organized fashion. The larger your database becomes, the more often you'll use filters so you can focus on key records while ignoring the hundreds or thousands of irrelevant ones. As well as reducing potentially distracting onscreen information, filters become almost mandatory when you're seeking all records that match a particular condition (like "all customers in Michigan" or "all new accounts generated in the last 30 days"), you're working with a database of more than 50 records, or you just need an answer fast.

Furthermore, you can use sorting and filtering in any combination. For example, after you filter for all Michigan customers, you can immediately use the steps on page 154 to sort those Michigan records by city, Zip code, last name, or whatever. If you've already sorted records by state, say, and then realize you want to print a list of only the Michigan customers, you can filter by state right then and there: Access hides all but the Michigan records. You can go on to sort *those* records by last name, and then filter by email address…you get the idea.

Access offers a number of ways to filter. Here they are in ascending order of speed and complexity:

▶ The **Filter for** shortcut menu option lets you quickly create a filter when you right-click that field (as shown in Figure 5-6).

▶ In **Filter by Selection** and **Filter Excluding Selection**, you highlight a particular bit of text or a field in your database (like a city name or a last name), and then create a filter based on whatever you've chosen. Filter by Selection looks for other records that match that text or field, while Filter Excluding Selection looks for all records that *do not* contain the chosen text or field.

▶ **Filter by Form** lets you set a filter by typing the text or values you want to search by.

▶ Use **Advanced Filter/Sort** when you want to do a more sophisticated search through your records, where you can filter on multiple fields at once or set up a specific sort order.

Note: Besides combining filters with sorting, you can use them as part of the query process that you'll learn in the next chapter. Basically, filters and queries often do very similar jobs. They both look up records based on criteria you set. Among other differences, though, Access automatically saves queries (as part of the Table view) when you save your database.

Because filters are pretty simple and straightforward to use and are usually pretty fast to perform, you can use them any time you're looking for results that target only specific files. (If you're working with an underpowered computer or a humongous database, you may find filtering goes as slow as molasses. See the box on page 166 for advice.)

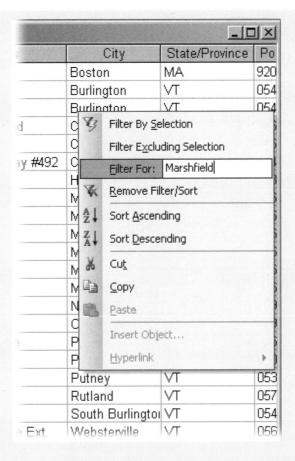

Figure 5-6. Access's filtering feature satisfies the need for instant gratification. Just right-click a field, select "Filter for...", type the text or value you want to filter for (in this case, Marshfield), and then press Enter. Access applies your filter and displays the results.

How to save or discard a filter

Access makes it a cinch to discard a filter or reapply it at any time you choose. The button you use to do this is actually a toggle switch: Click once and you remove, click again and you reapply the same filter again.

When Bad PCs Happen to Good People

Microsoft Office 2003 and Access can run on any system that runs Windows XP and has at least 128 MB of RAM memory installed. But that amount of memory is really just the minimum you want to use.

If your computer happens to have only 128 MB and you notice that, when working with especially large database files, your system seems about as responsive as mud in January, consider upgrading your memory to at least 256 MB. If you aren't sure how much memory you have, try this:

1. Open Control Panel.
2. Double-click the System icon.
3. Select the General tab and read what's listed near the bottom of the screen. You'll see your operating system version and PC's CPU speed listed there along with the amount of installed memory.

Also look at how much available hard disk space you have. Windows grabs a certain amount of hard disk space to convert into what's called *virtual memory* to use to move files onto and off your desktop. Too little hard disk space cuts down on available virtual memory and can slow down applications like Access.

Here's how you check your hard disk space:

1. Open My Computer.
2. Right-click your hard disk, and then choose Properties. A properties window appears, showing a graphical representation of your hard disk's level of fullness (pink is unused; blue is used).

Both PC memory and hard disks tend to be fairly inexpensive right now—certainly compared with even just a few years ago. But if money is tight, you can increase the level of Access's performance if you try to keep other applications closed while you're working with very large database files.

Whether you do a quick filter-on-the-fly, as you saw in Figure 5-6, or you use one of the more involved methods described in the next section, the way to remove—or rerun—a filter is exactly the same:

1. **On the Access toolbar, click the Remove Filter button (Figure 5-7) once to remove the applied filter.**

   You see your entire record set again. Click a second time to reapply the same filter.

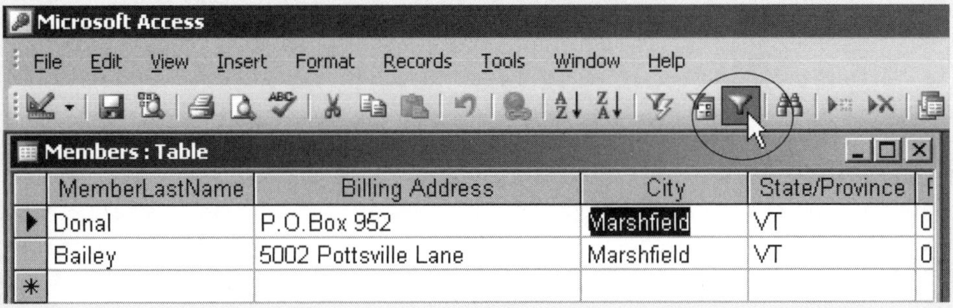

Figure 5-7. The Remove Filter button toggles between removing and reapplying your most recent filter.

It's almost as easy to save a filter to either your Datasheet or Form view so Access will keep track of the filter for your next session. You can save filters of all the types listed on page 164. Normally, Access assumes you want to save the filter unless you tell it otherwise. But if you want to be sure, there's an extra step you can take: Some people prefer to save the filter on the spot because then they don't have to worry about paying attention to the "Do you want to save…" dialog box when they close the file. (Everyone is guilty of occasionally pressing the Return key without bothering to read this warning.)

To save a filter, do any of the following:

▶ From the Access toolbar, click Save.

▶ Choose File → Save.

- Press Ctrl+S on your keyboard.

- Close the datasheet or form and, when prompted, click Yes to save the changes to your work.

 Tip: If you've saved a filter with your database when you close it, you can reapply the filter whenever you want by clicking the Remove Filter/Apply Filter icon from the Access toolbar.

Filtering by Selection: The Quick Way to Filter

After the "Filter for" method described on page 164, Filtering by Selection is the fastest and most common filter, where you're looking for all records that contain the text or value you want to find. To work through the following examples, have the OurClub database open to the Members table.

Adding a filter by selection

Using your fictional membership database, assume you want to limit your view of records to only those that contain the Vermont area code of 802. This filter will eliminate from your immediate view any members who are located out of state (Vermont is small and has a single area code).

1. **On the first listed record, right-click the Area Code field, and then, from the shortcut menu, choose Filter by Selection.**

   Alternatively, on Access's toolbar (the one with the little lightning bolt to its right), you can click the Filter by Selection icon.

You've just applied a filter based on the exact contacts of the area code field you clicked—802, in this example. All out-of-state records go away, so you see only those records with the 802 area code. You're not just limited to matching an entire field, though. You can filter just by a letter (or number) or two rather than the entire entry.

Say you want to look up all records where the member's last name starts with the first two letters "Ba," since you're not sure of the exact spelling of a name.

1. **On the toolbar, click the Remove Filter button.**

   You're doing a completely different filter this time, so you need to get all your records back first.

2. **In the MemberLastName column, locate the first field listed there that begins with "Ba." Highlight just those two letters, and then click the Filter by Selection toolbar button.**

   Simple as that. Figure 5-8 shows the results for all records where the last name starts with the letters "Ba."

Figure 5-8. You can also highlight characters other than the first or first few in an entry. For example, if you know you're looking for a member whose last name ends in "dorf," locate a record with "dorf" anywhere in the name. Next, highlight those four letters, and then click Filter by Selection from the toolbar (circled).

Tip: Don't scan laboriously down a long list of records when you're trying to find just part of a name. Instead, point to the field you want to use, like MemberLastName in this case, and then choose Edit → Find. Next, from the Find window, as shown in Figure 5-9, type in the characters you want to locate. Click Find Next to locate the first occurrence of your match in the listing.

Filtering by exclusion

Filter by Exclusion is sort of the mirror opposite of what you just did with Filtering by Selection. Here, you're excluding specifically all records that contain whatever text or value you select as the filter—for example, when you want to automatically filter out any records in the 05658 Zip code.

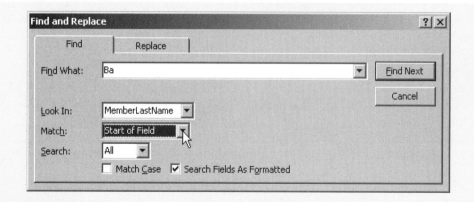

Figure 5-9. Note that the Find box lets you select a different field and match the Whole Field, Start of Field, or Any Part of Field. For this purpose, you would select Start of Field for the best result, since the last name starts with "Ba."

To try Filter by Exclusion in the Members table in the OurClub database, do the following:

1. **Choose Edit → Find.**

   A small Find box appears.

2. **Type *05658*, and then click Find Next.**

   Access takes you to the first record where this text appears.

3. **Right-click the field, and then select Filter by Exclusion (or, on the Access toolbar, click the icon of the same name).**

   You now see a display of records where the sole Zip code you excluded is nowhere to be found.

Using these same steps, you can select just some of the characters in the field as a point of exclusion rather than the entire field entry.

Filtering by Form

Performing a Filter by Form is just as simple as the others you've seen. And although the title has "form" in it, you can apply this filter in Datasheet view as well as Form view. The difference with this approach is that you open up a form that reflects the field IDs you've already established in your database. In it you can type conditions to match from one or more of those fields. This approach may be a more comfortable fit because it shows you the field IDs and lets you choose which one to filter by.

Adding filter criteria

To gain some experience using this type of filter in the OurClub database, open the Members table. Remember, you can work from Datasheet view, and this method works even if you haven't designed a form yet for data entry.

In this tutorial, you'll filter your records by which members are *not* currently serving on any of your organization's committees. Glance at the Members Table, and you see that the Committee Member field has just two types of responses listed: Y for yes and N for no. You want to look for the Ns so you can tap someone who currently isn't part of *any* committee to get more involved.

1. **In the Members table, from the Access toolbar, click Filter by Form. (Or right-click the table, and then choose Filter by Form.)**

   A form showing your field IDs appears. Click inside the Committee Member field.

2. **At the right of the field, a drop-down arrow appears. Click it, and then choose N (for no). Next, on the toolbar, click Apply Filter (Figure 5-10).**

   Access shows you the results for just those members without any committee assignment listed.

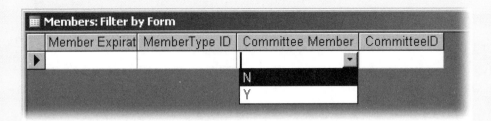

Figure 5-10. In the Filter by Form window, when you click in a field, you can choose from a drop-down menu of entries from all records. Filter by Form is a great choice when a field only has a few possible entries, like the one shown here. For fields like City that could have hundreds of different entries, Filter by Selection or Filter by Input are better options.

Filtering with Wildcards, Operators, and Expressions

So far, you've applied filters using specific entries like a full Zip code. But you're not always going to have that luxury. At times, you'll need to narrow—or expand—your search results to capture those records that match just *part* of an entry, like the first few numbers of a Zip code, the first letters of a name, or the last word in a product name. Other times, you may want to find records that meet two or more criteria you set based on two or more fields in your database.

Understanding the Variables at Work

When a bunch of different people (or one inconsistent one) are adding or editing records in your database, you have to be more creative with your filter conditions. For example, if you filter by *Robert* in the MemberFirst-Name field, and some slacker has been abbreviating the name as *Rob't*, then your Filter by Selection skips right over the records you need. This problem will crop up when you do queries as well, since queries typically utilize a filter to locate specific data.

Here are some ways you can make sure your filters catch all instances of what you're looking for:

* Select only part of a word to filter on (*Rob*, for example), to account for abbreviations.

* Use the Edit → Find command, as described on page 170, to try to pick up all variations on an entry. (You can then edit them for consistency—or make that slacker person do it.)

* Use wildcards in your filters (page 174) to allow for variations in spelling or format.

* Use input masks or lookups (page 80) where applicable to encourage consistent data entry.

Access also lets you set conditions for data entry, so that anyone entering information has to either type out the word in full or abbreviate it. If you're curious, you can read about this technique on page 329.

Access lets you use tools like *wildcards* (characters that stand in for text or other values) and *operators* (special words for combining search terms, like AND and OR). Access also understands *expressions,* where you use mathematical equations to look for either exact matches (like all members who joined on 1/1/2000) or comparisons (all members who joined on or after 1/1/2000 or whose membership type meets one condition or another).

All these examples show more complex types of filters and can be used with either the Filter by Form or Advanced Filter/Sort methods. They often aren't a good match for simpler searches using other types like Filter by Selection or Filter by Input.

 Tip: The use of wildcards, operators, and expressions can get pretty sophisticated and complex. In fact, the more you come to know about them, the more power you'll have in trying to find the exact records you want the first time, without having to go through a lot of chaff. While you've got the basics here, consider picking up a copy of *Access 2003 Personal Trainer* by CustomGuide (O'Reilly).

Using wildcards in filters

Wildcards give you both power and flexibility in performing searches and filters because you don't have to enter the full text or value. Instead, you can use a wildcard (like "*") to replace any letters that may be different. For example, you know that all the records you want to see have a Zip code that begins with the numbers 056. If you apply the filter 056*, the asterisk wildcard tells Access to look for every occurrence where the first three numbers of the Zip code match but the rest don't.

The most useful wildcards are:

▶ An asterisk (*) can substitute for any character or characters, as in the Zip code example above.

▶ A question mark (?) steps in for a single character only. Say you're looking for all records where the last name is Greenburg—or is it Greenberg? You would apply the filter like this: *Greenb?rg.*

▶ A pound sign (#) pinch-hits strictly for numerical characters, one-for-one. So if you want to search for all records where you have a four-digit street number in the Address field, use #### as the filter.

▶ A hyphen (-) acts as a range wildcard, and you can use it in combination with other ones. Say you want to look for all members with a last name between letters l and p. The filter would look like this: *[l-p]*.*

Using operators in filters

AND and OR are examples of operators, known in math circles as *logical* operators, because that's how they analyze the records you apply them to. In a filter, AND tells Access to look for records that meet *both* conditions on either side of it. For example, you can use AND to filter all members located in Vermont who *also* serve on a committee. With OR, you tell Access to look for records that meet either the first condition or second condition, but not both. For example you'd use OR to filter members residing in *either* Marshfield or Calais, Vermont.

Access also recognizes the following operators:

▶ > and < find records either greater than or less than a value; for example, greater than 10 or before M in the alphabet.

▶ = finds records *equal to* a value.

▶ **BETWEEN** finds records between two values; for instance, between 1/1/2005 and 6/30/2005.

▶ **LIKE** finds matches according to a pattern (like the 056* example on the previous page), with the help of wildcards.

Using expressions in filters

Expression is a technical term that simply refers to something you've been using throughout this chapter: It's whatever term you're looking for, like some text or a value. When you filter by a specific Zip code like "05681," the Zip code is the expression. Likewise, if you're looking for the name "Gomez," that name is the expression for the filter.

This expression then becomes the thing Access looks to match records against. That expression can be:

▶ **Exact** (like the name Gomez)

▶ **Nearly exact,** as when you replace some text or values with a wildcard (the 056* rather than 05681, for example)

▸ **Comparative,** where you're looking for records that meet or exceed a specific requirement like "all members who joined on or after January 1, 2000"

 Note: Chapter 6, where you dive into queries into your database, goes into more detail about constructing expressions and setting conditions for your filters.

Applying and removing filters

Now that you've got some theory under your belt, it's time to put a filter to work in a database. Returning to the OurClub database, perhaps you have a situation where you want to find all members named Gomez, as mentioned before. But from practical experience, you know that some people spell their name "Gomes."

To see it in action, apply a filter to the Members table with a wildcard that catches both Gomez and Gomes:

1. **In the Access toolbar, click Filter by Form.**

   Access opens an empty form, ready for you to type filter criteria.

2. **Click in the MemberLastName field and type *Gome** (*Gome?* would also work), and then press Return.**

   You've just typed an expression. As you can see in Figure 5-11, Access adds an operator (LIKE) to the MemberLastName field, because you've set a wildcard to get all matches close to (that is, *like*) this name.

3. **Click Apply Filter to see all the records that are like the expression you typed.**

   If you typed the expression correctly, you'll see records with the name spelled both ways. Click Remove Filter when you're ready to read on.

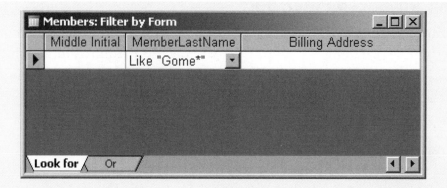

Figure 5-11. One of the best ways to learn the full range of what you can do with expressions and operators in Access is to simply try examples like this, and then check what the field displays after you press Return. This example tries to find members whose last names start with the letters "Gome".

Next, try something that builds on your success. This time, you'll locate someone with a name *like* Gomez who *also* lives in Vermont (some members live in Massachusetts and New York as well, but you're not looking for those).

Follow the steps on the previous page, with the following adjustments:

▸ After clearing the previous filter, click Filter by Form.

▸ In the MemberLastName field, type *Gome** or *Gome?*, and then press Return.

▸ In the State/Province field, type *VT* (or click the drop-down arrow and choose VT).

Then apply the filter.

Access uses the LIKE operator to look for records where the last name starts with "Gome," and the AND operator to filter only those who live in the state of Vermont. In the next section, you'll dive in a bit deeper as you go through what's involved with an Advanced Filter/Sort.

Using Advanced Filter/Sort

The Advanced Filter/Sort is your filter of choice when you need to do more than rather simple searching. This type gives you the tools required to set multiple conditions on multiple fields for what the filter searches through in your database. You've already gotten a little taste of this filtering method in the previous section, but you're about to get a heaping, yet still digestible, helping.

The Advanced Filter/Sort feature does one thing differently from the filters you've seen so far: It lets you both sort individual fields and select search criteria—all from the same window. No extra steps required. Instead, you see a targeted filter window in which you specify your requirements.

 Note: You can apply this type of filter in either Datasheet or Form view. It's also fairly flexible; you can apply it to tables, queries, or forms.

Adding filter criteria

Turning once more to the OurClub database, you'll give this tougher filter a trial run. Again, you'll use the Members table, but here you're going to filter based on three different fields: You want to see member records for all those who reside in Montpelier, Vermont, who *aren't* already on club committees.

To do this:

1. **Choose Records → Filter → Advanced Filter/Sort.**

   The filter design window appears. In the upper-left area of the window, you see a list of your table's fields.

2. **Point to City and drag it down into the first Field box in the QBE (Query by Example) Grid at the bottom of the window.**

   Figure 5-12 shows the drill.

3. **On the QBE grid, click the Sort field, and then select Sort Ascending.**

   You've just told Access to display its result in alphabetical order (A–Z).

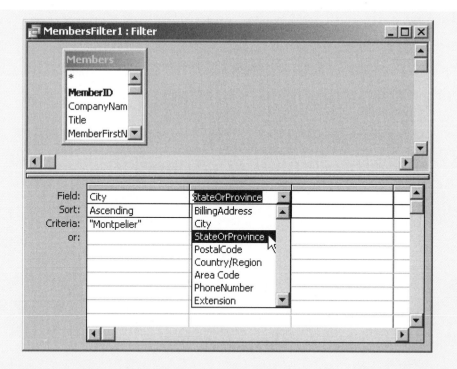

Figure 5-12. To select fields, you can also click the Field box, and, from the dropdown list box, choose the field you want If you make a mistake and drag or select the wrong field, just click inside the box, and then press the Delete key.

4. **In the Criteria box, type** *Montpelier.*

   You've just set one criteria. You want Access to show you only records whose city is Montpelier.

5. **Return to the field list at the top left of the window, select StateOrProvince, and then drag this down into the next available Field window so it sits side-by-side with "Montpelier." In the Criteria box, type** *VT.*

   Adding the StateOrProvince field makes the query more specific. You're only interested in members from Montpelier, *Vermont.*

6. **Go once more to the field list and drag Committee Member into the next open Field box. In the Criteria box, type *N* (for "no").**

   "No" means you're looking for folks *not* serving on committees. Your finished filter grid should look like that in Figure 5-13.

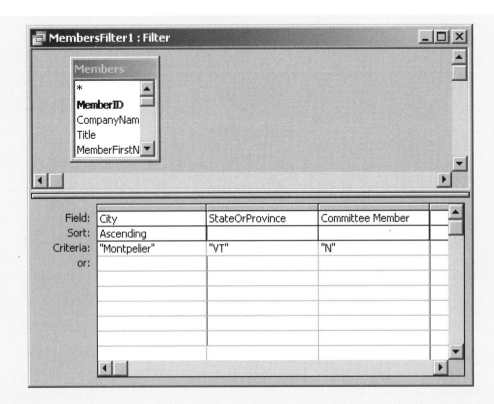

Figure 5-13. Not all filter fields require you to set a sort order. By default, ascending order is applied when Access sorts your records for viewing. Note, too, that when expressions are entered, Access automatically applies quotation marks around them.

Now it's time to apply the filter and do the sort. Because your database is so small, you'll get results instantaneously.

Applying and removing Filter/Sort

With your Advanced Filter/Sort criteria all set up, go ahead and apply the filter and its associated sort: In the toolbar, click Apply Filter. After you've done that, you'll see your results, which show just a single member in Montpelier who doesn't serve on a committee. When you're done and ready to remove the filter, click the Remove Filter toolbar icon.

POWER USERS' CLINIC

Saving Advanced Filter/Sort as a Query

Database filters are useful on their own, but they become even more powerful as part of a query, as you'll see in the next chapter. Either way, here's how to save a filter as a query.

While the Advanced Filter/Sort design window is still open (Figure 5-13), follow these steps:

1. From the Access toolbar, click Save as Query (or choose File → Save as Query, or right-click within the upper pane of the filter design window, and then select Save as Query).

2. Type a name for the query, like *Montpelier Committee Possibilities*.

3. Click OK.

With this filter/sort now saved, you can go back and run it any time you need. Every time you reopen your database, you'll see it right there on the list with your forms and tables and other queries, ready to select.

Best of all, you'll never have to go through all *that* work again—whether or not you end up using this filter in a query.

CHAPTER 6:
FINDING DATA WITH QUERIES

▶ Types of Queries

▶ Setting Query Properties

▶ Creating Queries with the Query Wizard

▶ Saving, Deleting, and Printing Queries

IF ALL YOU NEED TO DO is keep track of a bit of information and go back and look at those details again later, you don't need a database. A plain old spreadsheet program like Microsoft Excel, which lets you set up lists that work much like a simple database, can do most of the sorting and filtering tricks you learned in the previous chapter.

But you're not in Excel anymore. In Access, you can sift and scrutinize your information with much more power and flexibility. The key is *queries*—a database feature that uses a question-and-answer model to let you be very specific about what information you want to see and how you want to see it. Queries also let you make very selective changes to that information without having to change records individually.

For example, through careful crafting of queries, you can:

▶ Include or exclude specific rows and/or columns from a table.

▶ Combine tables (for example, if two tables in your database happen to contain all the essential ingredients you need, you can force the query to act like there's just one table that combines the information contained in both tables).

▶ Use the same table more than once in the same query.

▶ Sort rows.

▶ Collapse groups of rows to temporarily hide the contents of those rows from view.

Remember the club membership database you worked with in Chapter 5? In the Members table, you had one field that listed each person's membership expiration date. One thing you can do with a query, for example, is to look for all members whose registration expires next month (based on the date entered in that specific field) and come up with a printed reminder for them that it's time to renew their membership by sending in that check. That's a relatively easy query, and it takes a lot of the work off clerical staff (paid or volunteer) that would normally have to go digging through individual records to pull together a list. (You'll learn exactly how to do this query later in this chapter.)

How Queries Differ from Filters

Back in Chapter 5, you learned that filters do a bang-up job isolating your records to just those that meet certain criteria you set. And indeed, filters usually play a key role in developing and running queries to get the information you're seeking. Yet you may have noticed one limitation: A filter's results always show you the *entire* record for each match, even if all you really need to see are the details in a few fields of each record. There lies a chief difference between using a filter and using a query because a query gives you results that show *only* certain relevant fields from a record.

That's an important distinction when many different people have access to a database, and you don't want every single one of those people to be able to pull out more confidential or sensitive details. Or say you're the manager for a dentist's office and you want to be able to send reminders to patients when they're due for their regular check-up. You can create a query that pulls out only that relevant information and places it in a master file that you can use with a desktop

publishing program like Microsoft Publisher, where you can generate a spiffy-looking postcard. When it comes time to print the postcards, your Access query results can add the required information on the postcards and do everything but take the cards to the post office.

Unlike a filter, a query isn't limited to one table at a time. If you've got needed information stored in more than one table, which is typically the case with a well-designed database, only a query can get the results you need.

Finally, a query can create new calculated fields and automatically summarize and group your data. Suppose you need to check all accounts to find out which ones still owe you money more than 30 days after the first billing. If you use a filter alone, you can pull up all delinquent accounts and review them, but then you're going to have to summarize the aggregate information manually. A well-crafted query, though, can tell you instantly how many accounts are delinquent, how much each owes, and the total amount outstanding for all delinquent accounts.

Types of Queries

Access gives you the ability to *run*—that, is perform—a broad range of different query types. Choosing the right query can make all the difference in getting useful results, including the ability to check for and remove pesky duplicate records, update records automatically, or do something far more advanced, like calculate numbers or other values stored in your fields so you can get totals and subtotals, figure percentages, and more.

Select Query

The most commonly used type of query is called a *Select query*. It's also the type most similar to the filters you worked with in Chapter 5. A Select query gives you a fair amount of flexibility and capability, including ways to:

▶ Choose which fields you want to display and which you want to hide.

▶ Create new calculated fields (like when you want to total up all your accounts that are overdue in payment).

▶ Run a query that involves more than one table in your database.

▶ Summarize and group your data.

When you go through the Query Wizard in the next section, you'll get some hands-on experience developing and running a Select query a few different ways.

Crosstab Query

Presentation of data can play a huge role in how well people can understand what they're seeing. A *Crosstab query* offers an extremely effective way to do that by putting your record information into a totally different format from the standard look of Access records like you see in Table view. By pooling together important fields and displaying them in the rows-and-columns standard of a spreadsheet, you eliminate all the interposing, irrelevant fields so you can better assess and understand what the information means. This is true with sales figures, financial account information, and much more.

Parameter Query

You've no doubt heard the word *parameter* many times before. With queries, parameters serve as a placeholder of sorts of actual values. Using parameters, you can set up an extremely flexible query where you've got all the detail work established in advance, and then, using a parameter, substitute in different values all the time so you can look at the same information in a variety of different ways.

Suppose you have a database that lists every product your company offers, including the sales performance of each. Rather than set up a completely different query for each product (which involves way too much time for a busy person like you), you can create one query where the parameter acts as the placeholder in which you can swap in a different product name or category each time so that you can review the sales for each separately.

Action Query

Action queries get their name because they *do* something to the records in your database. The something they do can vary from inserting new records to deleting or purging old ones, or performing an update to a number of different records at once. Updating your records using an Action query can save serious time over going into individual records and making changes, one at a time.

Autolookup Query

Autolookup queries are typically used to save you both time and keystrokes. Lookup refers to Access's ability to automatically search and locate information you've previously entered elsewhere.

For example, you may have one table, named Employees, with each person's company ID number (used for personnel and payroll), as well as his name, home address, phone number, and pager number. As you create a new table in which you're listing emergency, off-hours contact details for each employee who pulls special on-call duty, you can specify that Access look up the previously entered fields, like cell phone and pager numbers, and automatically enter them into the appropriate fields of the record for you—so you don't have to type this information all over again.

The beauty of this type of query, besides saving you the time of repeat entries, is that if you later have to go back and update record information (say, if an employee changes her cell phone or pager number), all occurrences in all tables automatically get updated as well.

SQL Query

The chief difference between a *SQL query* and any of the other types of queries you can perform on your database is that SQL queries contain SQL statements or expressions. Because these kinds of queries use SQL, the native language your database understands, they're some of the most powerful and helpful queries you can run. With them, you can do just about anything to your data, including insert, delete, amend, and automatically update records. (For a quick intro to SQL, see the box on page 189.)

As a newcomer to Access and databases, you probably don't know much SQL. That's OK, because Access—at least, to some degree—guides you through the process of picking what you want to look for or do, and then transforms it into SQL just as if you had a tiny U.N. interpreter sitting there on your desktop. All this activity happens pretty much out of your sight.

 Tip: Want to become a little better acquainted with the SQL underlying your query? If so, Access offers a special SQL view to let you do that. To see this view, open your query in either Datasheet or Design view, and then, to the right of the Query view button, click the drop-down arrow (which opens a list box). Next, select SQL view. You may also choose View → SQL view rather than going through the list box.

What's a Dynaset? What's SQL?

When you're working with databases and queries—and the term *query* is used universally throughout database and database management and is not a term limited to Microsoft Access—you'll frequently hear words like *dynaset*, *recordset*, and *SQL*.

A recordset refers to any collection of records that you can treat as a single unit or object, usually because those records offer very similar information. A dynaset, by comparison, is a special type of recordset that can be dynamically updated—dynamic meaning they're updated without manual editing or other individual interaction by you as the records keeper.

Queries (and the filters you worked with in Chapter 5) usually result in recordsets; some offer up dynasets. Yet some of the queries discussed in this chapter can generate recordsets in which one, more, or all fields cannot be updated.

SQL is short for Structured Query Language. It's the native tongue of databases and the people who work with and manage them. SQL makes it possible for you to communicate with your database in more important ways than simply entering and looking up individual records. It's part of the great power of database management and runs throughout much of what you read in this chapter and beyond. Knowing a little SQL can help immeasurably in harnessing your data's power to inform and keep your business—whatever that is—humming along. (A great reference if you want to learn more about SQL is *Using Access 2003* by Roger Jennings [Que].)

Setting Query Properties

Query properties define and control both the appearance and the overall behavior of that query and the results you get from it. As you create a query, either on your own or through a wizard, certain properties are automatically assigned to the query.

You can view these properties at any time—that is, after you've created a query. You have three different options for opening a query's Properties window to see them:

▶ Click Properties.

▶ Choose View → Properties.

▶ Right-click anywhere in the Design window (except in the field lists themselves), and then select Properties from the shortcut menu.

Figure 6-1 shows the query properties for one of the queries you'll create in this chapter when you make and run a Find Unmatched query.

 Tip: Don't understand what a specific property listed means? Point your mouse to that property and press F1 from your keyboard. A description pops up telling you more.

Creating Queries with the Query Wizard

Just like elsewhere in Access, wizards help guide you through constructing queries that get you the results you want the first time and every time thereafter. In this section, you'll see when it's right to go with the wizard versus crafting your own from scratch in the Query Design window covered in the next chapter. Try your very first query using one of Access's ultra-helpful and wise wizards.

Using these wizards is a great way to get a feel for queries if you've never done one before. Access's query wizards include:

▶ **Simple Query Wizard.** This great starter wizard lets you run the most common database queries, called Select queries, discussed on page 186.

▶ **Crosstab Query Wizard.** Use this wizard to step through a specialized query that lets you organize information obtained from a table or query. You'll read more about this type later in this chapter.

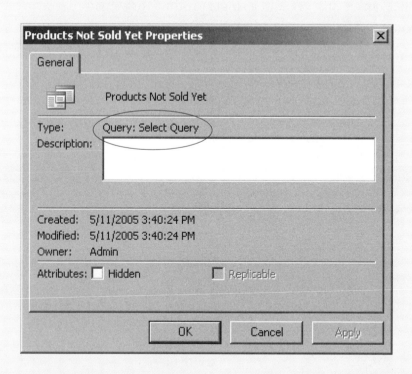

Figure 6-1. This properties window is very basic. Some query properties get far more advanced than this and display a great deal more information. Here, you can see that this properties window is based on a Select type of query (circled).

▶ **Find Duplicates Query Wizard.** Can you guess what this wizard does? Sure you can—and you'll find it highly useful, too, for spot-checking your database for duplicate entries, the bane of any database manager.

▶ **Find Unmatched Query Wizard.** Does your database have records in one table that have absolutely no matches in another table? This wizard creates a query to help you identify them, and can and should be used when you need to either see possible problems or locate records that need action. For example, perhaps you have a sales database where you're trying to determine which of your sales reps hasn't yet sold a single product, or a customer who has set up an account but has never ordered.

Yet you can also move beyond these wizards to design your own queries or modify ones you've started through the multiple wizards using the Query Design window covered in the next chapter. The more complex your query becomes, the more likely it is that you'll need to create it from scratch rather than going through one of the prepackaged query wizards.

Testing Your Database Design with Queries

Some wise database teachers say one of the very best ways to make sure your database is designed to get the results you need is to test it with a query. They recommend, in fact, running a query soon after you've begun entering information. The idea here is to keep from getting too far along in the process before you discover that the way you've set things up just isn't going to work when it comes time to actually find information you've stored.

This trick makes a lot of sense when you stop to consider how much tougher it is to make essential changes—like the need to add an additional table or break an existing table into two or more separate ones—that may require you to go back and enter additional data for each record.

So consider taking what you learn in the next section and beyond and applying it by creating a simple query to test a database you may have just started on your own. If you can't get the results you need back from the database, then it's time to consider changing your database design.

Don't be afraid to try multiple queries, each created to get different bits of information out of your records. Using multiple queries reduces your chances of getting clobbered later on if you just assume everything's fine and dandy because the first, and probably fairly limited, query you try works great, but further testing shows bigger problems the first query didn't catch.

Creating a Simple Query

Easy and simple is good, so why not start off your relationship with queries by performing a very basic one? Download (page 10) and open the OurClub2 database. (Yes, it's the same one as you used in the previous chapter, but just like a real-life database, it's undergone some slight changes from the first attempt). Start with the OurClub2 database open in the main Database window, as shown in Figure 6-2.

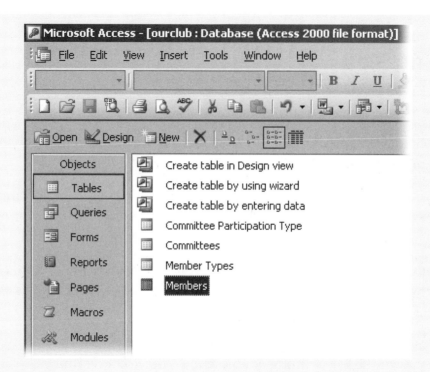

Figure 6-2. While the Database window always opens to the default view where the Tables option is selected, you're about to get a whole new view as you explore what's waiting for you when you select Queries from the left-hand Objects bar.

For this operation, you're going to use the Simple Query Wizard. Your first query will be super simple, and similar to what you've already mastered with filters: checking to see which of your members are located in Montpelier, Vermont. You want the first and last name of each of these members, along with the telephone number so you can call them, as needed.

Here's how to start:

1. **In the Objects bar, click Queries.**

   The Queries panel is where you start all new query work. It's also where, after you've created and saved queries, you can return to modify and run them.

2. **Double-click "Create query by using wizard."**

   The Simple Query Wizard opens.

3. **Click in the Tables/Queries list box (see Figure 6-3), and then choose Members.**

   In Access, you'll often see tables and queries grouped together in various windows. This setup makes sense because you run queries on tables, or on other queries, rather than on other types of objects like forms or reports.

4. **Under Available fields, select MemberFirstName, and press the single arrow button to add it to the currently empty list of chosen fields at the right.**

   The double arrow buttons let you select everything in the list at once, or, in the case of the left-pointing double arrows, deselect everything.

5. **Repeat Step 4 to add the MemberLastName field to the right-hand list until you have both fields selected, and then click Next.**

   Figure 6-4 shows exactly what these selections should look like to get the right result.

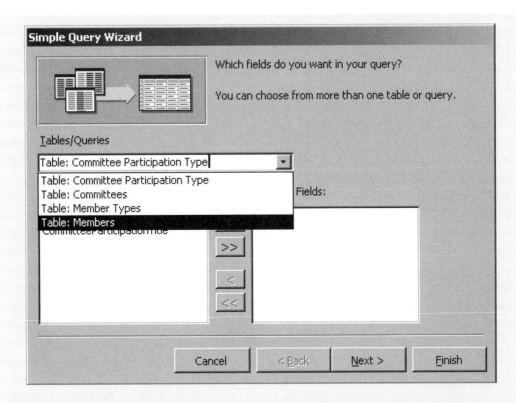

Figure 6-3. All the tables—and, if you've already created them, other queries— should be listed right there in the Tables/Queries list box. For a simple query, you're just choosing one table at a time.

6. **Choose Details from the next wizard screen, and then click Next.**

   When you choose Details, your results show every record that meets your query conditions. Your other option from this window is Summary. The Summary Options let you apply math functions like count or average (AVG) to a short, summary-style display of the records returned in the query.

   Next, the wizard asks you to name your query results.

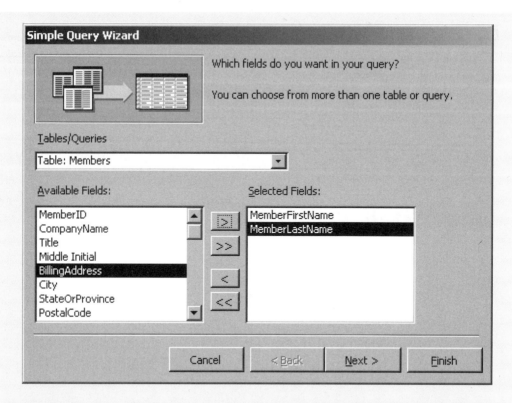

Figure 6-4. All the fields you've selected show up at the right side of the window, under Selected Fields. If you make a mistake and add a wrong field, just point to it on the right, and then click the left-hand single arrow to remove it from your list of selected fields.

7. **In the box at the top of the next wizard screen (see Figure 6-5), click to remove the text that's there, and then type:** *Montpelier VT Members.*

   Although you've just selected the fields to display, you haven't done anything yet to *limit* your results to just those members residing in Vermont's capitol city. You'll take care of that now using a filtering process. (However, you could also just click Finish now, and then go back later to modify the query design and rerun the query.)

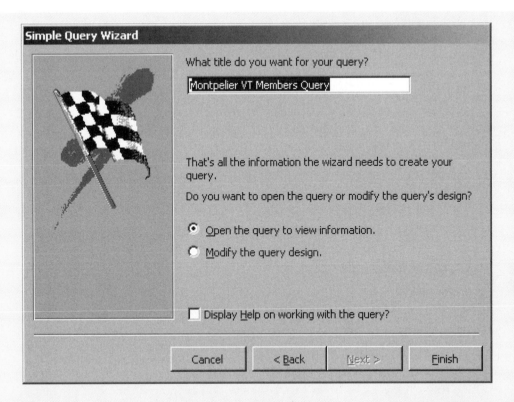

Figure 6-5. Give your query a short but uniquely descriptive name. Doing so helps you identify one query from another in case you end up with a long list of different queries or go a long time between running one.

8. **Turn on "Modify the query design," and** *then* **click Finish.**

If you select View rather than Modify, you can also go back at any time to make changes to the query design.

After you've wrapped up the wizard, the same type of window appears that you used to create filters in the last chapter (Figure 6-6). It now bears the prestigious title of Query Design window. You'll study and use this window in far more detail in Chapter 7. Here, the only criteria you need to set tells Access to limit the records returned to just those living in Montpelier, Vermont.

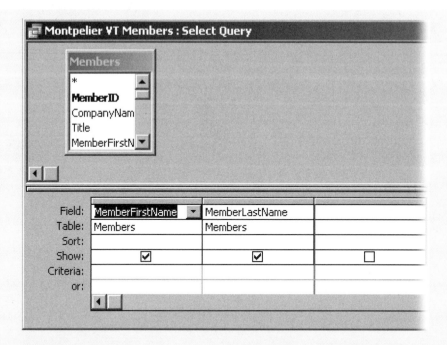

Figure 6-6. To learn far more about using the Query Design window, stay tuned for Chapter 7, where you'll work to create your own queries without the help of a wizard. Using this window rather than a wizard helps you accomplish some of the fancy moves and operations the wizards really aren't equipped to handle.

Here are the steps for applying a filter to the query for the city Montpelier.

1. **Click the first criteria field in the City column, and type *Montpelier*.**

   By setting this option, you're limiting records to only those where the city listed for the member is Vermont's capitol city.

2. **Under StateOrProvince, click the first criteria field, and then type *VT*.**

   Adding the state is a smart idea if there's any chance you have the same city name, or similar criteria, that could come up in a whole other state. In this case, you're working with a small database so you can get away with just dealing with a few extra records. But once you get into a sizeable database of hundreds or

thousands of records, you want to do everything possible to keep your work—
and results—sane and manageable.

3. **With your criteria now set to limit your record display, from the Access
toolbar, click Run (the red exclamation mark).**

You should see the Run icon on the toolbar whenever you're working with
Access in query mode. In fact, if you don't see that urgent-looking icon, it's a
sign you're not in query mode.

You can also choose Query → Run to start the query process and return your
results.

Immediately, the results from your query open up in a new window and, yes, as
you can see for yourself in Figure 6-7, you've got just those members from
Montpelier, Vermont listed. Nice work!

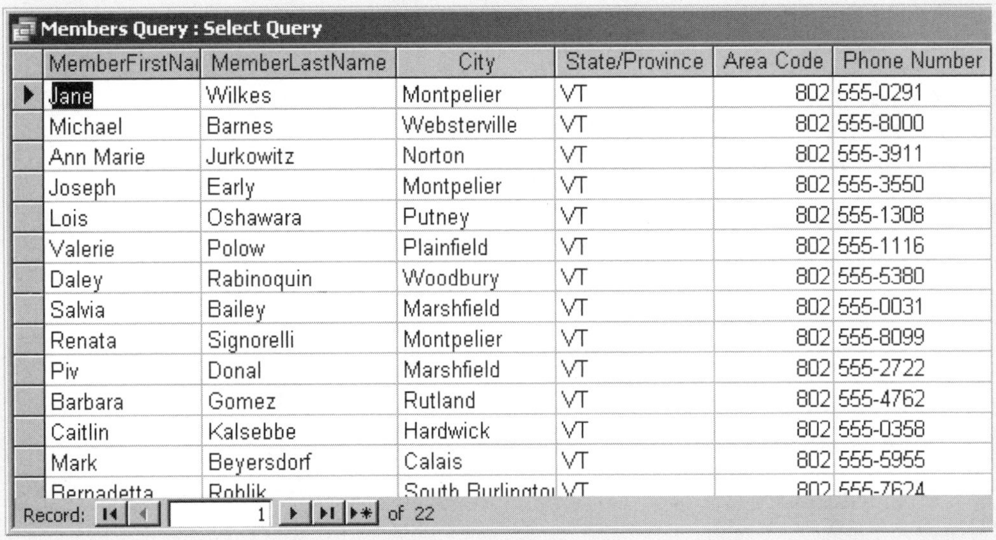

MemberFirstNar	MemberLastName	City	State/Province	Area Code	Phone Number
Jane	Wilkes	Montpelier	VT	802	555-0291
Michael	Barnes	Websterville	VT	802	555-8000
Ann Marie	Jurkowitz	Norton	VT	802	555-3911
Joseph	Early	Montpelier	VT	802	555-3550
Lois	Oshawara	Putney	VT	802	555-1308
Valerie	Polow	Plainfield	VT	802	555-1116
Daley	Rabinoquin	Woodbury	VT	802	555-5380
Salvia	Bailey	Marshfield	VT	802	555-0031
Renata	Signorelli	Montpelier	VT	802	555-8099
Piv	Donal	Marshfield	VT	802	555-2722
Barbara	Gomez	Rutland	VT	802	555-4762
Caitlin	Kalsebbe	Hardwick	VT	802	555-0358
Mark	Beyersdorf	Calais	VT	802	555-5955
Bernadetta	Roblik	South Burlingto	VT	802	555-7624

Members Query : Select Query
Record: 1 of 22

Figure 6-7. If you don't see the results you expect, then there's something wrong
with the way you framed the query, or there's a possibility your database design
needs work.

Northwind Database

Did you realize that Access includes a sample database with all the bells and whistles? Called the Northwind database, it's very professionally done, and it's a great tool to use both to experiment with creating queries and reports and to give you an example of what you can do as you get more skilled with Access. Later, when you reach the appendixes and learn about online help available for working with Access, you'll see that many of the Microsoft help articles refer to this sample in showing you how to do advanced operations with your own databases. Here, you're going to use Northwind, and the myriad information it contains, to create a specialized query.

Depending on how you installed Access, the sample database may or may not already be sitting on your hard disk. So have your Microsoft Access or Microsoft Office CD ready to pop into your CD or DVD drive in case Access has to go looking for the file. You'll see a message saying, "This feature is not currently installed; would you like to install it?" if the file isn't on your system already.

Creating a Crosstab Query

Crosstab queries begin a bit differently from the simple one you just created, because they take a different approach. They don't just filter and sort your data, they *summarize* it. Much like the summary reports you'll see in the next chapter, a crosstab query can add up, average, count, and group information so you can analyze and compare it much more easily. Unlike other queries, crosstab queries let you define rows as well as columns, which is what adds the extra summarizing power.

You'll use a different example file for this query, with good reason: Crosstab queries, at least the way your database may be set up, may not always be an easy fit for the wizard. Trying to force your information into the wizard to get the results you want can be an exercise in how much headache remedy you can consume without developing an ulcer. Fortunately, Access comes with a sample database that illustrates the concept perfectly. To open it, choose Help → Sample Databases → Northwind Sample Database. (If you see an error message, you probably didn't install the sample database. See the box on the previous page for more detail.) Click OK on the opening screen. When the Main Switchboard window opens, click DatabaseView.

 Note: If you don't get clean results when creating a Crosstab query in your own database with the wizard, then you can create a query from scratch using Design view. You can learn how to do that on page 220.

To start your query, open the Northwind database and go to the Queries panel in the Database window, as described on page 194. The database already contains some queries. You're going to add a new one that summarizes product sales by category.

1. **On the first Crosstab Wizard screen, select the Queries radio button (Figure 6-8). Then, in the Query list, click Sales by Category.**

   To calculate product sales by category, you need fields containing category, product name, and product sales. Fortunately, a query containing these fields already exists, so you've chosen it here. Click Next when you're done.

2. **Select the Category Name field, and then click the right arrow to add it to the Selected Fields list at right.**

   A crosstab query works much like a spreadsheet, performing calculations on rows and columns. In Access, the information in the rows and columns come from your fields. You've just told the wizard which field to use as the rows. As the preview shows, your query results will show each product category on its own row. The Crosstab Wizard calls this field the row heading. Click Next.

3. **In the list of remaining fields, select Product Name.**

   The preview shows that Product Name is the column heading. If your screen looks like Figure 6-9, you did it right. Click Next.

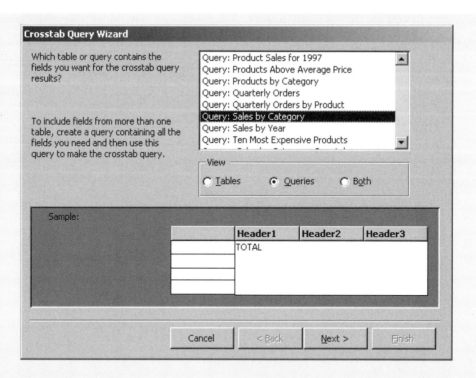

Figure 6-8. The Crosstab Wizard starts out by asking you to choose a table or query that contain the fields your query will filter and sort by. If you've already created a query containing all the fields you need, click the Queries radio button and choose it here.

Now the wizard needs to know what kind of calculation to perform for each category and product, and what field to get the numbers from.

4. **In the Fields list, click ProductSales. Then, in the Functions list, click Sum.**

   You can choose a number of common functions here, like the ones on page 245. You've chosen Sum here because you want the total sales of all products in each category. Click Next.

5. **On the final wizard screen, type a name for the Query, and then click Finish.**

   Access suggests *Sales by Category_Crosstab* because of the query you started out from.

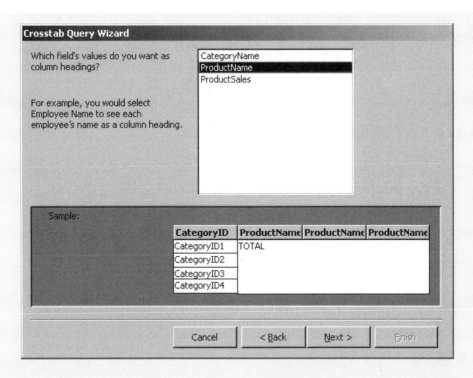

Figure 6-9. Once you've chosen row and column headings, the Crosstab Wizard shows a preview of the resulting arrangement. As shown here, you're going to do some kind of calculation based on products by category (represented by the word TOTAL in the middle of the box).

As you can see in Figure 6-10, this crosstab query shows the total sales in each category (in the Total Of Products column). As you scroll to the left, you see the sales broken down by individual product.

Using a Query to Check for Duplicate Records

Remember when you read that duplicates are the bane of any database manager? It's entirely too easy to create multiple copies of the same account, product, or even person. This problem comes up all the time when you enter records in chunks over a period of time or you have multiple people performing data entry.

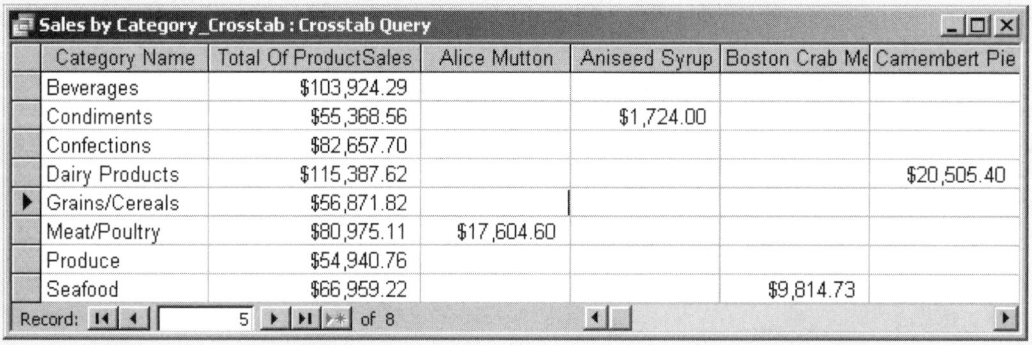

Category Name	Total Of ProductSales	Alice Mutton	Aniseed Syrup	Boston Crab Me	Camembert Pie
Beverages	$103,924.29				
Condiments	$55,368.56		$1,724.00		
Confections	$82,657.70				
Dairy Products	$115,387.62				$20,505.40
Grains/Cereals	$56,871.82				
Meat/Poultry	$80,975.11	$17,604.60			
Produce	$54,940.76				
Seafood	$66,959.22			$9,814.73	

Figure 6-10. A crosstab query looks much like a spreadsheet. Since you're using Access instead of, say, Excel to calculate these sales figures, the database always shows the most updated information every time you run the query. No retyping.

Duplicate records are more than just a mere inconvenience. For instance:

- You waste time when you enter the same information more than once.
- Duplicates take up space and, left unchecked, can make a large database into an unwieldy one.
- Worst of all, confusion can ensue when you update a record, but there's a duplicate hanging around that still contains the old information. Imagine a customer makes a payment on his account, and you record it in your database, but because there's a duplicate record for that customer that doesn't reflect the payment, the database sends him an annoying (and erroneous) collection notice.

Of course, with experience, you can use techniques like validation (page 329) to make Access check for and discourage duplicate entries. But even then, the possibility always exists that you'll end up with multiple records for the same John Smith guy, with slight variations in the name, like John Smith, Jon Smith, J.Q. Smith, and maybe even Jack Smith. You'll need a system you can use regularly to check for and remove duplicate entries. The query you're about to perform does just that. You can run it on a schedule (for example, once a day in a very busy and large database, or once a month for a personal system).

Access provides a wizard specifically for creating a query to look for duplicates. Once you've created a basic query, you can always go back and tweak it later, as necessary. This time, open the OurClub2 database, and then follow these steps to set up a duplicate checker.

1. **Open the Database window, and then in the Objects panel, click Queries. Click New, and then choose Find Duplicates Query Wizard. Click OK.**

   The Find Duplicates Query Wizard opens. Right off, you get to choose the table where you want to check for dupes.

2. **On the first wizard screen, select Members, and then click Next.**

   There's always the option of setting up a sophisticated query to check more than one table, or you can simply run the wizard again, choosing a different table each time. However, you'll find that certain types of tables are simply more apt to contain duplicates than others, and frequently these are the tables containing the greatest volume of records, like the Members table.

3. **On the next wizard screen, add the MemberFirstName and MemberLast-Name fields to the Selected Fields list at the right. Click Next.**

   First and last name fields for a table like this are likely suspects for duplicates. If you need help moving fields from the Available to the Selected field lists, review Figure 6-4.

 Tip: Any field that holds unique data—like a name, a phone number, an email address, or a street address—is a good candidate for duplicate checking.

4. **On the next screen, choose City in the Fields list, and then click the right-pointing single arrow to add it to Selected Fields (Figure 6-11). Click Next.**

   The fields you choose here are the ones you want Access to display. In addition to City, you could add additional fields, like State/Province or Phone Number. A good rule to use is that you want as few fields as possible while still making it easy to identify a dupe from a legitimate similar entry.

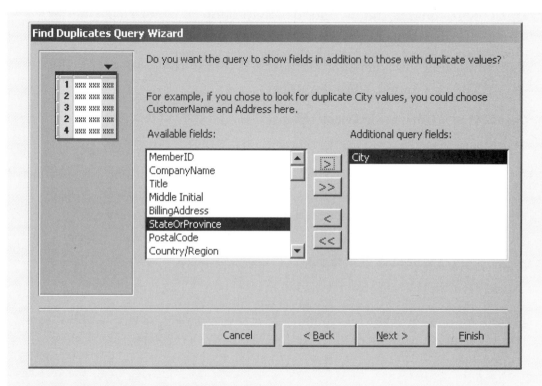

Figure 6-11. You can always change your mind and remove a selected field while in this screen. Highlight the entry to remove it in the right-hand Selected List, and then click the left-pointing single arrow to send it back to the left-hand list.

5. **On the final wizard screen, Access suggests a name for the query you've just created. Since "Find duplicates for Members" is good, leave it in place, and then, with "View the results automatically" selected below, click Finish.**

Showing its usual initiative, Access runs the new query and displays its results.

Look at your query results. You see that you indeed have two records from the Members table that appear to be identical, as shown in Figure 6-12. You have two Renata Signorellis in Montpelier. Is one a duplicate?

Find duplicates for Members : Select Query		
MemberFirstName	MemberLastName	City
Renata	Signorelli	Montpelier
Renata	Signorelli	Montpelier

Figure 6-12. The query results window displays exactly what you designated in setting up the query in the wizard: the first and last name, as well as the city.

Actually, right now, the question of whether this is a true duplicate is hard to answer. You may have a case of two people with identical first and last name spellings in the same city, which isn't impossible even with less-than-common names like this one. If you know for sure one isn't a duplicate, you can just close your query results and be done with it. But suppose you can't say for sure, at least not yet. You have two options:

▶ Go into the Members table and look for these duplicates, perhaps by using a filter.

▶ Modify the query to add a little more identifying information to help you establish whether you have a duplicate record.

Intrepid as ever, you decide to modify the query and run it again. First, close the query results window (by clicking its Close box, for example). Next, follow these steps to give your query an additional field to help decide whether you've found a true duplicate:

1. **If you've just gone through the Query Wizard as in the previous tutorial, the Database window probably shows the Queries panel. You're in the right place. In the Queries list, highlight "Find duplicates in Members"; in the toolbar, click the Design button.**

   The Design window opens, where you modify your query. The box at the top left lists the fields in the data source (Members table). Among these fields, an identical street address or phone number would help you differentiate a duplicate from a similar-but-not-same entry.

2. **Try adding the Phone Number field. Drag Phone Number from the Tables box into the first blank field listing below.**

   The result should look like Figure 6-13. Since you need to be able to find these records in the main table, and the table could contain many different records, it may help to add the unique Member ID number to the query as well. You'll add that next.

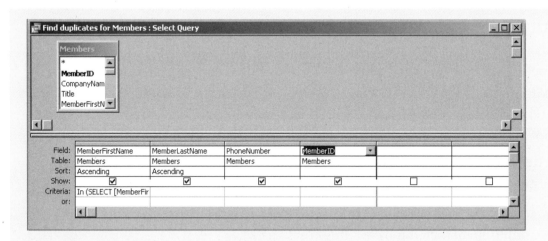

Figure 6-13. You can save your query changes before you close the Design window. To save, press Ctrl+S from your keyboard or select File → Save.

3. **Select Member ID from the Table list and drag it down to the next blank Field box to the right of the Phone Number you just added.**

   In the Sort row below each field, Access shows automatically ascending order. You're free to change the sort order, but in this case, ascending works just fine.

4. **With your changes made, close the Design view window.**

   As soon as you click the Close box, Access prompts you to save changes to the query you've just modified.

5. **Click Yes because you want those changes to stay.**

   Without wasting a moment, Access automatically runs the query again and displays the results in a fresh window.

You now get to see the results from your modified query. Since the phone numbers for both matching records are identical, you can assume that you've got a true-blue duplicate. Your next task is to delete one of them. Look at the Member ID field for the second occurrence of this member's name. The field identifies the duplicate record as #22. That's the one you want to find and kill in your Members table.

 Warning: At this point, you'll be tempted to right-click the second occurrence of Ms. Signorelli's record and choose Delete Record. However, this action deletes only the record from your query results and not from the Members table, which doesn't help much.

After committing the ID number to memory (or sticky note), close the query results window. Then follow these steps to get rid of record #22 once and for all:

1. **In the Database window's Objects panel, click Tables. From the list of tables in your database, double-click the Members table.**

   This step opens your Members table where you actually need to remove the duplicate record.

2. **Scroll down to Member ID 22. Click in the border to the left of the Member ID field to highlight the entire record.**

   You can also use the Edit → Find command to locate Member ID 22. That method may be faster than scrolling in a large database.

3. **With the record selected, right-click and select Delete Record (Figure 6-14).**

   Access asks you to confirm that you want to remove this record permanently. Click Yes to do the deed.

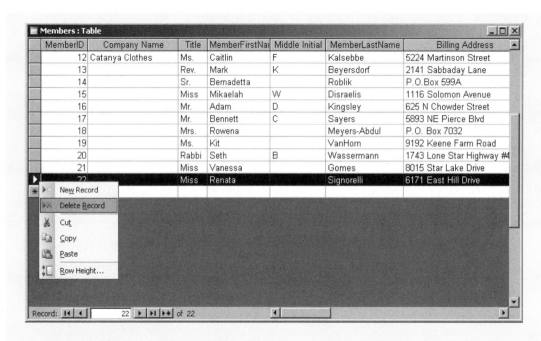

Figure 6-14. To remove the selected record, press the Delete key on your keyboard or choose Edit → Delete Record.

Creating a Find Unmatched Query

A special type of query you can run in Access 2003, and one already set up for you in wizard form, is the Find Unmatched Query. The job of this query type is to identify records that appear in one table but have no match in a related table where you may otherwise expect to see matching records. You may want to use this type of query in situations like the following:

▶ You want to identify which customers haven't placed orders yet with your company this year by comparing the records in your Customers table to the records of orders placed this year in your Orders table.

▶ You need to see which people in your Sales Rep table have made no product sales—because you can't find any matching records for them in the Sales Rep Orders Placed table.

▶ You must determine which employees contained in your employees table have a large backlog of unused vacation or sick time that must be used up or will be lost by the end of the year by comparing your Employees table against a table that tracks who has applied for or taken a vacation or sick leave over the past year.

The key ingredient in all these situations is that the two tables are related to each other. For example, you would normally expect to find orders placed by a customer or sales rep, or vacation time requested by an employee. Understanding this, you can then apply this type of query to other situations where you have a similar situation.

For this exercise, you get to do some role-playing. You'll be one of the many folks who make a living by placing goods up for auction on a site like eBay. You've set up a simple database in which two of your tables keep track of the items you're selling (Products) and of the customers who win the bid to purchase them (Auction Customers). But you've been so busy that you're no longer sure how many of the goodies you're offering online remain unsold. So you're going to run a Find Unmatched query to determine just that.

Download (page 10), open the eBayProducts database, and proceed as follows:

1. **Make sure you're in the Database window. In the Objects panel, click Queries.**

   Since it's your first time doing this type of query, you want to start with the wizard, although the Queries panel shows you lots of other tools as well.

2. **In the toolbar, click New. When the Query Wizard Options window opens, select Find Unmatched Query Wizard. Click OK.**

   The appropriate wizard opens so you can begin your work and, ultimately, get the information you need from your little database.

3. **On the first wizard screen, select Table: Products, and then click Next.**

   The Products table contains the records you want to see in your query results. This table holds a list of all products, sold and unsold, that you're auctioning online.

4. **On the next wizard screen, choose Tables: Auction Customers, and then click Next.**

   You've just told Access which table contains the related records, as shown in Figure 6-15. The Auction Customers table not only lists contact information for each of the buyers, but it also contains the Product ID field—also found in the Products table—to specify which product they purchased. As you learned in Chapter 4, Product ID is the common field that links these two different tables.

5. **On the next screen, select Product ID, and then click the double-arrowed button.**

   The double-arrowed button simply indicates that the same field exists in both tables. Next, you'll select the fields you want to display in your query results.

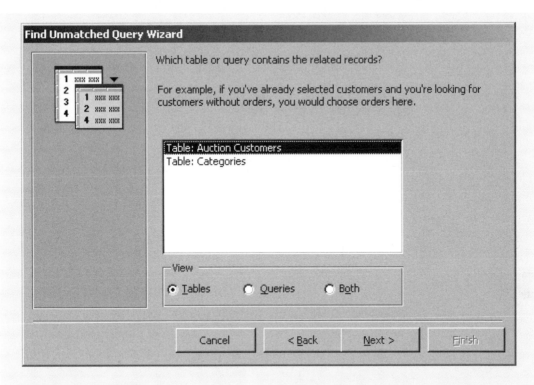

Figure 6-15. When choosing tables for an unmatched records query, always check in advance to be sure a related field exists between them.

6. **Choose Product ID, and click the right-pointing arrow (Figure 6-16). Repeat this step to choose the Product Name and Suggested Product Price fields.**

   The idea here is to choose fields that, when viewed as part of the result, give you a fairly good picture of what you're looking at without (necessarily) opening the Products table to find out.

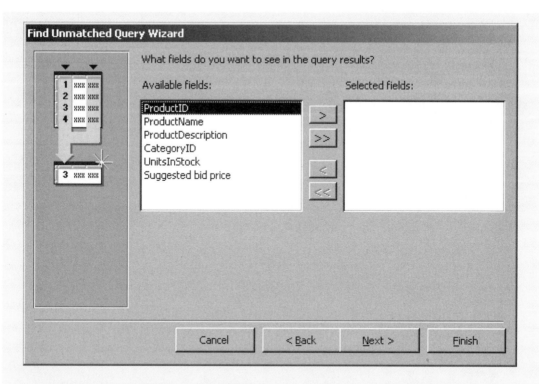

Find Unmatched Query Wizard

What fields do you want to see in the query results?

Available fields:

ProductID
ProductName
ProductDescription
CategoryID
UnitsInStock
Suggested bid price

Selected fields:

>
>>
<
<<

Cancel   < Back   Next >   Finish

Figure 6-16. Normally, you don't need to see all the fields in a table in query results. Select only those necessary to give you a picture of the situation. After clicking a field name (ProductID in this case), click the right arrow to select it.

7. **In the final wizard screen, click inside the name box to delete the suggested name, type *Products Not Sold Yet*, and then, with "View the results" already checked, click Finish.**

The new name you've provided here is just a little more readily identifiable than what the wizard automatically offered. If you wanted it better still, you could add the date to the title when you type it to help you identify the date of the query when you last checked how many products were left unsold.

Look at your results; they should match what you see displayed in Figure 6-17. You see a fairly complete picture of the goodies you've yet to sell, and you don't have to open the original tables to get this.

Product ID	Product Name	Product Descri	Category ID	Units In Stock	Suggested bid price
6M02	Guitar Amplifier	Special edition,	3	1	$500.00
6A02	Framed Art - Roger Bedell	Signed lithograp	4	1	$450.00
6C01	Original IBM XT PC	One of the first	1	1	$1,200.00
6G01	Psychodelia The Game	Created in 2002	5	1	$300.00
6E01	Zenith Color TV console	1958 Original is	6	1	$7,800.00

Figure 6-17. Your query shows just what you need to know, including your suggested bid price, which may be the reason these products haven't sold as quickly as others.

Tip: Need to stop a query before it's finished? Normally, you should let a query run through to completion whenever possible. But if you absolutely must stop during the process, press Ctrl+Break from your keyboard.

Saving, Deleting, and Printing Queries

Without you having to do a thing, Access automatically saves your queries to the Queries list available when, from the Database view you see when you first open your database, you click Queries under Objects. Figure 6-18 shows an example list of queries for the OurClub2 database you've worked with several times already.

When you modify an existing query and then go to close it, you'll be asked whether to save your changes. But you can also select File → Save to save the file before you close it.

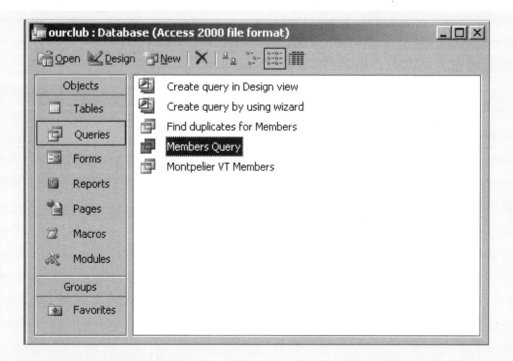

Figure 6-18. Access lists the queries you create yourself in the Database window—the Members Query in this example. To modify a query, select it and click Open.

To remove a query you don't plan to use again, just highlight it in the Queries list, and do one of the following:

▶ Press your keyboard's Delete key.

▶ Right-click and select Delete.

▶ Choose Edit → Delete.

Whichever of these you try, you'll get a prompt asking if you're sure you really do want to kill that query. Click Yes, and the query disappears from your list.

You can print your query results right from the results window. Select File → Print or press Ctrl+P. Either method opens your Printer window and lets you set properties, or simply click OK to print a hard copy immediately.

You've learned a lot in this chapter, but there's much more to know about queries. Turn to Chapter 7, where you'll take queries to a whole new level, starting with the Query Design window and moving right through to the setting of specific criteria and adding calculated fields to give you more details.

CHAPTER 7: CREATING CUSTOM QUERIES

7

▶ Creating Queries in the Query Design Window

IN THE PREVIOUS CHAPTER, you learned everything you need to construct queries, but the ones you've seen so far have been fairly simple ones. After all, you were only asking the database simple questions. Next, to paraphrase that popular TV chef, you're gonna kick it up a notch—by creating queries that ask tougher questions. You're also going to learn how to extract information from your database that isn't explicitly stated there—that is, you'll learn how to build *calculations* in Access that add, multiply, divide, and process your information to generate new data right in the query.

But first, you're going to work outside those helpful but sometimes limiting Access wizards to create your own queries using the Query Design window. The more complex and powerful your queries get, the more likely you'll need the flexibility the design window offers over a wizard.

Creating Queries in the Query Design Window

The Query Design window, as shown in Figure 7-1, isn't a completely foreign critter to you: It looks very much like the Database Design window used for creating filters. The table or tables used as the data source for a query appear in the upper half of the Query Design window. If only one table is used, a box listing the fields available in that table appears at the top left; if multiple tables are used, then each table gets its own listing box spread out across the top half of the window. The lower half of the window—called the Query by Example (QBE) section or QBE grid—sits below.

As you've done before, you can choose a field from the table list and drag it down, and then drop it into an empty Field box, or you can click within a Field box, and then select a table field from the drop-down menu. Once your query is complete, you click the Run (red exclamation mark) button in the toolbar or select Query → Run.

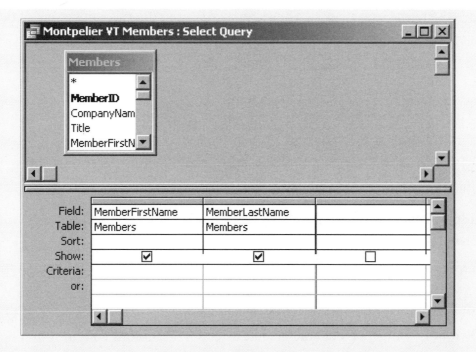

Figure 7-1. The Query Design window looks just like some Query Wizard screens. At its bottom, you can give Access a Query by Example by choosing fields, the tables for Access to take the field from, a sort order, and filtering criteria. You'll also find a Show checkbox where you can tell Access whether to display each field.

But first, you need to be familiar with all the options you can designate here as part of your query. It's time to review, and expand on, the criteria, expressions, and operators you first tackled at the end of Chapter 5.

Using Criteria in Queries

Criteria, also referred to as *selection criteria*, help you target only those records in your database that meet one or more specific conditions you set, just as you saw before with filters. You may recall that back when you worked with filters, you heard the term "expression." The criteria you set in queries can be one of two major types:

▶ **A simple value,** where you provide a straightforward name, number, and date for the query to match.

▶ **An expression,** which combines a number of different elements, including simple values, functions, and calculations.

Expressions are made up of different entities or a combination of elements, including:

▶ **Identifiers.** Specific values of a field; a common type of identifier is the actual name of a field, like MemberLastName or City.

▶ **Operators.** Either words or symbols used to indicate what kind of operation (example: a math operation like multiplication) is going to be performed on one or more parts of the expression.

▶ **Symbols.** Designated characters like asterisks (*), colons (:), question mark wildcards (?), and quotation marks ("), as well as special characters (page 174).

▶ **Values.** Simple, literal values like the name of a city or a person, a designated number (like 100), a date, a mathematical constant (a preset value that doesn't change, like a True or False flag on a record), the result of a function or calculation (like adding two values together and dividing them by another number), or an identifier.

Through setting criteria, you've already been able to find just those members in your OurClub database that live in a particular city, as an example of a fairly simple selection process where you're filtering records based on a single criterion (records have to match the city you specify). You can also set multiple criteria, just as you did when you searched the Our Club database for both a particular city name and state. Then you used wildcards, which are symbols, to match just part of a name to help you locate records even when someone may have misspelled a name or address when entering the record.

But you can get far more sophisticated when establishing criteria. For example, you can perform calculations you provide in the Field box that then add, multiply, divide, subtract, count, or average (to name a few possibilities) all records that match the condition you set in the Criteria field. You can also use criteria to look for only the top or bottom performers or the average grade for all students taking a particular test.

To give you a better idea of what's involved, you'll build some custom queries using the Query Design window, set up criteria and calculations and craft your expressions. After that, you can run the queries and see the results for yourself.

 Tip: If you've used Microsoft Excel, you're probably familiar with formulas, which are the way you tell Excel to perform calculations. Formulas in Excel are basically the same thing as expressions in Access databases. Just be aware that the *syntax* (the structure of the calculation) in Access may be different.

Crafting a Custom Query Using the Query Design Window

In the OurClub database you worked with in the past couple chapters, you may have noticed that the main Members table includes a field detailing information on when each person's membership expires. One common type of database query determines who needs to be contacted at a particular time with a reminder notice. In this case, the query would look for everyone whose membership expires this month so you can send them a renewal notice. But this same kind of query works if you're working in a busy medical or dental office and you want to remind people that it's time for their regular checkup or, for a vet's office, tell the owners that it's time to get Fido or Fluffy his yearly shots.

Oh No! It's Math!

Don't get bogged down with terms like "expression" (page 175), thinking you're getting out of your comfort zone. While nearly everyone professes a mental allergy to math, in reality, much of what you'll do with Access, queries, and expressions isn't much different than what you do in the real world all the time.

You create and use expressions all the time, like when you're figuring your share of a lunch tab or calculating the tip to pay. You also create them in your head when you're standing at the Express Checkout at the supermarket with $20 in your pocket, doing a quick calculation to be sure you've got enough to cover the cost of the items in your shopping basket.

All you're really doing is putting your basic math skills to work for you in your database. But unlike the old

pen-paper-calculator method, where a simple change means you have to recalculate everything all over again, you can set up expressions in your queries so that you can run them again and again, and the results will change automatically when the information in your database changes.

Also, as you're about to see, Access includes a helpful tool called Expression Builder to help you create an expression to fit the situation you may want to set up. Combine this tool with a little room for trial-and-error until you get exactly what you want, and you trade off a little time here with time saved over calculating all this stuff yourself the old fashioned way.

Later in this chapter, you'll work with Expression Builder in the Northwind sample database that comes with Access.

To learn how to create this kind of query yourself, download the example folder for this chapter from the Missing Manuals Web site (page 10), and open the OurClub3 database. Next, follow these steps:

1. **In the Database window's Objects bar, click Queries.**

   You can also select View → Database Objects → Queries as another way to open the Queries panel.

2. In the toolbar, click Design, as shown in Figure 7-2.

When clicked, the Design tool opens the Query Design window.

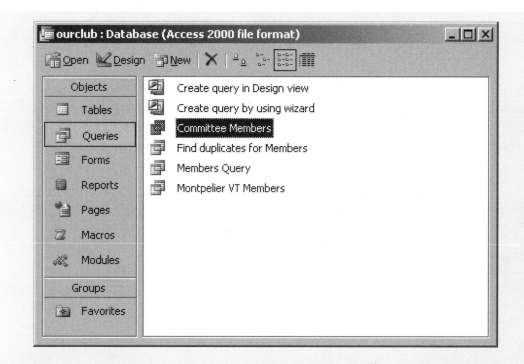

Figure 7-2. When you create a new query, Access starts by asking you to choose a table as a data source. As explained in step 3 below, you can find all members whose subscriptions need renewing just from the information in the Members table. For more complex queries, you can choose additional tables here and click Add.

3. When the Show Table window opens, select the Members table, and then click Add (see Figure 7-3).

Here, you're working only from a single table. To reach the Query Design window proper, in the Show Table window, click Close.

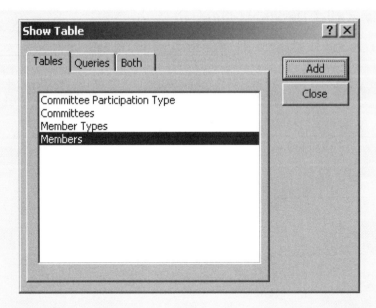

Figure 7-3. If you need to add additional tables (or even another query) as a data source for your query design, select the next table, and then click Add again, and continue until you have all your data sources chosen. To choose both tables and queries, select the Both tab, and then click Close when you're ready to move to the Query Design window proper.

4. **From the Table fields list at the top left, select MemberFirstName, and then drag it down to the first blank Field box. (You can also double-click the field, and then move it down.)**

Since you want to see the full name and mailing address, along with the membership expiration date for all records that match the criteria you set later in these steps, repeat this step to add the MemberLast Name field to the next available Field box and so on, until you've added BillingAddress, City, State/Province, Postal Code, and Member Expiration Date, in that order, to each available Field box. The end result should look like Figure 7-4.

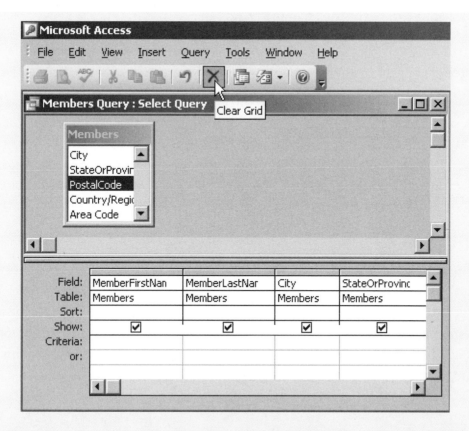

Figure 7-4. If you accidentally drag or select the wrong field and drop it into a Field box, you can simply click the erroneous entry in the Field box, and then click Delete (Clear Grid) to remove it. This example shows the PostalCode field being deleted.

5. **Locate the empty Criteria box beneath the column starting Member Expiration Date. Click inside it and type: *02/28/2006*.**

By typing this date, you're setting a simple value of a date to look for all members whose member registration expires on the last day of February 2006. Also, note that dates in Access are set off by the pound (#) sign.

6. **In the Access toolbar, click Run (the red exclamation mark icon).**

You can also select Query → Run to start your query. The query runs and results appear in a new window.

 Note: If you happen to have other queries set up and saved for your database, and one of them is selected in Query view when you open Design view, the selected query is what opens on your Access desktop. While you can always edit the existing query, you may not want to do that. Instead, you may prefer a spanking new query you're about to design. To avoid opening an existing query in the list, from the Queries menu, simply double-click "Create a query in Design view."

Assuming you followed the directions to the letter, your results should show two members who are due for your friendly renewal notice, as shown in Figure 7-5. Look at the title bar at the top of your results window and you'll see the query doesn't have a very distinctive name (here, *Query1*, and it's identified as a Select query). This default name occurs because you didn't specify a name for this customized query, which then becomes the name of the customized query results.

	MemberFirstNar	MemberLastName	Billing Address	City	State/Province	Postal Code	Member Expir
▶	Bennett	Sayers	5893 NE Pierce Blvd	Plattsburgh	NY	12098	2/28/200
	Ann Marie	Jurkowitz	2343 N Main Street	Norton	VT	05907	2/28/200
*							

Query 1 : Select Query

Record: 14 ◀ 1 ▶ ▶I ▶* of 2

Figure 7-5. Your query results provide everything you need to send renewal notices.

If you want to save your actual query results using a different name, select File → Save As (see Figure 7-6) with your query results window still open. Next, click inside the Save Query: Query 1 box, type instead *Feb06 Renewals*, and click OK.

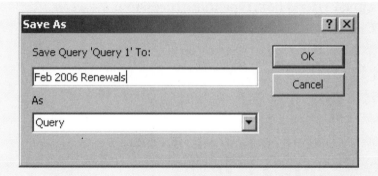

Figure 7-6. Once you rename the query or query results, as you're doing here in the Save As window, you can automatically save any minor changes you subsequently make by pressing Ctrl+S.

Tweaking Your Custom Query

With the last exercise fresh in your mind, suppose you want to locate all members whose memberships expire this month *and* over the next *90 days*. You need to tweak your query criteria slightly. In the Query Design window, just edit the date criteria from the simple, specific date of 02/28/2006 to an expression that gives a range of dates between 02/28/2006 and 05/31/2006.

Here's how to create the expression and rerun your query in the OurClub database:

1. **Click Query to open the Query view, and then double-click Feb06 Renewals.**

   This step opens your existing query in Query Design view, where you can make the necessary change to the dates you filter for.

2. **Click inside the Criteria field in the Member Expiration Date field column, and delete the existing criteria.**

   Next, since you're still using the set date of 02/28/2006, you could just leave the text in place and edit the field to add the rest of the expression. Do whichever causes you the least finger fatigue.

3. **In the same Criteria box, type this expression:** *Between #02/28/2006# And #05/31/2006#.*

Figure 7-7 illustrates the expression. It's a formal way of telling Access, "Look for and display any records where the expiration dates occur between the last day of February and the last day of May 2006."

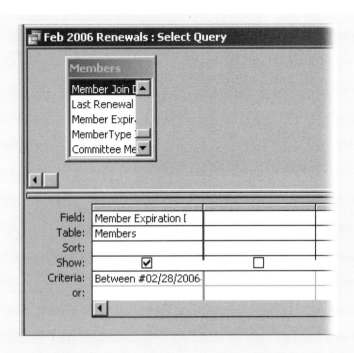

Figure 7-7. The pound signs on either side of the dates in the Criteria box serve as brackets, enclosing a specific value. (If you can't see them, right-click the box and click Zoom.) Access adds these symbols automatically when you create queries using a wizard.

4. **Select File → Save As, and rename this query** *Feb-May 2006 Renewals.*

By saving the query with a new name here, you aren't overwriting the first query where you looked for just those records expiring in February 2006. You also changed the query name to more accurately reflect what the query does, so you could use it later as the basis for yet *another* newly tweaked query where you look for all members up for renewal, say, between June and August 2006.

5. **On the toolbar, click the Run button.**

Access runs your query and returns results that include the two additional months you specified when you changed the specific date of 02/28/2006 to a range of dates from that last day of February until the final day of May 2006.

If you glance back at Figure 7-7 (or you were watching your screen when you typed the expression), you may have noticed that the expression is larger than the Criteria box, so you can't see the entire expression at a glance. That's inconvenient, and makes it more likely you'll make an error that you can't see. Fortunately, there's a way to zoom in on the box and see the entire contents at once. To do so, right-click the box and choose Zoom. A separate window opens and shows you the exact contents of this box, as shown in Figure 7-8. When you're done viewing the contents of the window, click OK or Close to return to the Query Design window proper.

Getting Sums, Totals, and Averages from Your Database

You've already gotten a hint of Access's calculation capacity. Once you get into Expression Builder in the next section, you'll see how you can perform just about any math function on your data to get cumulative information you just can't get from viewing each record in your database individually.

With calculation capabilities in mind, you can have Access:

▶ Count the number of records that fit your criteria so you know how many you have that fit a category you're looking at.

▶ Identify the top or bottom performers overall or in a segment of data (example: looking at top or bottom students in an entire class or in a portion of a class).

Figure 7-8. You can also edit a criteria's expression by typing right in the Zoom window. Right-click the Criteria box (Figure 7-7) to open it.

▶ Add up records and calculate averages either for the total or a group of records.

▶ Calculate a subtotal or a grand total.

▶ Create totals by a group of records.

▶ Add up a running sum.

▶ Add up two or more columns and have the results appear in a new row.

Right now, it's easier for you to appreciate how all this calculating works if you try some real-life examples. While the following calculations focus on simple and straightforward math, you can take the ball and run with it to do more advanced work as your skills with Access grow.

When to Query, When to Report

Are queries the best way to cull information from my database? Don't most people use their databases to run reports?

That's a smart question. Here's the general rule: If you need to get answers to questions for your own needs, then a query is probably the best way to go. You may not need to display the results a certain way or to package them up with additional information, so a query works just fine.

However, when you need to present database results to other people, go the report route. With reports, you can formalize the results and present the information in a way that works best for a broader audience.

Working with queries is good experience, though, since you use some similar concepts to generate reports.

Calculating averages

Calculating an average for a group of records is a cinch. To try it, download and open the ClassGrades database (page 10). Assume for a moment you're a teacher, and you've set up a small database where student information is in one table (Students) and their grades for various tests, quizzes, projects, and class participation are in a separate table (Individual Grades).

Say you want to figure out the average grade for each of the four tests your students took. You have that information in the Individual Grades table, but there's no record that shows it explicitly, since the table lists each grade for each test by StudentID. Instead, you must sit with a calculator and work it out yourself by adding up all the grades for each test and then dividing them by the number of students. Or, you can let Access do the job for you. Here's how to create the query:

1. **In the Database window's Objects bar, click Queries, and then double-click "Create query in Design view."**

   Again, opening Query Design view this way makes sense because if you have other queries established for this database, you'll end up opening an existing query by mistake if you click Design from the toolbar instead.

2. **When the Show Table window appears, click the Tables tab, select Individual Grades, and then click Add. Click Close.**

   If you want to add actual student information to this query, click Add *again* before closing the Show Table window, so you can include the Students table as well. But here, you just want averages without details by student. Once Show Table closes, you're back in Query Design.

3. **In the top left Tables field list, click Test1 and drag it down to the first blank field in the QBE grid. Repeat to add Test2, Test3, and Test 4 to the next three blank fields.**

   Since you're just looking for averages, there's no need to establish a Sort order. Remember, too, that you can also click a blank field to choose the table fields rather than dragging and dropping.

4. **On the Access toolbar, click the Greek E (Sum) icon.**

   Once you do this, look back at the QBE grid and you'll see a new row has been added, labeled "Grouped by."

5. **On the right side of the "Group by" box beneath Test 1, click the down-pointing arrow, and then choose Avg, as shown in Figure 7-9. Repeat this step for the "Group by" boxes beneath Test2, Test3, and Test4.**

   This step tells Access to calculate the grades for each of the tests and divide each total by the number of students taking the test to provide you with the average grade. Glance again at the "Group by" field and you'll see a number of other functions you could also choose, like Count (which would show you 16 students took this test), Min (to see the lowest grade), Max (to view the highest test grade received), and so on.

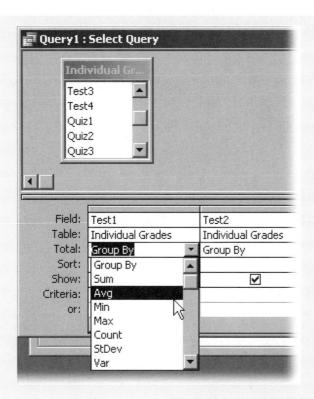

Figure 7-9. The Total → "Group by" field lets you perform a number of different common functions without the need for putting together an expression yourself or getting too complicated within the query design. For example, you can just choose Avg instead of typing out an expression that averages all students' grades.

6. **From the toolbar, click Run, or select Query → Run.**

After the query runs and delivers the results (see Figure 7-10), you've got the answers you need. Clearly, this approach is much faster than adding up four different columns of 16 grades each, and then performing division to reach the average grade for each of the four tests. If a grade happens to change (because a student begs you for a retest, for example), you can rerun the query and get updated results far faster than you can if you work manually.

Test1	AvgOfTest2	AvgOfTest3	AvgOfTest4
38	54	68	72
48	56	64	72
50	62	70	72
62	71	68	80
66	62	54	76
68	72	78	74
72	94	86	90
74	78	64	80
78	88	55	66
86	90	77	84
90	100	96	92
92	98	94	90
98	89	87	92
100	87	81	88

Figure 7-10. One huge advantage here is that Access gives you the correct results the first time and every time. If you were to do the calculations yourself, you may key in the wrong number, forget one number altogether, or mistakenly add the same grade twice without realizing it.

Using the numbers in two columns to create a third one

One thing you may have done frequently in spreadsheet software like Microsoft Excel, as well as on paper is to take the figures found in two columns and produce a third column that's the result of multiplying, adding, dividing, or subtracting the first two. You can do the same thing using a query. You can, for example:

- Add the cost of a product to the shipping price or tax for the product to get a final price.

- Calculate sales tax (where the price is in one column and the tax rate in the second).

- Multiply the number of hours it took to complete a project by your hourly labor rate.

- Determine the value of your on-hand inventory by multiplying the cost or price of the products against the number of units you have on hand.

Let's use that last example as the basis for your next query. Download (page 10) and open the FarmShopProducts database. Assume you're creating records to document the products sold by a small farm stand (the kind that opens along roadsides across the country in the spring). The information contained in the database includes the retail prices for each item this stand sells, along with the units in stock for each.

One detail the shop must know as it opens is the value of the product inventory it has on hand. You're going to create a query that lets you multiply the retail price found in one field in each product record by the number of units in stock. The result will give you a by-each-product value in a new column in your query. Later, you'll total all these individual products to get the full value of the inventory.

The query you're about to create is very general purpose. As you work, consider the ways in which you can apply this kind of query in your own databases. Here are the steps to create the initial query:

1. **In the Database window's Objects bar, click Queries, and then, in the toolbar, click Design.**

   The Show Table window opens. The FarmShopProducts database has only one table set up. It also has no existing queries. You're going to add the first one.

2. **In the Show Table window, select Products, click Add, and then click Close.**

   At last, Query Design view appears, ready for you to set up your query.

3. **In the Products table, select Product Name and drag and drop it into the first blank Field box in the QBE grid. Do the same to add Units in Stock to the second blank Field box and Unit Price to the third blank Field box.**

You added the Product Name because it's the easiest way to differentiate one product from another in the query results you'll get at the end of the process.

4. **Right-click the next blank field column (the fourth column), and then choose Zoom.**

The Zoom window opens, making it easier to see the entire expression as you're typing it. Otherwise, part of the expression disappears from view as it grows too long for the Field box.

5. **In the Zoom window, type:** *Today's Inventory: ([Units in Stock]*[Unit Price]).* **Click OK.**

Your expression should look identical to that shown in Figure 7-11. Here's what each detail means:

Today's Inventory sets up the name that will appear on this newly created column in your query results.

The **parentheses** tell Access that you're going to group certain fields together for calculation; in a more complex expression, you may have two or more groupings and sets of parentheses, each specifying to Access what fields go together for calculation.

The **brackets** are used to identify field names found in your database records and the query.

The **asterisk** (*) is the symbol for multiplication, telling Access to multiply the value of the Units in Stock field against the value of the Unit Price field.

6. **Click Run from the Access toolbar, or select Query → Run.**

You've done everything right, so the query will run and display your results, as shown in Figure 7-12. If you made a mistake in your expression, you may

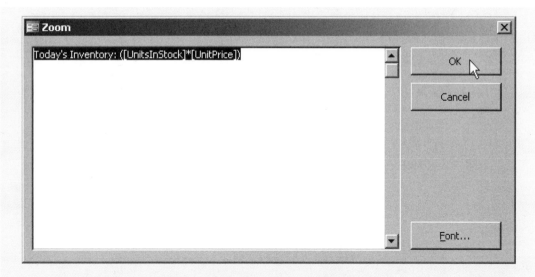

Figure 7-11. When you type expressions, make sure that every left-side bracket or parenthesis has a close (right-side) one, as in the example shown here. This expression multiplies the number of products in inventory by the unit price of each, as discussed on the previous page.

get an error message. The error message basically tells you to go back, review your expression, and make changes to get it to run properly. Unfortunately, the error messages don't give you much indication of what's wrong.

Next, save and name your query results. Here's how:

1. **Select File → Save As.**

   The Save As window opens, where you can supply a personalized name for your query and its results.

2. **Click inside the top box, delete the existing name, and type:** *Current Inventory*. **Click OK.**

   When you go back to look at your Queries list for this database, you'll see the query listed there with the name you specified.

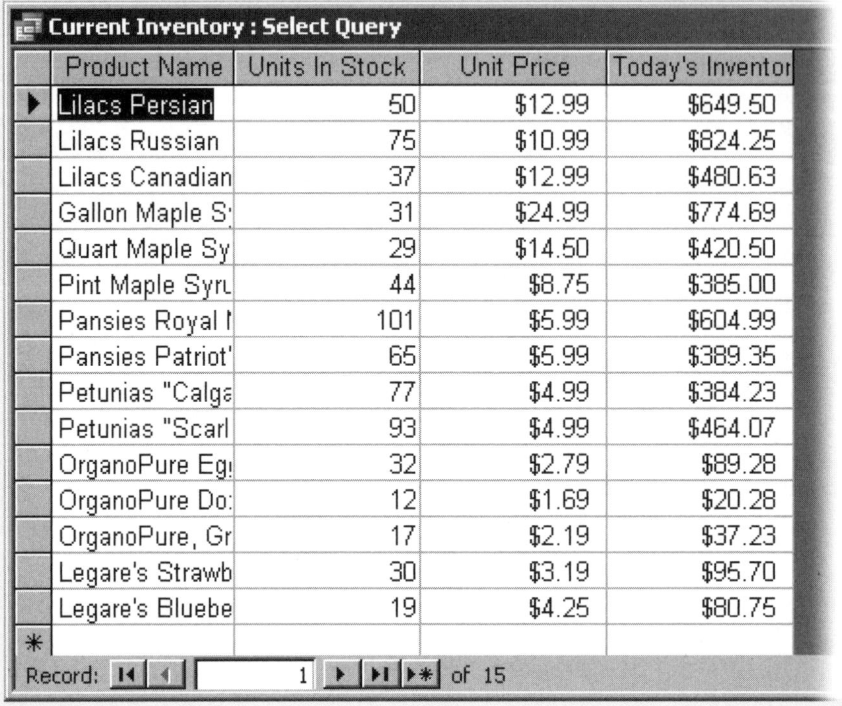

Current Inventory : Select Query

Product Name	Units In Stock	Unit Price	Today's Inventor
Lilacs Persian	50	$12.99	$649.50
Lilacs Russian	75	$10.99	$824.25
Lilacs Canadian	37	$12.99	$480.63
Gallon Maple S:	31	$24.99	$774.69
Quart Maple Sy	29	$14.50	$420.50
Pint Maple Syru	44	$8.75	$385.00
Pansies Royal I	101	$5.99	$604.99
Pansies Patriot'	65	$5.99	$389.35
Petunias "Calga	77	$4.99	$384.23
Petunias "Scarl	93	$4.99	$464.07
OrganoPure Eg:	32	$2.79	$89.28
OrganoPure Do:	12	$1.69	$20.28
OrganoPure, Gr	17	$2.19	$37.23
Legare's Strawb	30	$3.19	$95.70
Legare's Bluebe	19	$4.25	$80.75

Record: 1 of 15

Figure 7-12. As you see, your efforts created a whole new column in your query results. This column's values aren't added to your database records, but the column provides a needed summary in your query.

3. **Close the query results by clicking the Close box at the top-right corner of the window.**

   This step returns you to the Queries view on your Access desktop.

Creating a subtotal, total, or grand total

For this example, you'll use the Northwind sample database that comes free with every copy of Access (see the box on page 200). Select Help → Sample Databases → Northwind Sample Database (see Figure 7-13). Either the file will open directly, or, if it's not installed, Access will pull it off your Access or Office installation CD, and then open it on your desktop. Once you see the opening screen, click OK. When a window opens called Main Switchboard, select Database View. The main Access window opens in Tables view, giving you an idea of how well developed this sample is with its many tables.

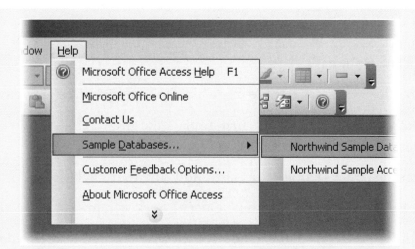

Figure 7-13. While this database was created by Microsoft several years ago (which you may notice if you look at the order dates listed in some of the tables), the functionality still works well today. The advantage of using this database is that it gives you an excellent view of a professional style database with many related tables, sample queries, forms, and reports that you can learn from in developing your own Access skills and database results.

You're going to use Northwind to look up a specific piece of information: how much one particular customer spent on her last order through Northwind. If you went through the various tables of the database, you could get different pieces of the puzzle, like how many of one particular product this person ordered, but you want to see a subtotal of how much they spent overall.

The fastest way to get the subtotal is to create a custom query that performs a calculation of records stored in the Order Details table. You limit the search to just the OrderID for the customer's last order, and then add up all the different products (and quantities) in that order. For the sake of argument, assume you've looked up this customer's last OrderID—11066. Next, follow these steps:

1. **In the Objects bar, from the Objects menu, click Queries.**

   You'll see that the Northwind database has a whole slew of existing queries, which you can (later) explore at will. For now, you're going to create your own just looking up the records associated with a particular Order ID and calculate a subtotal.

2. **In the Queries panel, double-click "Create a query in Design view."**

   As you've seen before, Access first displays the Show Tables window with its three tabs. You're interested in Tables.

3. **Select the Order Details table, click Add, and then click Close.**

   This step opens the now-familiar Query Design window.

4. **In the Order Details table window, click OrderID and drag this down to the first field in the QBE grid.**

   You've chosen this field from this table because it lets you look just at the piece of information you have: the unique OrderID. Next, you'll limit your records to the OrderID you want to subtotal.

5. **In the Criteria box below Order ID, type *11066*, as shown in Figure 7-14.**

   Although a horde of other orders are listed in this database, you're telling Access to pay attention only to those products and prices detailed for this one OrderID.

6. **To the right of Order ID, right-click in the blank field, and select Zoom.**

   Remember the column you added to your query in the previous exercise? You're going to do something similar here to add a subtotal column that's not available anywhere else in this database, to report back how much this customer spent on this order.

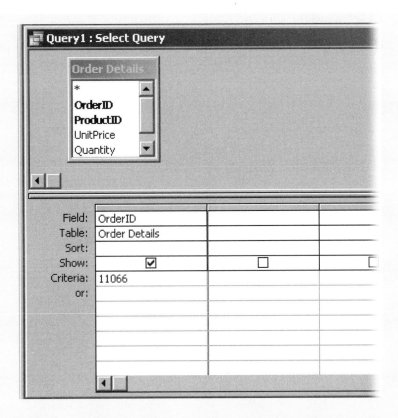

Figure 7-14. Typing *11066* in the Criteria field for OrderID means that your query is only interested in getting a subtotal for that one order number.

7. **Type *Subtotal: Sum(CCur([UnitPrice]*[Quantity]))*.**

With this expression (see Figure 7-15), you're creating a new column labeled **Subtotal** (with a colon just to its right telling Access this is a new column title) that sums up (**Sum**) your subtotal from the values of the **Unit Price** field (in brackets) multiplied (*) by the **Quantity** ordered field (also in brackets).

The **CCur** part tells Access to return the results in currency format so you see the $ and decimal points separating dollars from cents. Notice that there's a parenthesis before CCur, which creates a general grouping around the expression here, and after CCur to close it out, as well as a set of parentheses grouping the math operation that multiplies the two different table fields.

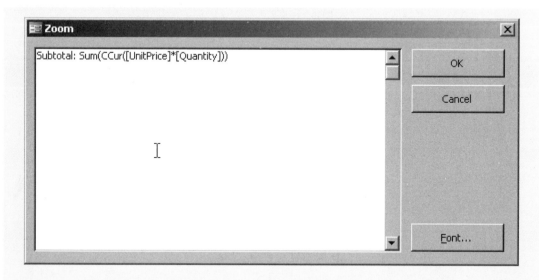

Figure 7-15. The Zoom window (page 238) gives you more room to see what you're typing.

8. **On the toolbar, click the E (Sum) button.**

   Access adds a Total row. While you've created an expression to do the math required for your subtotal, you need to inform Access to treat it as an expression, which you'll do next.

9. **Click in the "Group by" listing in the Total row in your new Subtotal column, and select Expression.**

   If you omitted this step, it's very likely you'll receive an error message from Access if you try to run the query.

10. On the toolbar, click the Run button, or choose Query → Run.

Your query instantly finds the specific OrderID you've listed and returns your results, as shown in Figure 7-16. You have your answer—the customer tied to OrderID 11066 spent $928.75 (a nice chunk of change).

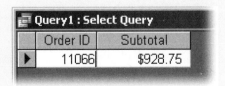

Figure 7-16. Whatever you've typed before the colon in your expression is what will appear as the column label in your query results. You can easily substitute terms like "Total" or "Grand Total" or "Order Total" for the "Subtotal" shown here, depending on exactly what it is you're calculating. Also, if you can't see the entire column label in the results, just right-click the column, select Column Width, and then click Best Fit. The column adjusts to fit the column's longer-than-its-contents name.

Since you probably won't need either this query or its results again, you can close the query results window and, when prompted whether to save it, click No.

 Tip: From the query results window, you can right-click any of the existing queries in Northwind, select Design view, and see how these queries were set up, including the expressions used to perform various types of calculations. This tool will be of great use as you create your own queries.

Using Expression Builder

Expression Builder (see Figure 7-17) is a special tool found on Access's toolbar (it's the icon with a magic wand called Build) to help you create expressions using buttons labeled for commonly used operators like greater than (>), less than (<), AND, OR, LIKE, and math operators like add (+), subtract (-), divide (/), and multiply (*).

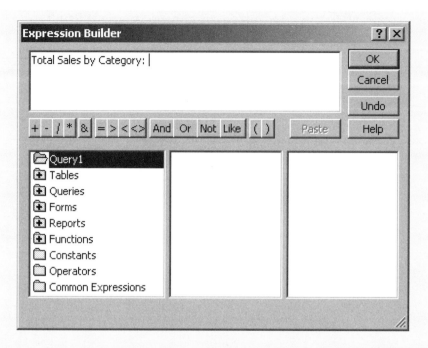

Figure 7-17. The more complicated your expression becomes and the less familiar you are with creating calculations, the more you should rely on this list-and-button approach that Expression Builder offers. This window lets you choose, rather than type, the elements to add to your expression, cutting down on typos.

To give you some experience using Expression Builder, you're going to use the Northwind database again. If Northwind is still open on your Access desktop, you're set to go. If not, reopen it by selecting Help → Sample databases → Northwind sample database.

Once you get a chance to really explore the Northwind database, you'll notice that this phantom company sells food products, including beverages, condiments, seafood, and dairy products. Each of these has its own category ID, and most categories feature several different items. Using Expression Builder, you're going to design two different queries:

- One that creates a total for sales in three different categories for all products in each of those categories.

- One that totals up all sales for a particular date for all the products Northwind sells.

You'll start by creating the by-category totals using Expression Builder where you look specifically at sales totals for three categories: Dairy (Category ID 4, according to the Categories table), Meat and Poultry (Category ID 6), and Seafood (Category ID 8). Here's the procedure:

1. **In the Database window's Objects bar, click Queries, and then double-click "Create query in Design view."**

   For this exercise, you need to create a new query from scratch.

2. **In the Show Tables window, select Order Details, and click Add. Next, choose Products, and click Add again. Then click Close.**

   When the Query Design window opens, you'll see both tables listed above the QBE grid.

3. **From the Products table list, drag the Category ID field down and drop it into the first Field box in the first column.**

   You make this selection first because your primary job here is to identify and limit your results to specific categories.

4. **Click in the Criteria box below Category ID, and type *=4 Or 6 Or 8* (see Figure 7-18).**

   These values correspond to the Category ID for each of the designated products you're targeting. In targeting specific categories, you won't include sales for other categories like Condiments, Beverages, or Produce.

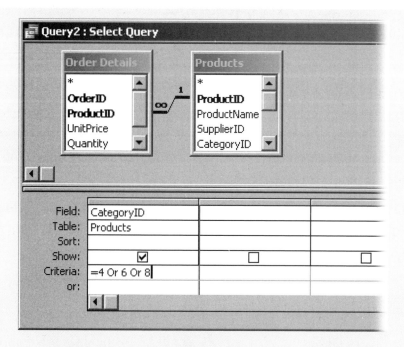

Figure 7-18. Syntax with expressions and criteria can make all the difference in how you get your results. If you substituted the "And" logical operator for "Or," the results would combine all the sales figures for each of these three categories into a single total, instead of three separate per-category totals.

5. **At the top of the second column, click the blank field, and then click the Build icon on the Access toolbar.**

   With this step, you're creating a new column to display in your query results, which will list the sales totals, and opening the Expression Builder to help you in designing the expression you need to arrive at your total sales for each specified category.

6. **First, in the top window in Expression Builder, type the label that you'll use for this new column:** *Total Sales by Category.*

   The colon separates the label from the expression itself.

7. **Using the labeled buttons in Expression Builder, typing where you don't see a listed character, build this expression:** *(1-[Order Details]![Discount]/100)*([Order Details]![UnitPrice]*[Order Details]![Quantity]).*

   Access adds the brackets around tables and field names automatically when you select a field. If you need help cobbling this expression together, see the box on page 250.

   Also, the reason you have the leading "1" and the division by 100 (/100) is that the Northwind database figures in discounts for certain customers buying in quantity.

8. **Next, in the "Group by" box in the Total row beneath your Total Sales by Category column, click to open the drop-down menu, and select Sum.**

   When you constructed your expression, one thing you didn't do was specify the end result of the math operation to be performed, which is the summary of all sales. Specifying Sum in the "Group by" box takes care of that.

9. **Click Run, or select Query → Run.**

   The results appear, as shown in Figure 7-19. The Total Sales by Category listing isn't formatted for currency, as it should be; the result is some wild decimal places. You'll fix that next.

10. **To the right of the View button at the far left of the Access toolbar, click the down arrow and choose Design view to return to the Query Design window.**

    This step is necessary because you can't change the formatting of this column in the Datasheet view you see once your query runs.

11. **Right-click anywhere in the Total Sales by Category column, and select Properties.**

    The Properties window opens, from which you set special conditions for the field, including the formatting.

Bracket Coverage

The expression you're building to calculate sales category totals differs from the expression you created in the last section because you have more than one table. Just as with the Zoom window, you can easily edit your expression by clicking in the box where your expression appears and inserting or deleting characters. Instead of just listing the field name, you need to add the Table name "[Order Details]" followed by the field name, like "[Discount]." Here's how to do it.

In Expression Builder, double-click the Tables option in the first column to expand it to show all tables, and then click the table name to expand its list of fields in the second column. Next, in the second column, double-click the appropriate field to automatically add both the table name and the field name, in

brackets, to the main expression window. Access automatically separates the table and field names with an exclamation mark (!), as shown here. You can also type a period between the table and field name.

Click OK when you're done to close Expression Builder and add the newly created expression to the Field box at the top of the first column. If you close the Expression window without clicking OK, anything you've created there is lost.

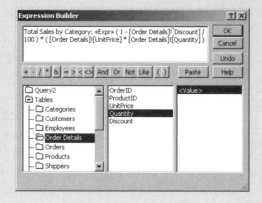

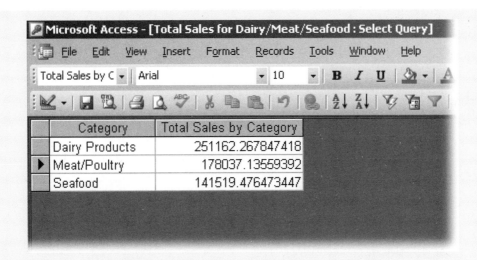

Figure 7-19. When your query runs and you get the results, Access quietly switches you from Query Design to Datasheet view. These results show the total sales for Dairy Products, Meat/Poultry, and Seafood.

12. In the Properties window, click in the box to the right of Format, and select Currency (see Figure 7-20). Close the Properties window.

Access reruns your query.

13. Select File → Save As, and save your query with the name: *Total Sales for Dairy/Meat/Seafood*.

When you view your results again, you should now see the figures as they're supposed to look, with a dollar sign and just two decimal places.

Note: Beyond changing the format choice to currency from the Properties window, you can also add the *CCur* specifier to the beginning of your expression, much as you did on page 243 when you created a subtotal. Either choice sets your results to display as currency.

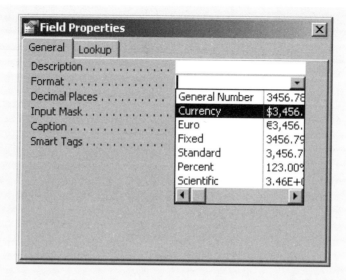

Figure 7-20. To check a field's format and other properties, right-click its column and choose Properties from the shortcut menu. The format type becomes particularly important whenever you're performing calculations. If you try to perform a math operation on a field that isn't formatted for either of those types, you'll receive a data mismatch error when you run the query.

Looking at total sales for a specific date

Here's one more example of a calculated query that shows you both how to limit your records to those matching a specific criteria—a date in the history of the database records—and how to summarize all the sales made on that date. Again, the Northwind database lends itself to the exercise.

As you work, there's an important point to keep in mind—one that can save you from going mad and tearing your hair out. Access, as you may have already noticed, is very finicky about syntax; it's far fussier than any teacher you had in elementary school. Get the syntax in an expression or criteria wrong, even with a slight typo, and you aren't going to get what you want. For example, if you use the field named UnitPrice in your expression but spell it with a space between the two words, your sales totals don't show up.

Resentment Builder?

Some people who use Access all the time swear by Expression Builder because they think it makes it easier to focus in on the kind of operations they need to perform. Others, who aren't as skilled in Access, like Expression Builder because they say that having everything available to them from the tool window is much simpler than trying to dream up the right expression all on their own.

But not everyone likes it. Some, in fact, wonder aloud why the tool even exists.

In truth, Expression Builder doesn't do a lot more than provide a focused window with little buttons reminding you of the symbols for math

opertions and other operators like And, Or, or Like, and lets you see the table(s) and fields available. The tool doesn't even give you a way to test your expression to see if it works without leaving the expression window.

In this section, you're getting a chance to try your hand at Expression Builder. While it's worth these trial runs, use it only if you find it makes your work easier. If it doesn't, don't feel bad if you never open the window again. Fast, accurate typists often don't see much advantage in using Expression Builder over the Zoom window you've used elsewhere. Who knows, someday Microsoft will develop this tool into something more powerful and helpful.

Here, you're going to look for and calculate all sales performed on a specific date, which, because the Northwind database has stood the test of time, happens to be February 6, 1998. When you set the criteria in the following tutorial, how you type the date will very much matter. What you set as criteria absolutely must match how the date is formatted when the records were created, which happens to display this date as 06-Feb-1998. If you type *2-6-1998*, you'll see an error message. So follow the steps exactly.

If you've still got Northwind open, you're ready to go. If you don't, reopen it from the Help → Sample Databases menu. Next, go ahead and open it up to Queries panel.

1. **Click "Create query in Design view."**

   The Show Tables window appears, right on schedule.

2. **Select the Orders table, and then click Add. Next, select Order Details, click Add, and then click Close.**

   Why put two tables here? Because while most of the information you need is contained in the Order Details table, only the Order table provides the date on which the order was placed and the sale was made. Therefore, without the Order table, you can't limit your records search to just the date.

3. **In the Orders table list, drag the Order Date field and drop it into the empty Field box in the first column.**

   Next, you need to specify the order date you're targeting. To avoid errors, remember the warning about syntax.

4. **Click in the Criteria box below Order date and type: *#06-Feb-1998#*. Press Enter.**

   Access automatically changes the date into the more common "2-6-1998." You've told Access to look only for records where sales were made or orders were placed on this date, so you're ready to craft your expression.

5. **Right-click in the Field box at the top of the second column, which, in your query results, will display the sales total for all orders on that date, and choose Build (another way of opening Expression Builder).**

   If you've sworn off Expression Builder, you can select Zoom instead and simply type the expression shown in the next step.

6. **Build, or type, the following:** *Total Sales: (1-[Order Details].[Discount]/ 100)*([Order Details].[UnitPrice]*[Order Details].[Quantity]).*

If you're using Expression Builder and you get an exclamation mark rather than a period between the table name and field name brackets, that's fine. You don't need to change them. Click OK to close either Expression Builder or the Zoom window. Access adds your newly crafted expression to the second column's Field box.

7. **Click Total on the Access toolbar. With the Total row added, click in the "Group by" box in the second column, and select Sum.**

You've just told Access to calculate all the sales together based on your formula. Ah, but remember the currency formatting problem you saw on page 249? Take care of this issue before you run the query.

8. **Right-click anywhere in the second column and choose Properties. Click inside the box to the right of Format, select Currency, and then close the Properties window. Click the Run button.**

When your results appear in Datasheet view (Figure 7-21), you see the newly created column and the sales total you wanted. Congratulations!

9. **Select File → Save As, and rename this query from its default name to:** *Feb6 1998 Sales.*

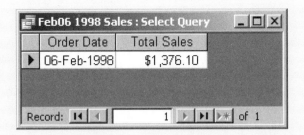

Figure 7-21. Here, you're seeing just a single date and its sales total. But you could create a single query that lists sales totals for a number of different dates, much as you did in creating the sales totals for the different product categories on page 247.

Actually, that last step isn't absolutely necessary. But if you save the query, you can go back and look at your query details when you're puzzling out your own expressions and query setup for the customized queries you design for your own databases.

Obviously, you can create many more types of queries—either from scratch or using one of the Access query wizards. The ones covered here just begin to scratch the surface of the possibilities. Hopefully, however, you have a good sense of how you can customize your queries and add calculations to your results, so you can take what you learned here and build on it for your unique circumstances.

In the next chapter, you're going to pick up where you left off by taking your questions and answers and turning them into a prime-time presentation in the form of reports that you can readily share with fellow team or committee members, your boss, or even the loan manager at your local bank (you know, the one you're trying to impress with your track record or project planning into giving you a business loan).

CHAPTER 8:
GENERATING REPORTS

▶ Report Basics

▶ Parts of a Report

▶ Using the Report Wizard

UNTIL NOW, BEYOND DESIGNING YOUR DATABASE and entering records into it, the focus in this book has been on how to get information out of your data by using filters and queries to locate and answer specific questions. You've learned a number of different ways to extract certain details depending on what you need to locate or what types of answers you're looking for.

But what should you do when someone other than you needs to know some of the details found only in your database? Sure, you could run queries and either print out the results or copy them into email or publish them to a Web page where others can read those details. Perhaps, however, you need something more comprehensive and professional-looking, a more formal entity that's ready for prime time and suitable for showing to your boss or a client, to members of a committee or other organization, or in a public presentation.

When it comes to pulling together details from your database for public consumption, reports are the way to go. As you'll discover in this chapter, Access lets you create reports that can paint the broadest possible picture of whatever information you're keeping or zero in on very specific details. With Access, your reports can be as short and simple as a bunch of mailing labels, or as professional and polished as an annual report, a comprehensive directory, or even a book-length manuscript. In this chapter, you'll learn how to create reports either through one of the step-by-step wizards that do some of the work for you, or through a design you make up all on your own.

Report Basics

A *report*, by definition, details information you've collected for dissemination to a wider audience. A good report can cover an incredible amount of ground in a reasonably short space and offer its readers key details while also presenting a broader picture of the subject as a whole.

In this section, you're going to get a crash course in Data Reporting 101, including the many tools available within Access to help you create reports, the assortment of report types Access lets you put together, as well as the steps involved in viewing and printing reports. From there, you'll move along rapidly to the features included in different report types, you'll learn how to use the Access report wizards or design your own report style, and then you'll get some hands-on experience putting together different reports and getting them out to others.

How Reports Differ from Forms

In most respects, forms are an internal tool, used by people who have direct access to the database for entering and viewing data. Reports are used for much wider distribution of your data, often to external audiences. Since reports lend themselves to printing, people don't even need a computer to appreciate them. But don't make the mistake of thinking that reports are necessary only when you have to get essential details out to hundreds or thousands of people. Even if you only need to share information with a few other people, a report may be the best way to present it.

Types of Access Reports

Just as there isn't one single reason to keep a database or only one type of data, there isn't just one type of report. Stop and think for a moment, and you can probably identify a few report types right off the top of your head, including annual reports, individual subcommittee or committee reports, overall performance summaries, and yes, even the much-feared report card.

Access is designed to create a number of different report types, ranging from mailing labels only to very formal data presentation. Report types include:

▶ **Columnar (Vertical).** In this form (see Figure 8-1), a report shows each field on a separate line with a label to its left. This style is effective when you want to clearly identify certain information, like a product or program list.

▶ **Tabular.** One of the most common report types, the Tabular form shows a new record on each row, with field labels at the very top of the report. This type is good to use in situations where you want to display a number of records on a single page where the data fields are fairly short or narrow.

Special Reports

Not so long ago, having a database required a great deal of time and money. The computer used to handle the database cost hundreds of thousands of dollars (if not millions) and filled a good-sized room. The people who worked with them were all specially trained, down to the clerks who keyed in the individual records. Thankfully, times have changed. The computer on your desktop is much smaller but far more powerful than many of those humongous old room-sized systems. Database management software like Access is easy enough for non-pros to use and inexpensive enough that you can go buy a copy and start your database the same day.

If you're coming to Access as a small business owner or even as a hobbyist who passionately collects information about a particular subject, you may wonder if you need to do any reporting at all. But reports can come in very handy whenever you want to share some details with others, even if your audience is just a few other people.

Amateur astronomers, horticulturists, collectors, and chefs have been known to keep databases primarily for their own reference that they then later share with others (when teaching a class, for example).

Neighborhood crime prevention volunteer groups sometimes keep a database to keep track of suspicious behavior or specific problems in their area. A report helps make their case for increased police patrols or documents their efforts.

Access even helps you to publish your results to a Web page. You can let customers, students, and fellow committee members view and edit information right on the Web page.

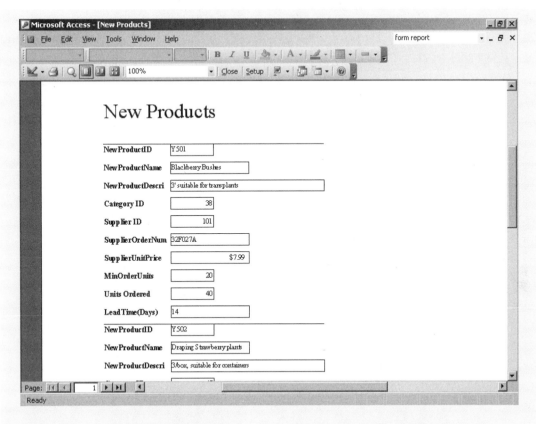

Figure 8-1. This example shows what a columnar or vertical report may look like, depending on the material you're presenting. It's ideal for reviewing inventory and prices and examining a product list and similar types of material.

▶ **Groups/Totals.** This report type organizes larger quantities of information into groups similar to the Tabular form but allows for more data, and for the addition of functions like sums or totals, percentages, averages, and minimum/maximum values.

▶ **Summary.** Similar to the Groups/Total type with the ability to offer counts, totals, averages, and more, the Summary form usually features less detail about individual differences between the various groups presented.

- ▶ **Charts.** This type converts data from raw or grouped numbers into graphical displays, which are far more effective for presenting some types of information for quick review.

- ▶ **Mailing labels.** Use this type (via the Label Wizard) to turn your individual employee/customer/student/subscriber address records into printed labels using an office-standard label like the Avery brand. (See Figure 8-2.)

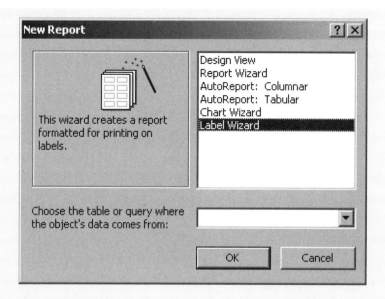

Figure 8-2. Not every type of report you can create and generate is available through the wizard list shown here. To see the available wizards or start a report, select Insert → Report.

 Tip: You can convert an existing query or filter you've created and saved into a report. To do so, open the query, choose File → Save As, and then choose Report from the drop-down menu.

One Size Doesn't Always Fit All

As you work with the Access report wizards, you may be surprised both by how helpful they are in letting you produce very professional results in less time than you may have hoped and mildly irritated that the wizards aren't always terribly flexible.

In the beginning, you may want to rely on the wizards to get your initial results. But once you become familiar with the process, creating your own specialized report style may make more sense. You can even create your own templates so that the toil and creativity you pour into getting everything right in a first "from scratch" report can be used by you, and others, again and again in the future.

If you know others working with Access or other types of database software, and you happen to notice they're producing great-looking reports that strike you as a better solution than your own, ask these folks how they did it. If they're using a report template, see if they'll give you a copy you can review and maybe adapt for your own use.

You can also sometimes find online report templates available for downloading, for example, the Microsoft Office online site. Visit *http://www.microsoft.com/access* (while Microsoft-based Web addresses frequently change, this URL redirects you to the Access resource site) and explore. Even if one template doesn't offer you everything you want and need in terms of style and format, you may be able to pick and choose elements from two or more different templates in crafting your very own.

Two Ways to Create Reports

By now, you know the drill: Access always gives you at least two different ways to do anything, and the same holds true with reports. You can either use Access's packaged report wizards to create, and, in some areas, customize your reports both during and after the wizard's work, or you can design your own from the bottom up using the Report Design window. (See the box on page 263 for more info.)

Wizards

Access includes different wizards for all the styles you learned about on pages 259–262. These wizards step you through every phase of the process, including:

▶ Choosing your report type

▶ Selecting the data source used and the fields you want presented

▶ Grouping and sorting the information selected

▶ Deciding on a report layout and style to apply throughout

▶ Adding a title and other elements like page numbers

Design window

Much as you've done already with creating your own databases and their tables, queries, and forms, you can use a specialized Report Design window (Figure 8-3) to draft a report style that's uniquely yours, with elements, layout, and style that fit your own situation to a tee. But you can also use the Design window to customize a report type that you first generate using a wizard and then want to adapt to your special needs.

Displaying and Printing Reports

Why tackle the subject of displaying and printing reports now before you've even created one, rather than after? Because you want both to be prepared as you put the report together to make certain it displays properly (see Figure 8-4, which shows a columnar style report in Print Preview mode) and to be sure you think ahead to how you want the report to be printed.

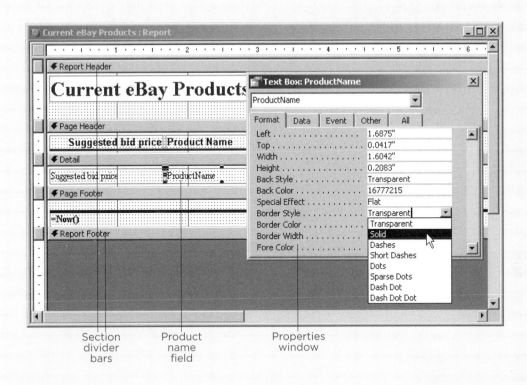

Figure 8-3. Just like the Form Design window in Chapter 3, you can use the Report Design window to change fonts, text, or background colors, and the arrangement of items on the page. For example, to add a border around a field (here, ProductName), right-click it and choose from the Border Style menu in the Properties window.

When creating a mailing label report, for example, you need to know what labels you need for the type of print job you'll run. Access supports most common types of Avery brand printable labels. But even if you're printing a more standard report, you want to consider the paper you'll use and whether you plan to create a color or black-and-white presentation. If you need multiple copies, decide whether your desktop printer is up to the job.

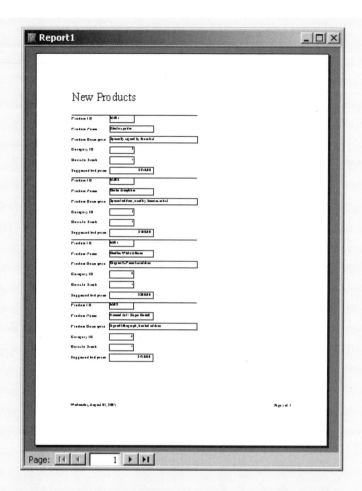

Figure 8-4. You can check the display of your report as it should appear when printed by selecting File → Print Preview. But you can also do a quick assessment of how the report should print if you click View on the Access toolbar, and select Print View.

Keep in mind that most consumer printers aren't designed with volume printing in mind. Most print anywhere between 4 and 12 pages per minute in decent quality; "best" quality printing is much slower. Also, the printer may begin to fuss or eat paper if it's suddenly charged with printing out 100 to 200 pages.

If you face a large print job, you want to take your work to a professional print shop for best results. Because of the high price of inkjet toner), it may cost you little more to professionally print. In some cases, you actually save money and get a better document copy.

 Tip: See the box on page 268 for special tips related to printing and report legibility. You'd be amazed at how many people decide to create color-based charts, for example, and then print everything in one color so that the color-coding on the charts is rendered useless.

Parts of a Report

Most reports have a few features in common. You may use all of them or just a few. The following pages take each part of a report one-by-one, so you can start thinking about which ones your report needs.

Report Design Sections

Access reports are typically broken down into sections or parts, some of which appear outside the actual information furnished as part of the details within the report. When you're in Print View or Print Preview, for example, you'll see that these sections are labeled on the screen for you, as you saw back in Figure 8-4. Depending on your goals and audience, you may be able to do without some of these features and still deliver the goods effectively.

Every report has a Detail section, which displays the information from your database, as organized and processed by the report. The next most frequently used type of sections are headers and footers. If you've got any experience with creating formal documents in Microsoft Word or another word processing program, the concept of headers and footers isn't new to you. If you've never heard the terms before, here's a brief rundown:

▶ **Headers** are small capsules of information that appear at the top of a page, a document, or a data grouping. Headers often include titles, the report creator's name, and perhaps a few words of description.

The Secret of Great Reports

What makes one report fall flat while the other seems so compelling and clear?

Chances are, the difference is in the presentation. Whether the news they deliver is good or bad, the best reports provide the most important need-to-know details in a brief, concise package that's easy for folks to read and understand.

While Access makes it easy to produce reports, it's up to you to be sure that what you present is delivered in a way that makes sense to the reader. To achieve this result, you need to plan ahead, before you run the Access wizard or design your own report.

As you plan, think about these issues:

* What's the objective or desired result of the report? Make sure that your end product meets this goal.

* Present all necessary information but be selective. Too much information may leave your audience afloat in a sea of data so they don't understand what they're looking at, while too little can make your audience wonder what they aren't seeing.

* Where possible, represent information in a visual format like a chart, but be sure the charts are clearly labeled so the readers understand what they're looking at.

* Legibility counts. Print the report using a good quality printer and very decent paper. Use highly readable fonts and, if you choose colored paper, be sure the contrast is good. If you have to copy the report, make sure the copies are as readable as the original.

* Have one or more objective people review your report, looking for everything from typos to bigger problems like missing data. The more important the report is, the more vital having test readers becomes.

▶ **Footers** are predesigned chunks of information displayed at the bottom, or foot, of a page, document, or data group. Footers provide a great place for page numbers, the date the report was generated, and other details that aren't as attention-getting as header information.

Report header and footer

Just as their names imply, a report header appears at the very beginning of a report while a report footer displays at the very (although hopefully not bitter) end of the report. If you decide you don't want to use headers and footers, toggle them off by selecting View → Report Header/Footer.

Page header and footer

These sections should be pressed into service when you think your report should have a header and footer on every single page of the document. Page footers, for example, are great placeholders for page numbers and the date the report was created. Access automatically adds page footers to every new report. You can toggle them off again, and then back on, should you choose, if you select View → Page Header/Footer.

Every page header or footer repeats the details of the first; you can't vary the information between pages. For this reason, use headers and footers only when you're absolutely sure your report, and its audience, will benefit from seeing the same details again and again.

 Tip: One good case for using page headers and footers is when you're distributing a report of a few pages or more that's collated (put together in proper page order) but not permanently bound. The reasoning here is that if a page gets loose from the report, the header and footer identify what it is·and where it belongs.

Group header and footer

More specialized than the other types, these sections, when turned on, appear at the start and finish of every data group within the report. They're optional, so you can turn them on and off using View → Group Header/Footer from Design view.

Detail section

The Detail section is where the real meat-and-potatoes of the report appears—your actual database information.

Challenging Boundaries

Here's a design trick you can use to modify either reports generated by a wizard or those you craft yourself. You can increase or decrease the length of any type of page section by moving the boundaries. Look toward the bottom of the page layout, not the bottom of the window. You'll see a double-headed arrow with a crossbar; the normal cursor transforms into this configuration when it approaches the edge of a page section as you press your mouse button. This crossbar lets you resize the page section to make it shorter or longer to fit your layout preference.

Design view, as shown here, clearly distinguishes the different page sections for you and makes it simple to make changes quickly. However, if you tweak something and don't like the results, you can immediately revert back to the previous appearance if you select Edit → Undo. Also, the Undo tool works sequentially backward through history, so if you make two or three other changes before you realize you want to revert back, click Undo two or three times, reversing all the subsequent changes, until you hit the one change you made before.

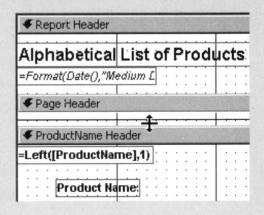

Using the Report Wizard

While Access gives you several report-generating wizards, Report Wizard is the general-purpose helper to use when you don't want one of the specialty wizards like Chart or Label Wizard. Since Report Wizard is also likely to be the wizard you're most often going to use, you should go through the wizard once so you can get a feel for what's expected and the steps involved.

Here's one important detail that some folks overlook, at least until they get an annoying onscreen nag message: Every report, regardless of whether you use a wizard or create your own, requires the database you're basing the report on to be open on your Access desktop.

 Tip: If you happen to have multiple databases and have more than one open on your desktop, consider closing all but the one you're using to create your report. Doing so can save your sanity as well as your time; you don't want to accidentally switch into the wrong database and spend 10 minutes or more creating a report where you don't need one.

Starting the Wizard

Before starting the wizard, open a database file to work in. You can either choose one of your own or download the example files from the "Missing CD" page (page 10). For this tutorial, you can use eBay Products2.

You can initiate a fresh report in a number of other ways. You can:

▶ From the Object menu from Database view, double-click Reports, and then select New.

▶ Select Objects → Tables (or Queries) → Report.

▶ From the Access toolbar, click the New Object button, and choose Report.

You can also choose the same Insert → Report from any database table or query one already open in Datasheet view or from just about any other Object page. For this example, choose Insert → Report. The first wizard screen appears.

Tip: As an alternative, you can launch the Report Wizard from the Objects bar by clicking Reports, and then double-clicking "Create report by using wizard."

Choosing the Report Type

From the New Report window shown in Figure 8-5, Access gives you six different ways you can go about creating your report, including:

- **Design view.** When you want to work from scratch.

- **Report Wizard.** That's what you'll use in this example.

- **AutoReport: Columnar.** Available when you want to fashion a columnar-style report or create one to use as the basis for modifying into a Summary style report.

- **AutoReport: Tabular.** A great choice for getting a lot of record information together on a single page.

- **Chart Wizard.** Creates a chart, just like the ones you can make in a spreadsheet program like Excel, which take your database information and display it in the form of a graph, pie chart, and so on.

- **Label Wizard.** A superb choice addresses labels and mailing lists, as described on page 262.

Select Report Wizard and read on to the next section. But *don't* click OK yet—you still need to choose your data source.

Tip: If you happen to change your mind at any point in the wizard, you can exit by clicking Cancel. Or click Back to reverse course and return to an earlier step.

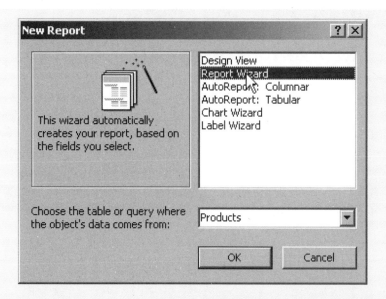

Figure 8-5. If you click each of the options listed here, you'll notice the drawing and the test at the left side of the window change. These provide visual cues to what you're choosing to do.

Choosing the Data Source

Data source refers to whatever entity—a table or a saved query or filter—you want to use as the foundation for this report. If you're using the eBay Products database, the primary table is named Products. Click the down-pointing arrow at the right side of the Tables/Queries box, and select Products. Next, click OK and then follow the steps in the next section.

Choosing the Fields

Under most circumstances, you don't need to use every field in a selected table in your report. Select those fields that are pertinent to what you're presenting and omit anything that your audience doesn't need to know. For example, if you're creating a mailing list, then you don't want anything that doesn't belong on an address label.

Creating Report Snapshots

Report snapshots give you a way to distribute Access reports in a cost-effective way whether you're printing the results or sending them through email or posting them to a Web site. These snapshots let you send the report information using the exact same fonts, colors, charts, and other types of embedded objects as in your Access files.

To create an Access report snapshot, start from the Database window, and then follow these steps:

1. In the Database window, click the name of the report for which you want to create a snapshot.

2. Select File → Export. When you create a snapshot, you're actually exporting the existing report into a different format that's saved with the file extension *.snp. This export will include any of the charts, graphs, or embedded objected contained in the original report.

3. From the Save As window, click the drop-down menu next to File Type and choose Snapshot Format.

4. Click within the File Name box and modify the existing report name, if desired.

5. Click Export. If you want to be able to open the snapshot automatically when you or others click it, from the Save As window, select AutoStart before you click Export.

A really helpful aspect of these snapshots is that the person who gets an electronic copy of the report snapshot does *not* need a copy of Access to open and view it, as they would with a full electronic Access report.

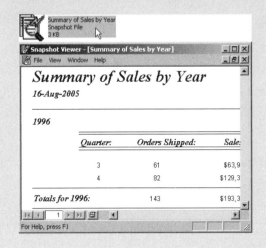

For the eBay Products database:

1. **Choose Product ID, and then click the right-pointing single arrow button to move it into the selected field column at the right.**

   If you were going to choose all fields, you would simply click the double arrows pointing to the right to move them all instantly.

2. **Repeat step 1 to add Product Name, Category ID, UnitsInStock, and Suggested Bid Price.**

   After completing these steps, you have all the fields you want to include in your report. Click Next to move on unless you need to add more table(s) or a query to the report details.

Remember that in the first wizard screen, where you selected the wizard type, you were only given a choice of a single table or a query. But in the screen here, you have the option of adding another data source by clicking in the Tables/Queries box and choosing another object, as shown in Figure 8-6. For this report, though, you don't need to.

Grouping the Report Data

Grouping refers to how the information appears together in the report. Everything you selected in the previous wizard screen is grouped together automatically, with nothing called out or given special emphasis.

If you want to call attention to a particular field, like the Suggested Bid Price field, in the left-hand list, select the field, and then click the right-pointing single arrow. When you do that, you see that this field name moves up to the top of the window, as shown in Figure 8-7. When you print the report, you'll see this field appear at the very start of the listing for that record.

Sorting the Report Data

Do you want to establish a sort order for one or more (up to four) of your fields, in either Ascending (the automatic choice) or Descending order? If so, click in the

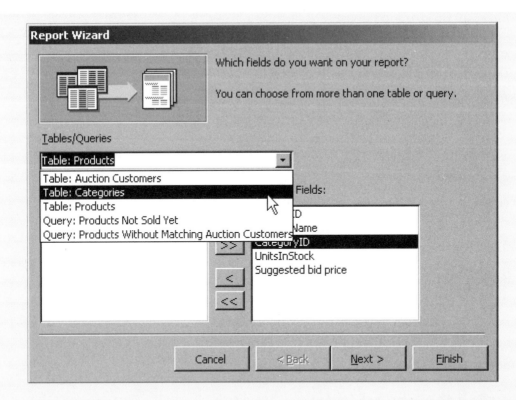

Figure 8-6. You can use more than one table or query in a report. Just choose one at a time and then select the fields. Your additional field choices would join the others at the right under Selected Fields.

first field box and choose the field to sort. If you want a Descending rather than an Ascending order of display, click Ascending and watch it change. You can repeat this action up to three more times to select additional fields for sorting.

Here, choose ProductName as the primary sort choice and leave it as Ascending, as shown in Figure 8-8.

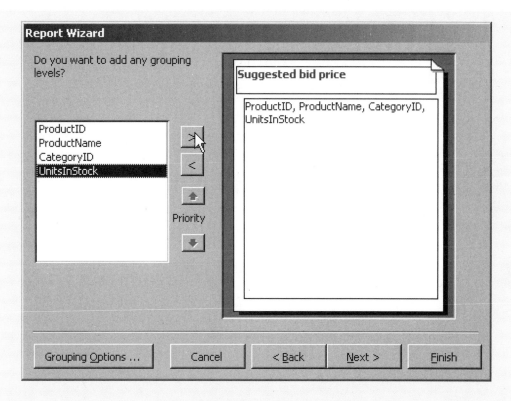

Figure 8-7. Creating grouping levels determines the order in which fields appear on your report. The first field you select in the left column ("Suggested bid price" in this case) appears at the top of each record in the report, as you can see in the preview on the right.

Tip: You can click the Summary Options button if you want Access to display a count of the records, calculate an average, or show Max(imum) or Min(imum) results. Turn on the ones you want in the window, as shown in Figure 8-9.

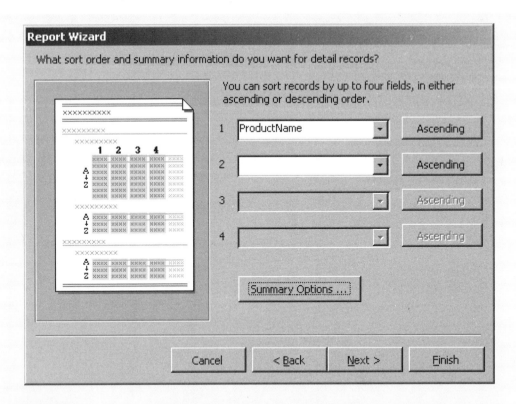

Figure 8-8. No matter how records are sorted in your database (page 154), you can choose a separate sort order for a report. If you choose multiple fields on which to sort, the first item selected in the top box establishes the first sort order, and then so on down the list.

In some types of reports, the already checkmarked option, "Calculate percent of total for sums," may be useful (for example, if you need to show what percentage of total sales a listed item represents). In this case, since you want a simple list of Products, turn it off (Figure 8-9).

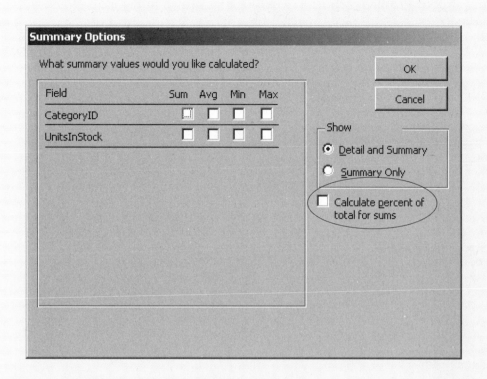

Figure 8-9. Access reports the details for anything you turn on in the Summary Options window. Only the "Calculate percent of total for sums" option (circled) comes turned on automatically. If you don't want it in your report, click to turn it off before you click OK.

Choosing a Report Layout

Next, you get to select the overall layout style that you believe will work best for the type of data you're reporting. If you've got a number of selected fields, look through the choices to find the one that will display the information for the least crowded appearance. As you work through the options, in the left side of the window, you'll see a diagram of the layout style differences.

For the eBay Products report, select Block, as shown in Figure 8-10. Next, look at the right side of the window under Orientation. Say you want the report to print out horizontally across a page rather than vertically down a page as you have with the standard Portrait style. To make this change, click Landscape to select it. Click Next to move along to select a report style.

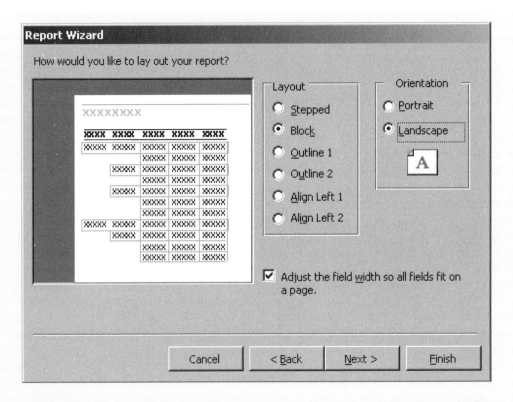

Figure 8-10. The Report Wizard makes you choose a layout type. If you later regret your choice, you can always go back and tweak your design choices later using the Report Design window.

Choosing a Report Style

A style can set the tone for your report, just as your choice of attire can set the tone for a meeting. Access provides more than a half-dozen selections, ranging from Casual to Corporate. Some of the options are colorized, which only works well if you're planning to print the report using color (or copy it using a color-capable photocopier). If your own reports use color, factor that into your decision because you'll want results that translate well in monotone printing or copying.

Select each option, one at a time, to view the differences between them in the left side of the window. For this report, where you may go the color route, choose Bold, and then click Next.

Adding a Report Title

Finally! You've reached your last wizard screen. Here you'll notice that the wizard has automatically added the name of the primary table or query you selected as a data source as the title of your report. But that's not necessarily what you want to appear in big, bold typeface across the top of your printed report.

For this database, click inside the Title dialog box and type: *My Current eBay Product Listings*. You've got two choices below: the automatically selected Preview to open your report in preview mode or Modify to tweak your wizard-generated design. Leave Preview selected, and click Finish.

Figure 8-11 shows the glorious results of your labor. But if you see anything you don't like, you can always modify it using the Report Design window (page 264).

Using Other Programs to Create Reports

If you're creating a larger report that will include many different elements beyond what Access can create for you—for example, an annual report that includes large and/or multiple sections of narrative text, photographs and other types of artwork, and/or information normally contained in spreadsheets rather than your database—then you can call in help from another program.

For example, you may want to create the majority of your work using word processing or desktop publishing software (Microsoft Word fits both requirements quite nicely), and then simply import relevant information from Access. Or you can use Access to export data to another program or, at least, into a format that another program can read.

Since Access is part of the Microsoft Office family of products, it works well with Word, Excel, and even Power-Point presentation software. In fact, when you finish creating a report using Report Wizard and get a chance to see the result, a "Publish with" option becomes available on the toolbar. You can choose to send this report to, say, Microsoft Word for further modification and printing.

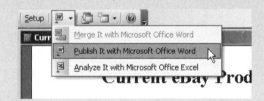

Current eBay products

Suggested bid price	Product Name	Product ID	Category ID	Units In Stock
$250	Electric guitar	6M01	3	1
$300	Psychodelia The Game	6G01	5	1
$450	Framed Art - Roger Bedell	6A02	4	1
$500	Guitar Amplifier	6M02	3	1
$800	"The Elements of Style" Book	6B01	2	1
	Beatles White Album	6A01	4	1
$1,200	Original IBM XT PC	6C01	1	1
$3,300	1980 Political ad pack	6N01	8	1
$4,500	"Alice in Wonderland"	6B02	2	1
$7,800	Zenith Color TV console	6E01	6	1
$15,500	Patriot Silver teaset	6K01	7	1

Figure 8-11. Printing a single copy (press Ctrl+P from your keyboard, or select File → Print) is a great way to proofread a report. Sometimes the human eye can spot little problems on paper that it can't detect on screen.

PART THREE: APPENDIXES

APPENDIX A:
HELP AND INSTALLATION

▶ Installing Access 2003

▶ Access Help

▶ Visiting Microsoft Office Online

Installing Access 2003

Like all Microsoft Office programs, Access is pretty simple to install. The hardest part may be typing that 25-digit Product Key number (and making sure you don't lose it in case you ever have to reinstall). If you have Microsoft Office 2003 on your computer, you probably already have Access 2003. To check, click Start menu → All Programs → Microsoft Office, and see if Access is on the submenu.

 Note: To install Access 2003, your computer has to run on Windows 2000 or Windows XP. If you're on Windows 2000, Microsoft recommends installing Service Pack 3 and any subsequent updates first. Choose Start → All Programs → Windows Update to check for and install updates. You can also search for updates at *www.microsoft.com/windows*.

Installing Office

If you're upgrading or installing Office 2003, you're best off doing a full install or upgrade, which gives you a clean, fresh copy of all Office programs, auxiliary programs, and files. Nothing breaks up your workflow like getting an error message saying that Access needs you to install additional software.

To install all Office programs and components:

1. **Exit all running programs, and then insert the Office 2003 CD.**

   The CD launches its own setup and install program. (If it doesn't, double-click the Setup icon.) You may see messages like "Preparing to Install."

2. **In the first Setup screen, type your Product Key.**

   If you make a mistake, you get to keep trying.

3. **Next, the Setup program asks for your name and initials. When you're done typing them, click Next.**

   Access (and other Office programs) uses this as the Author information in the File → Properties box for all files you create. Microsoft pledges not to reveal any personal information you type into its software.

4. **Turn on "I accept the terms in the License Agreement" and click Next again. On the next screen, select an installation type.**

   Install Now (or Upgrade Now) is your best bet, especially if you choose the option to remove older versions, which saves space on your computer's hard drive.

5. **When the setup program lets you know it's done, click OK.**

Installing Access Only

If you didn't install Access when you first installed Office, you can simply add it, as long as you have the CD and Product Key. Here's how to get Access onto your computer.

1. **Insert the Office 2003 CD. Next, choose Start → Control Panel → Add or Remove programs.**

   The Add or Remove Programs window opens (Figure A-1).

2. **In the left panel, click the Add New Programs icon. In the panel that opens, click the CD or Floppy button.**

   Your computer locates the Office 2003 CD. The Run Installation Program box should open and show SETUP.EXE. If so, click Finish. If not, click Browse, and choose your CD drive.

3. **When the setup program launches, follow the installation instructions above and choose the Custom Install option. Click Next.**

   You'll see a screen that lets you choose which Office components to install. Click the plus (+) signs to expand each heading and see all the individual programs, plug-ins, and example files you can choose to install or remove.

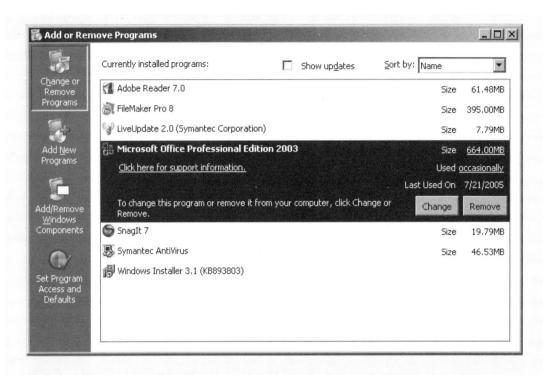

Figure A-1. You can add Office programs you haven't installed before, or remove ones you never use, by running the Office Setup program. To get started, click Start → Control Panel → Add or Remove Programs.

 Tip: This book refers to some examples in the Northwind sample database, so make sure you install that database along with Access.

4. **When you're done customizing, click Next.**

   The setup program installs Access. Click OK to close Setup and get back to work.

Access Help

In Access, help is never far away. Some forms of help show up unbidden, like the Tip of the Day that pops up every time you open the program, and the screen tips that appear when you point to a button or toolbar. In addition to the help that's right on the screen in front of you, help documents are stored on your computer, and Microsoft Office Online features an entire Web site full of resources.

In this appendix, you'll see how to visit the online support site, download Access templates, get advanced training through tutorials, and post questions for other people who use Access, including experts designated as Microsoft Most Valued Professionals (MVPs) because of their wealth of experience with products like Access.

Where to Look for Help

The best answer is usually the one you get first, so here (in order from quickest and simplest to most time-consuming and complex) are the ways you can summon Access's help system (see Figure A-2).

Screen tips

The quickest way to get help on a feature is to point to it. A small, yellow screen tip identifies the toolbar or icon under your mouse pointer. Often, that's enough of a clue. If it's not, type the name of the feature in the menu bar search field or Office Assistant, as described next.

Menu bar

The box at the upper right of Figure A-2 is actually a help search field. Type a word or two of what you're curious about and press Enter. The task pane opens (Figure A-3), showing the list of related help documents on your computer (and on Microsoft's Web site, if you're connected to the Internet).

Office Assistant

So many people complained about "Clippy," the annoyingly helpful Office Assistant character, that Microsoft no longer has him appear automatically. You have to turn him on by choosing Help → Show the Office Assistant.

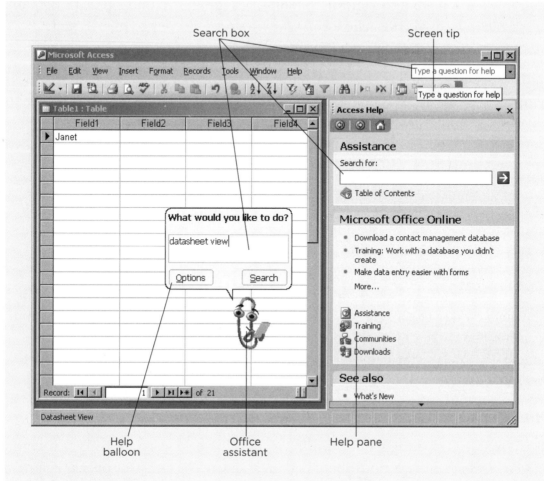

Figure A-2. You may never see them all at once like this, but here are all the help features you'll find arrayed around the Access screen. If you can't think straight with all this clutter, then close the task pane, turn off the Assistant (page 291), and rely solely on the little search field in the upper right of the screen.

Figure A-3. When you search help, Access displays a list of potentially helpful help screens in the task pane. Each links to a brief help article stored on Microsoft's Web site or on your computer. Often, you'll have to read two or three of these screens to get the full story.

When the Assistant is on your screen, error messages show up in a speech balloon instead of in a boring message box. These messages often include a link to a corresponding help page. Also, occasionally the Assistant notices what you're trying to do in Access and offers advice and more help links. If you can't stand this behavior, choose Help → Hide the Office Assistant to turn it off. You can always search for help, when you're good and ready, in the task pane, described next.

 Tip: If you like having an onscreen assistant, but just don't like Clippy, you can choose another character. Click the Assistant to display his help balloon, and then click Options. Click the Gallery tab to see all the Assistants installed on your computer. (And if you don't see any additional Assistants, refer to the installation section at the beginning of this appendix.)

Help Task Pane

The Access task pane has a help panel (Figure A-3). It opens whenever you summon it from the Assistant or the search field in the menu bar (page 291). If the task pane is open, click its top bar and, from the pop-up menu, choose Help to get to the help pane. You can also choose Help → Microsoft Access Help to display it.

Whenever you search for help using any of the methods described in this appendix, Access automatically searches the online help screens (if your computer is currently connected the Internet) and a smaller set of help screens installed on your computer and displays the results on the task pane. You can tell the difference by the question mark (online) and book (on-your-computer) icons next to each link. Click one of the links to read the full article in the task pane.

 Note: When you click one of the offline topics, it pops up in a separate window to the right of the task pane. (In general, Access gives preference to the online help information, since it's newer and freshly written.)

When you're using Help, the task pane has all the navigation features you need in one place. As shown in Figure A-3, here are the highlights:

- The **Search** pop-up menu is where you enter the keywords or a question. Click the arrow button next to it or hit Enter to start the search. If you can't seem to come up with the right search term to find the information you're hoping for, try the Table of Contents link.

- Clicking the **Table of Contents** link displays all the help pages both on your PC and online, organized by category. When you click a category, a list of pages and subcategories opens up beneath it.

> **Tip:** If you're not connected to the Internet, browsing this index of all help files on your PC is a quick way to zero in on information.

- **Contact us** opens up the contact Web page for Microsoft Office products. This page mostly offers links to parts of the Office Web site described in the next section. If you click "Contact a support professional" because you actually want to talk to someone, you'll probably end up paying money for the privilege.

- **Online Content Settings** opens up a very simple Options window for the help system. You can turn online help on and off (forcing help searches to look only in the installed help pages), choose to include any relevant templates (page 306) in help results, and so on.

- The **Accessibility Help** link opens a page of instructions for navigating the Help system with keyboard shortcuts, a more legible font size and color, and so on.

> **Tip:** For more information on Windows' accessibility features, see *Windows XP for Starters: The Missing Manual*, by David Pogue.

- **Can't find it?** After Access performs a search and shows your results (Figure A-4), this link appears at the bottom of the task pane. Clicking it opens up a page with hints on improving your search techniques.

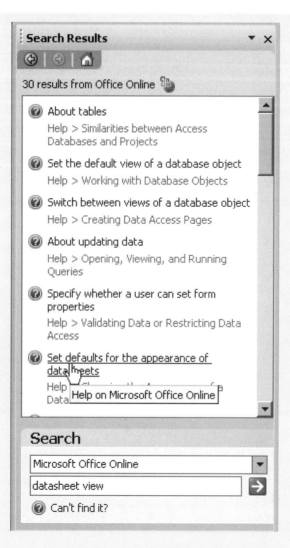

Figure A-4. The four links at the bottom of the Microsoft Office Online panel in the middle of the Help task pane (Help → Microsoft Access Help) go directly to pages in Microsoft Office Online. You'll learn how to use the Assistance, Training, and Communities features later in this appendix.

Visiting Microsoft Office Online

You can choose a few ways to get to Microsoft Office Online. You can go directly through your Web browser by typing *www.microsoft.com/office* (this address redirects you to the actual site, the address of which sometimes changes). But if you're already working in Access, and your Internet connection is up and running, it's quicker to choose Help → Microsoft Office Online, or, on the task pane, click the Connect to Microsoft Office Online link.

Either way, you see the main screen shown in Figure A-5, at the left. Scroll down and you'll see links to a host of specialty areas that:

▶ Give you access to online tips, help articles, how-to steps, and tutorials on databases in general and Access in particular.

▶ Let you check for updates to the software.

▶ Test your Access knowledge through pop quizzes.

▶ Offer the opportunity to view and download templates for different types of Access databases, forms, and reports—these can help you see how others are using the program to create solutions and more powerful record-keeping.

▶ Connect you to a packed library, called the Microsoft Design Gallery Live, of clip art and photographs you can download and use to enrich—or simply "jazz up"— your forms and reports.

▶ Provide demos for other Office products and give you the option to download free 60-day trial versions of other Microsoft programs.

▶ Guide you into Web-based newsgroups where you can post questions, read tips, and get answers to the questions you ask.

 Tip: To go directly to the Access page shown at front in Figure A-5, you can also type *www.microsoft.com/access* in your browser's address bar.

Figure A-5. Whether you surf to Microsoft Office Online in your Web browser or get there through Access, you get to the same site. Don't worry if it looks a little different from what's pictured here: Microsoft adds to and updates this material several times a month.

You'll see Access mentioned several times on the Office Online home page. Those links take you to articles and tutorials, as discussed later in this appendix. In fact, since Office programs work well together, you may get some idea of new ways of using Access by skimming this main page. However, to get to the Access help material you came here for, you have a little more clicking to do:

▶ **In the Office Online home page's left panel, click Assistance.** Again, the Assistance page offers some Access resources, but they're mixed in with information about all the other office programs, too. Halfway down that page, under the Browse Assistance heading, click Access 2003.

▸ **Or, in the Office Online home page's left panel under Products, click Access (Figure A-6, right).** The Access main page has all kinds of Access information, but to get to help pages, scroll down to the Browse Access heading, and click "2003 assistance."

Either way, the Access 2003 Assistance page opens, as shown in Figure A-6. This dry, no-nonsense page is a sort of index to the online help articles you can read in the task pane in Access. The benefit of looking at them here online is that you can read them in full-sized browser windows and have more than one page open at a time. Also, you may find it easier to navigate from one help page to the next and jump to other parts of the site.

 Tip: At the top of the left panel, click Home whenever you want to return to the glitzier Office Online main page.

Here's an example of how to locate and read featured help articles:

1. **On the Access Assistance page, as shown in Figure A-6, left, scroll down to the Expressions heading. Under it, click the Creating Expressions link.**

   A new page opens, with links related to the topic of expressions in Access (Figure A-6, right). In this book, expressions come up on pages 175 (Chapter 5) and 222 (Chapter 6).

2. **Click the "Create an expression" link.**

   Finally! The "Create an expression" page opens, as shown in Figure A-7. This article is long, so you'll have to scroll to read it all. Or, use the list of links that Microsoft thoughtfully provided under the heading "In this article."

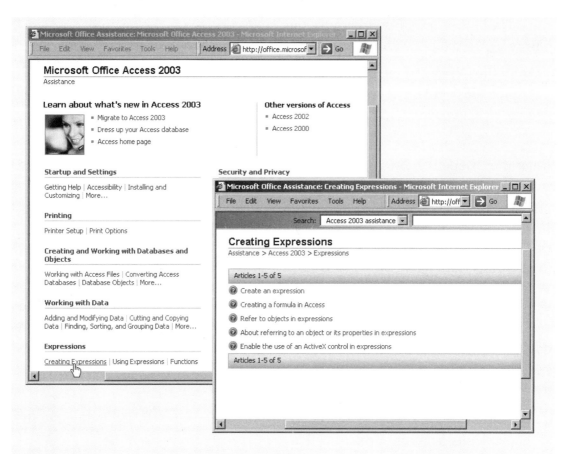

Figure A-6. You can get to the Access 2003 Assistance page (left) using either of the methods listed on pages 298–299. Click any of these links to see a list of more specific links related to the topic (right).

3. **Click "Where and how to use expressions."**

   This section of the article discusses the process of adding expressions to your database and provides a step-by-step example. If you scroll down to step 5, you'll see the words "Expression Builder" are in a different color, indicating that they're a link.

Figure A-7. The links under "In this article" on some of the longer help Web pages let you jump directly to specific subtopics. The See Also box at the upper right links you to pages about similar and related features, which can help you fill in gaps in your knowledge.

4. **Click the Expression Builder link.**

   The page jumps to the "Using the Expression Builder" section of the same article. Stop and read, if you wish.

5. **At the end of the Expression Builder passage, click the <back to top> link.**

   At the end of each section, a <back to top> link takes you back to the beginning of the article. Next, look at the upper right of the page. The See Also box contains links to related articles.

For example, here you can surmise that expressions have something to do with reports, so if you feel you need more about reports, now's your chance.

6. **Click the "Counting in reports" link.**

   The "Counting in reports" page is a different kind of article than a typical help screen; you can see by the name and date that a real live person wrote it (Figure A-8, back). If you scroll down, you'll see links that reveal more step-by-step tutorials.

7. **Click the "See all 'Get it done with Access' columns" link.**

   The "Get it done with Access" page lists, by date written, several columns written by experts in the field. These pages supplement the usual help screens, and may cover exactly the issue you're dealing with.

By now you have an idea of the vast sea of online help you're dealing with. To return to dry land, you can use your Back button, or click Assistance in the left-hand panel.

Learning with Tutorials

Did that stuff about expressions in the previous section leave your head spinning? Performing calculations on your database records really lets you use your information to the fullest in Access, but it's a topic many people find challenging. Microsoft understands. If help pages are too dry for your taste, you can try the Training tutorials on Microsoft Office Online, complete with audio to guide you along the way, sort of like a virtual classroom.

 Tip: Since the tutorials contain audio, make sure your computer's speakers are turned on, with the volume adjusted to a comfortable level. Better yet, you may want to plug in a set of headphones so you can listen in private, even if you're doing this from home in the same room where others are talking or watching TV.

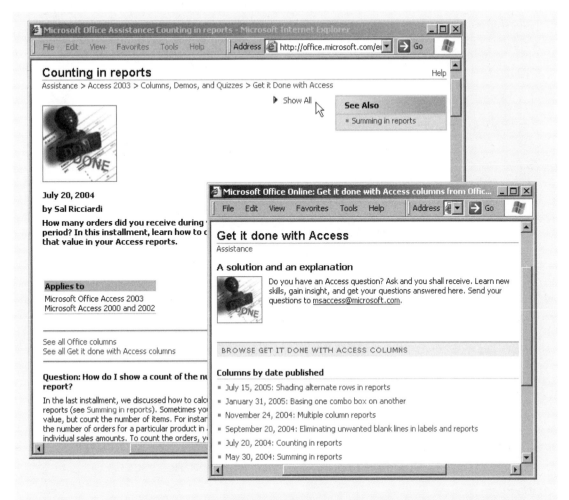

Figure A-8. When you see the author's name on an online help page, you're looking at an article that an Access expert wrote in response to reader questions. To submit your own questions, email them to *msaccess@microsoft.com*.

You'll often see Training tutorials on Microsoft Office Online's home page, under Featured Courses. You can always get to them by clicking Training in the left panel of any page of the site, and then, under the heading Browse Training Courses, clicking Access. You'll see a list of courses, as shown in Figure A-9.

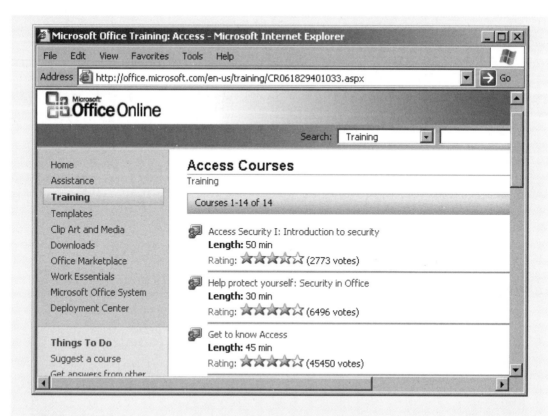

Figure A-9. Stars at the right of each listing report the "poor to great" rating given to each tutorial by the people who've gone through the modules. You can use these ratings as a guide but you usually won't find a module listed here unless it's passed rigorous testing to be sure it provides solid information and assistance.

The training session then opens in your browser (Figure A-10), and you can proceed along at your own speed. Many of these modules pause to let you try examples of the information being presented as a way to test your skill.

At the top of the page, click the Next arrow to move forward (or the back-pointing arrow to review). A little control bar lets you play, pause, and adjust the audio volume.

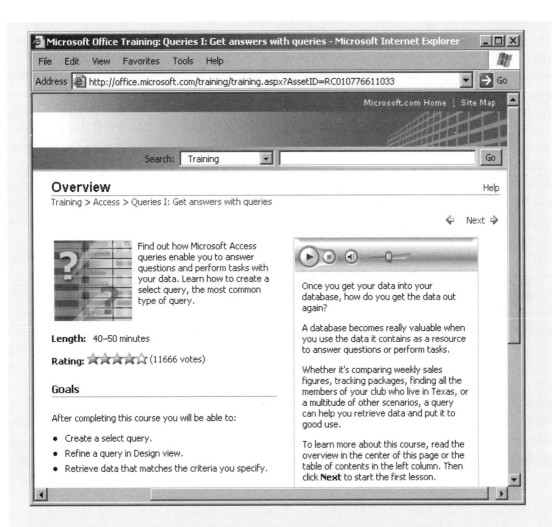

Figure A-10. Within seconds after the page opens, the tutorial's audio begins to play over your speakers or through your headphones; if you don't hear anything, check your volume. Notice, too, that navigation controls on each page of the module let you go back or move forward, as needed.

Finding Help Articles and Training Tutorials Not Listed

Just about every page on the Microsoft Office Online site features a search tool that lets you type in a topic or click within the Search window to choose from an overall category. You can see one in the top right of Figure A-9, for example.

Suppose you're taking a Training course on Forms but want to know if the site has an Assistance article on the same subject. Follow these steps to use the search tool:

1. **Click in the list box to the immediate right of Search, and choose either Assistance or All Microsoft Office Online.**

   The first possibility restricts your search to just those articles appearing in the Assistance area, while the second performs a search throughout the Office site.

2. **Click within the second, right-most window in the Search tool and type** *Access Forms* **(see Figure A-11). Click Go.**

   When the search is complete, your browser opens to a search results page.

Locating and Downloading Access Templates

Members of the Office Online community frequently share templates or copies of special documents, databases, and other files they've developed. You can browse these templates to see if any of them look like they hold a solution for you, and then download them. Once they're on your computer, you can use them just like any of the templates that came with Access. Best of all, you can tinker with their design to better suit your own information.

1. **On the Access toolbar, select File → New, or click New.**

   One of the options when creating a new database is to use a template for an already existing one—either on your computer or available from the Microsoft Office Online site.

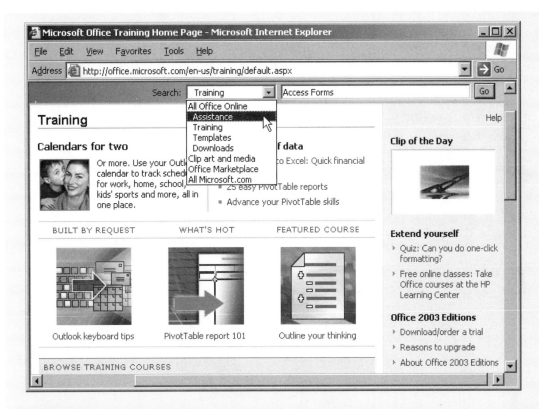

Figure A-11. Type the item you need help with in the Search field, like "Access Forms" shown here. Also, while the search tool is pretty smart, try your best to spell the phrase correctly; this helps you get the best possible matches.

2. **When the task pane opens, on Microsoft Office Online, click Templates, as shown in Figure A-12.**

   So long as your Internet connection is open and active, your Web browser opens automatically and whisks you to the Templates library online. (The stars are a user-rating system, as described in Figure A-9.)

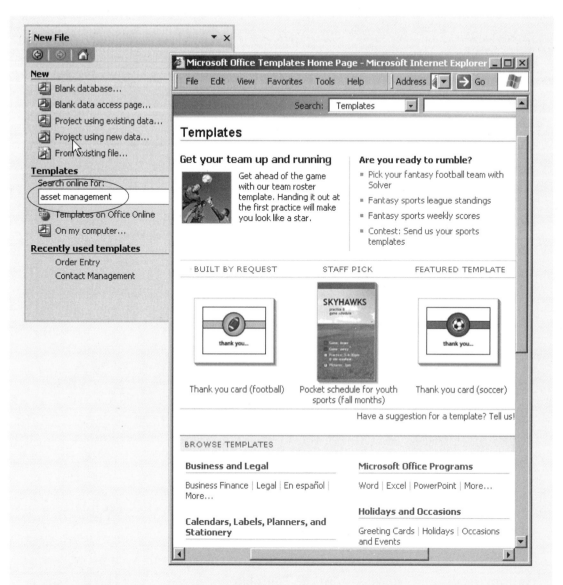

Figure A-12. On Microsoft Office Online, when you click Templates, Access launches your Web browser and takes you straight to the list. Typing the kind of template you're looking for in the task pane (circled) is another way to search online.

Tip: If you're browsing Microsoft Office online, you'll see templates listed on the main page and all over the place. In the left panel, click the Templates link to see them all in one place. Click Microsoft Office Programs to see them listed by program, so you can pick out the ones that are specifically for Access.

3. **Click the name of a template to see a full-page description.**

    The page usually includes images of the forms in the database template, so you can see what you get.

4. **When you've inspected a template online and want it, click Download Now.**

    Follow the onscreen instructions to save the template on your hard drive. You can keep it in your My Documents folder, so you can double-click its icon to open it, or with the other Access templates in the My Computer → Local Disk (C:) → Program Files → Microsoft Office → Templates → 1033 folder.

Asking Questions and Finding Answers

Newsgroups and Web-based message boards are a popular way for people to either post messages seeking help or offering a tip or trick, or to reply with answers to previously asked questions. Microsoft Office Online offers a broad range of newsgroups and message boards, often including several for different aspects of their many products.

You've read this book, used the help options from Access, and maybe even browsed through some of the online resources already covered here, and you're still stumped. Another alternative is to post a question stating your problem to one of the Access message boards to see if someone can give you a hand.

Follow these steps to post a question (or a tip or trick of your own):

1. **Go to the Microsoft Office Online Access area using any of the methods already discussed. Click the Discussion Groups link.**

    Depending on the speed of your Internet connection, it may take a few moments for the next Web page to open, displaying a list of available discussion groups/message boards. The page automatically opens to the Access General message area, as shown in Figure A-13.

 Tip: To see what other discussion groups are available for Access besides this general one, go to Access Databases at left, click the arrow, and then click to open a different group page.

2. **Click New → Question.**

    To post, you need to sign in using your Microsoft Passport account. If you don't have one, you'll be taken to another Web page where you click Register and fill out the required information, including your email address and password, to create an account. If you have a Microsoft Passport account, you'll be prompted to sign in using your email address and password. After you're signed in, you end up back on the Discussion Group page, where you may need to click New → Question again.

    Pop-up boxes and onscreen prompts may ask you to enter a profile, as well.

 Tip: if you use Microsoft Hotmail (the free Web-based email service) or Windows/MSN Messenger, you likely have an MSN Passport. Just sign in using the email address and password you use to access one of those other account types.

3. **When you get to the New Question screen, type a subject line and your question.**

    Be as clear and concise as you can about what you're asking. And yes, you may see little more legalese on this screen. Turn on "I accept" to agree to Microsoft's terms, which basically say that they get to use any great ideas you send in.

4. **If you wish, turn on the "Notify me of replies" checkbox, so that you'll get an email when someone answers your question.**

    If you don't turn this on, you'll have to remember to keep checking back on your own, as described next.

5. Click Post when you're done.

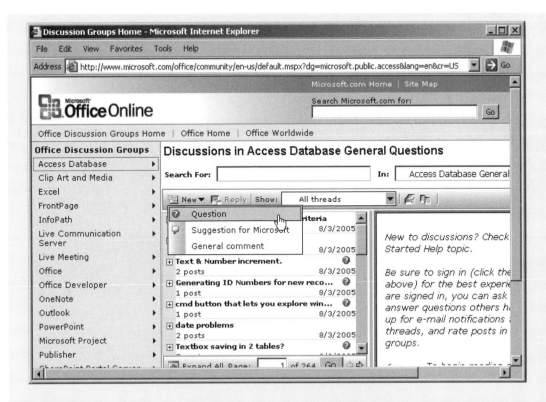

Figure A-13. As you post questions and comments, helpful information appears in the panel at the right side of your screen.

Later, when you want to go back and see if anyone has posted a reply to your message, simply return to the Discussion Group where you left your message following these same basic steps. Browse through the messages listed until you find yours. Click the plus (+) sign next to your message to expand it and show any replies. Next, click a reply and follow onscreen prompts to read and respond to your reply.

APPENDIX B:
ACCESS FAQ

▶ Importing and Exporting

▶ Validation

▶ Finding Find

THIS BOOK COVERS ALL THE BASICS of creating and using Access databases, but there's plenty more to be curious about. You may not need to swap files between Access and, say, Word or Excel very often, but it's good to know you can. And the fields in your database probably work just fine, but there's a way to make extra sure that you're entering information correctly. This appendix covers these burning issues and more.

Importing and Exporting

Q: I've already done a fair amount of work in other Office programs like Microsoft Word and Excel. Now that I've gotten Access, how can I move this information over to Access without having to enter all the information all over again?

A: Excellent question! Actually, you can move information, including text and numbers, between other programs and Access in any number of ways. This is especially true for Access and other programs in the Microsoft Office product line, such as Excel, PowerPoint, and Word. (You got a hint of this in Chapter 8 where you learned about Access reports.)

For example, you can take records or query results from Access and import them into Word where you may be preparing a whole document—say, for a monthly or annual report. You could also take a list you've been keeping in Word and use it as the start of a new Access database; you could do the same with information stored in an Excel spreadsheet.

The best way to get a feel for the import and export process is to try it. For these examples, you'll go through two of the more common operations: importing a Word file into Access, and taking information stored in Excel and bringing it into Access.

Importing a Word File into Access

If you have Microsoft Word on your computer, you can get an idea of how you can move a table of information in a Word document and import it into Microsoft

Access with the following exercise. Download (page 10) and, in Word, open the file Group Members.doc.

This document contains contact information for members of an organization in Word's table format. You've decided that it makes more sense to keep this contact list in a table in Access, but you don't want to have to create all these individual records yourself manually; rather, you'd like to import the information directly from Word.

Here's how to import a Word table into Access:

1. **Open Microsoft Access and choose File → New.**

   Here, you're creating a brand new database to start tracking information about these members.

2. **Select Blank Database and, when prompted to save the new file, save it with the name:** *New Group Members.*

   Notice that the new database is stored automatically in your My Documents folder, which is where you'll find it when you want to open it again.

3. **Next, switch back to the Word document you have open.**

   You need to make some changes to the Word document to prepare for it to be easily read by Access.

4. **Delete all the text in the Word document that appears outside the table. The finished result should display only the table, as shown in Figure B-1.**

   The note above the table isn't something you want to bring into your Access database. By deleting this text, you don't have to worry about it later during the import process.

5. **Highlight all fields in the table, and then select Table → Convert → Table to Text.**

   Access can't properly read inside the table grid. In this step, you're changing the listings from the table to straight text.

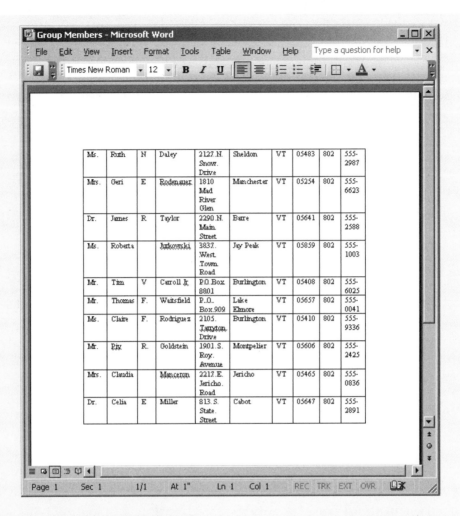

Figure B-1. Since anything contained in the Word document will be treated by Access as something it should import, you need to get rid of anything you don't want. For example, if you're importing a table, delete any text that's not part of the table.

Tip: Don't see the Convert option from the Table menu? If that's the case, you're probably just seeing an abbreviated menu listing. At the bottom of the menu, click the double down-pointing arrows to expand it.

6. **From the Convert Table window, you need to choose a character type to tell Word how to separate the various fields in the table (see Figure B-2). Choose Tabs, and then click OK.**

   Access can read the different fields as unique if they're separated by different types of characters, like the Tab key that's used to move between fields in the table. You've just instructed Word to use tabs to separate them.

Figure B-2. You're choosing Tabs here because, as you set up a table like this in Word, you press the Tab key to move between fields. But you could also select Commas if you had all fields separated by a comma instead.

7. **Choose File → Save As. Click inside the File Name window, and type *Existing-Members*. Next, click inside the Save as File Type list box, and choose Plain Text, as shown in Figure B-3. Click Save.**

   Because Word documents contain special formatting normally hidden from your view—but which will be very apparent, as well as problematic, to Access—you need to save the file as a text file. This is what you've just done. You may be prompted that by changing the file type, you'll lose all formatting, which is exactly what you want. Click OK.

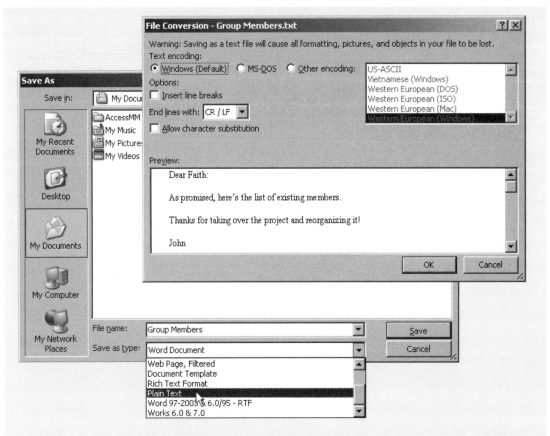

Figure B-3. After you select plain text as the file type (back), Access may ask you to specify exactly what kind of plain text, like MS-DOS or other system. Windows (default) is usually your best bet.

8. Close Word and any open files.

With your work done in Word, close Word and any files open in it. This step is necessary because Access won't be able to open your newly created text file if it's already open in Word.

You've just completed the first part of your work. You're now ready to return to Access to perform the second phase of the operation.

Follow these steps to proceed:

1. **Switch back to Access and the blank new database you created.**

   The new database should be open in Database view with Tables selected from the Objects menu. If it isn't, click Tables.

   This action is necessary because you're actually going to add a table to the new, blank database by importing that table-turned-to-text in the text file you converted a few steps ago.

2. **Select File → Get External Data → Import, as shown in Figure B-4.**

   You'll be prompted next to specify the file type (text) and then the actual filename of the document you converted to a text file.

3. **In the Files of Type box, select Text Files.**

   Here, you tell Access you're going to import a text file.

4. **Locate and select the text file ExistingMembers, and then click Import.**

   Once you specify the exact file to use to import, or bring into, Access, the Import Text Wizard opens.

5. **Select Delimited, and click Next.**

   You've told Access to expect a separator (or delimiter) between the fields.

    Note: *Delimited* is a fancy term for any character that separates each field. Common separators or delimiters are tabs, commas, and (with Word and other word processors) paragraph marks. For table conversion, usually Tabs is the best choice.

6. **Choose the delimiter type Tabs. Click Next.**

   Tabs are the separators you chose when you converted the Word table earlier. Next, Access asks where to store the information it's about to import.

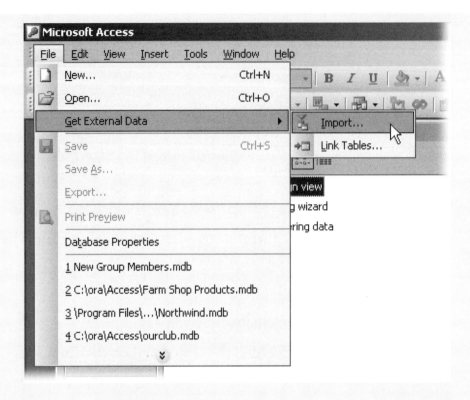

Figure B-4. The Import option is the one you'll use whenever you're using information available in an outside data source, like a table in a Word document or a list in Excel, to bring into Access. The opposite operation to Import is Export, which transfers Access data to other formats.

7. **Select New Table. Click Next.**

This step tells Access to create a whole new table to store the imported fields because you don't have any existing tables.

Note: In the table you're importing here, you don't have any column names identifying each field in a row. If these columns are there, turn on "First row contains field names," and Access treats that first row as labels for your table fields.

8. **In the window shown in Figure B-5, you can specify details about each of the different fields you're importing. Here, however, that's not necessary, so click Next.**

Since the table you had in your Word document didn't label the different fields, you're seeing automatically set field names used here like Field1, Field2, and so on. You can change these field names later by renaming them after you finish the importing process.

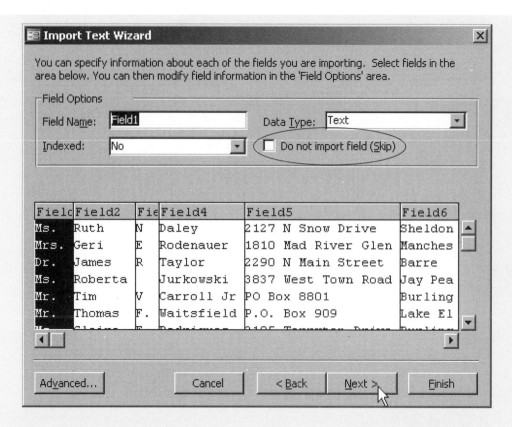

Figure B-5. In this window, if you want to avoid importing a particular field, you can turn on the Do not import field (circled). You can also specify details about each field, like text or number formatting.

9. **On the next screen, you see that Access automatically adds an "ID" field to the imported table that will serve as the table's primary key if you want to use it. This works for you, so click Next.**

   If you had a different field you wanted to use as primary key, you would choose to set your own primary key instead.

10. **In the final Import Text Wizard screen, click inside the Import to Table field, and type a new name for your document.**

    Or just accept Access's suggested name, which is the name of the text file you imported. When you're done, click Finish to close the wizard.

To see how well your importing job did, click to open ExistingMembers to see the newly created table. You should see that the result is pretty clean. But you'll notice that you've got the automatically set field names of Field 1 and so on. You'll probably want to change the names for each of the fields.

Right-click Field 1 and select Rename, as shown in Figure B-6. Next, click inside Field1, press Delete to remove the preset name, and type *Title*. Repeat this action to change the other fields to *First Name*, *Last Name*, and so on, right through to *Phone No*.

While you went through several steps to convert the existing table from the Word document into the table in Access you now have, this process is still probably faster than having to print out a copy of the table and create a new table in Access where you type in all these individual records. The more records you import, the more time you save.

Importing an Excel Spreadsheet into Access

Microsoft Excel, the world's bestselling spreadsheet program, isn't always used to crunch numbers. People often create a spreadsheet—called a *worksheet* in Excel—to keep track of information, including details for a project and even a contact list.

In fact, you can create a list in Excel that acts very much like a basic database. If you're new to Access but not to Excel, you may have already created a list in Excel,

Figure B-6. You can rename any field label at any time by right-clicking the field heading and choosing Rename Column. Also, you may want to adjust the field's width so you don't waste space. Right-click the field again, choose Column Width, and select Best Fit.

but now, with the addition of Access to your desktop, you may want to use that Excel list as the start of a new Access database. That's what you're going to do here.

Download (page 10) and open the Excel workbook MonthlyProductionTotals.xls. In this spreadsheet the first worksheet tracks the production totals by employee for each month in 2006. The range of cells, A4:M19, has already been set up as a list, which can work something like a database. Much like the tables you've already seen in Access, an Excel list has labels identifying each field contained in the first row. In this spreadsheet, the person who prepared the list also named the range A4:M19 "ProductionList" to help differentiate this list from anything else contained in the workbook, which will make your job of importing the list easier.

After you've looked at the list, choose File → Save As and save it with the same file-name in your My Documents folder. Next, close this file because Access can't open the file and import the list if it's open in Excel.

To import the list from this spreadsheet into Access:

1. **In Access, create a new blank database and save it with the name *Production*.**

   Access suggests you save it in the My Documents folder.

2. **In the Objects bar, select Tables.**

   Since you'll be importing the list from Excel as a new table in this new database, you want to start from the Tables view, just as you did when you imported a table from Word.

3. **Select File → Get External Data → Import.**

   The Import window opens, where you'll choose the file you want to import into Access.

4. **In the Import window, next to Files of Type, click in the list box and choose Microsoft Excel, as shown in Figure B-7. Next, from the main Import window, double-click Monthly Production Totals to open it.**

   After you specify the Excel file type, you'll see only those files created with Excel listed in the main window of the Import window. Next, the Import Spreadsheet Wizard opens.

5. **Click Named Ranges to display a list of named ranges in this spreadsheet. When the list appears, select ProductionList (see Figure B-8), and click Next.**

   You could also choose an individual spreadsheet (this workbook contains two) from this first wizard screen. But the named range limits the importing to just the records contained in the list.

Figure B-7. When you choose your file type to import, your options include Lotus 1-2-3 (a really old spreadsheet program), HTML (Web page), Paradox (a database program), and Microsoft Excel, as shown here.

6. **When the next wizard screen opens, make sure First Row Contains Column Headings is turned on. If it isn't, click to turn it on. Click Next.**

   This setting is important, because the table you're importing has its own column headings, and you want to make sure the wizard uses those as the field names in Access.

7. **On the next screen, select New Table, and then click Next.**

   You're starting with a blank database, so you don't have an existing table to choose here. On the next screen, you can select one or more fields to exclude (or Skip) when importing. You don't want to make any changes, so click Next again.

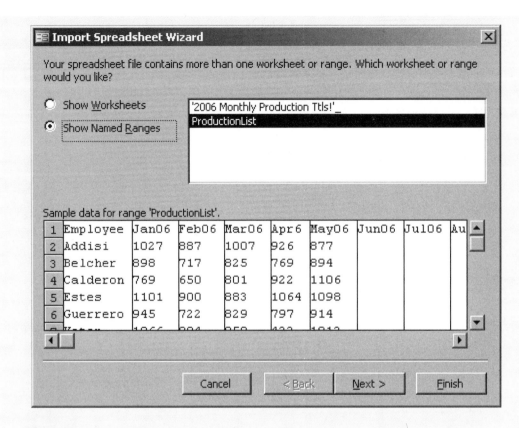

Figure B-8. The big advantage to using a named range in an Excel spreadsheet you're importing is that you don't have to worry about importing superfluous information. Here the Production List range contains exactly the information you want.

Note: If you want to skip a field, you can click the down arrow next to Field, select the field name you want to exclude, and then click to turn on "Skip this field" before you click Next.

8. **Below Import to Table, click in the box, delete any existing text, and type** *2006 Monthly Production Totals.* **Click Finish.**

Your new database table, based on the Excel data, appears in the Tables list in Database view.

To double-check that everything went beautifully and resulted in a perfect new table based on the Excel list, open the newly created table. As you can see in Figure B-9, as well as on your screen, the results are fabulous.

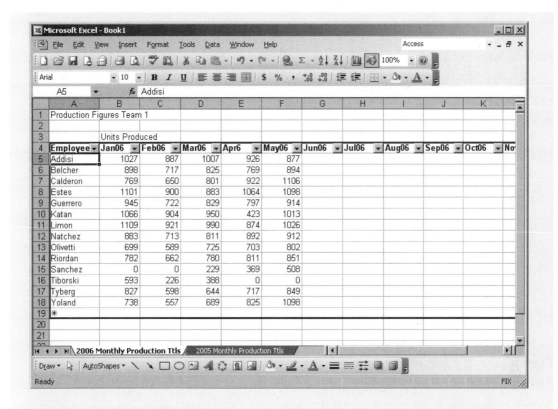

Figure B-9. Unlike the Word table you imported where none of the columns were labeled, here you were able to bring in the column labels along with the imported fields. You won't have to rename these fields unless you have a special reason to do so.

Q: Besides importing whole blocks of information into Access from other programs, how easy is it to simply copy smaller bits of information between Access and my word processor or another application?

A: Actually, that's usually very easy to do. You just need to have both files open, like the Access database and a Word document. For example, suppose you want to copy a street address from a Word document into an address field in an Access record in table view.

First, select the information you want to copy from the Word document, and then choose Edit → Copy (or press Ctrl+Insert). Next, move your cursor to the field in the Access table (or other Access object) where you want to place this copied information, and choose Edit → Paste (or press Shift+Insert) to drop the copied address into place.

Q: *This book hints that Access can import and export information directly to Web pages and Web sites. How about a little more information on this?*

A: Just about all the Microsoft Office programs are *Web friendly*, meaning they let you both import information from the Web and save your own files as Web pages. That lets you upload them to a Web server just like any other Web site, where your friends (and enemies) can visit them. Next, when you save a Word document as a Web page, it looks and works pretty much the same on the Internet as on your own screen. Not so with Access databases.

Making an Access file Web-worthy usually involves the creation of special files called *Data access pages*, in which you can either simply report data from your database on a Web site or let visitors add data directly or download information into their own copies of Access. Data access pages are a subject unto themselves, well beyond the scope of this book, but if you're game, try a book like *Microsoft Access 2003 Professional Results* by Noel Jerke (McGraw-Hill), which focuses on Access's Web side.

Q: *Every time I read something about creating Web pages, I see the term XML. What is it?*

A: XML stands for *Extensible Markup Language*, which is the universal data format of the Web. Many databases and spreadsheets store information in what's called a *proprietary format*, meaning that when you get a data file from someone else, you often have to have the same program they use in order to open the file. XML changes all that, because most modern database programs—in fact, all kinds of programs—can understand XML documents.

Access can read XML files and save information in XML format. Data access pages, as described above, use some XML. XML is a programming language, and you don't have to learn XML in order to use it. If anyone asks for a copy of your data in XML format, just open up your table, choose File → Export, type a name for the new file, and choose XML from the "Save as type" menu.

Validation

Q: Even when I'm the only one adding records to my database, I find I'm not always consistent. For example, I may misspell a name, or I abbreviate an entry in one place but not in another. Other times, I forget and leave fields blank that I didn't intend to skip. How can I make Access be more demanding so that I don't create these inconsistencies?

A: What you're talking about actually involves *validation*, or making certain that what you enter in a field meets the condition(s) you establish for that data. As part of this validation, you can also tell Access not to allow a field to be left blank or skipped.

Also, there are two major types of validation:

▶ **Field validation.** With this type of validation, you're specifying the values, or a range of values, that can be entered into a specific field. You can tell Access that a field's valid entries can be any number between 0–10, for example.

▶ **Record validation.** This validation is used when you have a reason to force Access to check the contents entered into one field against another field in the same record to determine if the value entered is legitimate. Here's an example: Say you have one field that specifies the maximum credit limit allowed for an account holder. If someone then tried to enter a credit purchase that is greater than the amount of the remaining credit amount, that person would see an error message (in the Validation text field under a field's properties).

It's time to try some examples. Open the ClassGrades2 database (page 10). This database is the starter database you used in an earlier example when you did some basic calculations. Two forms have been created with this database to allow for data entry. You're going to change the properties of one of the forms to make certain that a field can't be left blank and that whatever is entered into a field meets conditions you set.

To do this:

1. **From Database view, from the Objects menu, click Forms.**

   Since you'll most often use forms to enter data, it makes sense to change the form attached to a table. You can, however, apply validation to a table using the same steps outlined here.

2. **From the Forms menu, select Grades, and then, from the Database toolbar, click Design.**

   The Grades form opens in Design view, as shown in Figure B-10.

3. **Right-click inside the field labeled Test1, and choose Properties.**

   When you choose Properties here, you're opening the Properties window for a specific field, with the name of the field at the top of the window.

4. **Select the All tab.**

   Here you set validation rules and test for a field.

5. **To the right of Validation Rule, click inside the dialog box, and type the expression: *>=0 AND <=100*, also shown in Figure B-10.**

   What this expression means is that the value provided must be 0 or greater but no higher than 100, since all grade values fall between 0 and 100.

6. **Next, to the right of Validation Text, click in the dialog box, and type *The value entered must be between 0 and 100.***

   By providing this text, you're telling Access to pop up an error window, whenever someone tries to enter a value that doesn't fit this field, that instructs them what the valid field values are.

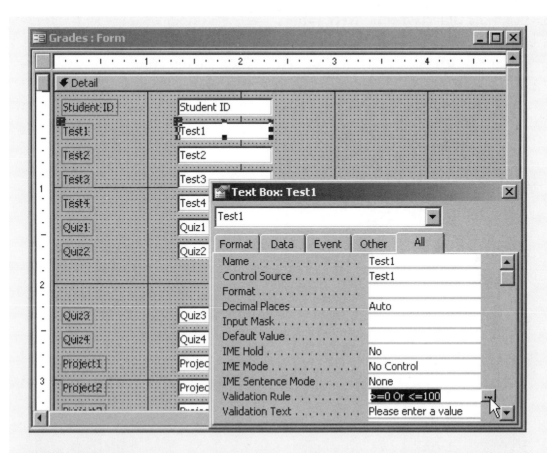

Figure B-10. When you have a form open in Design view (top), you can click the edge of a field box and, holding your mouse button down, drag the hand to resize it, like the Test1 field shown here. Right-click a field and choose Properties for more precise settings (bottom).

7. **Close the Properties window and, when prompted, save the changes to the form.**

   You're not done yet because you also want to require some value to be typed in this field, rather than skipped. For that, you'll switch to the Tables view.

8. **From the Objects menu, select Tables.**

   Next, you'll choose the table where this information would be entered.

9. **Select Individual Grades, and then, from the Database toolbar, click Design view.**

10. **When you do this, the table opens up using the Design window you've used before.**

    Click within the field Test1. Specific information for this field opens, as shown in Figure B-11.

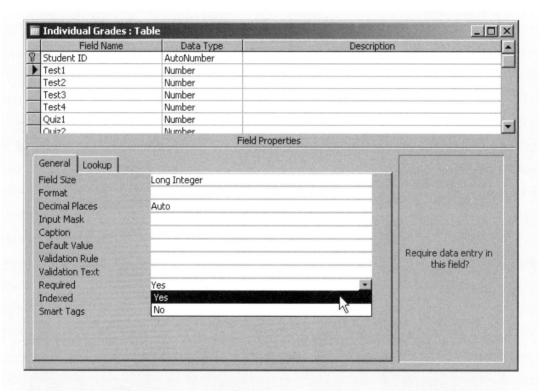

Figure B-11. Be selective. Don't make all fields required unless you expect that a particular field will apply to every record. For example, if you provide two address fields, for primary and secondary addresses, you may only need the primary one.

11. **At the bottom of the window, click in the field next to Required, and select Yes.**

You've now made it mandatory that someone enters something in this field and can't leave it blank. You can now close the field and table and save the changes, when prompted to do so.

Understand that validation can get far fancier and more sophisticated than what you've seen here. But this example gives you a sense for what you can do and how you can control your data entry, regardless of how many different people are adding or editing records and the level of consistency they generally use in working with them.

Q: *I've heard of something called a lookup list that you can use for a type of validation. What's a lookup list?*

A: You're undoubtedly thinking of a method of data entry where folks can choose entries from a list that pops up onscreen, rather than typing the whole word or phrase. Access actually has two ways of outfitting your database with this type of list—*value lists* and *lookup lists*. Both are quite easy to implement with a wizard, and both can look and act the same for the person entering the data. Both kinds of lists are attached to a *lookup field*, which actually goes and *looks up* information stored elsewhere in your database to display on the list. A lookup list is a better option when you don't know in advance exactly what the data will be: To change what's on the list, you just edit the field in its table. In fact, the list is updated automatically when anyone adds or edits the field's values in, say, another form in your database. A value list is better when the data to be entered is unchanging, like a list of the 50 United States (although you can go back and edit a value list later).

To add either kind of list to your database, you can start either in Form Design view or Table Design view. In Table Design view, click the field you want a list for (State, for example), and choose Lookup Wizard in the Data Type column. The Lookup Wizard opens.

To create a value list, choose "I will type in the values I want." The next screen gives you a one-column table to enter the list items (Figure B-12). Type a list of states, for example. Lastly, the wizard asks you to type a label, if desired, that will appear when you use the field on a form.

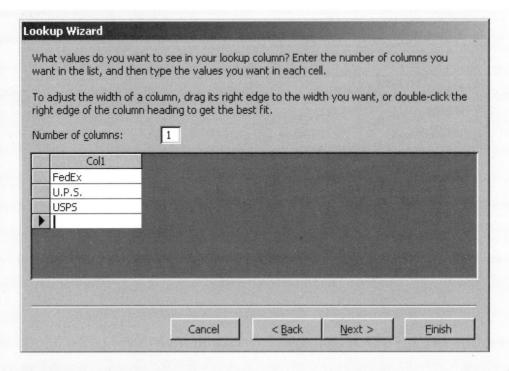

Figure B-12. When you're creating a value list in the Lookup Wizard, type the items that you want your database's users to be able to choose from.

To create a lookup list, choose "I want the lookup column to look up the values in a table or query" on the first wizard screen. On the next screen, you get to choose the table and field that holds the information you want on the list. For example, in the first and last name fields on the orders table, you may want data-entry people to choose from names that are already in the Customers table. In a related database, the wizard gives you a chance to hide the CustomerID number, so that data-entry people only see the name.

Note: You can also create a value list or lookup list in Form Design view. Start by clicking the Control Wizards button on the Toolbox, and click the List Box button. Drag the field on your form design. When you let go of the mouse, the List Box Wizard opens, offering much the same choices as the Lookup Wizard, just not in the same order.

Finding Find

Q: Chapter 3 is all about finding information in Access, so why is there so little mention of the Find dialog box?

A: Actually, that's two questions. But the same answer covers both. You won't see Access's Find and Replace dialog box very often since you don't need it very often. Most of the time, in a database, you're searching for records; the Find and Replace dialog box searches for text. You might use it when, for example, you have a table open in datasheet view and want to find all the records in a field that begin with "Ma," because the boss is named "Mr. Mazel" and think someone might have spelled his name differently. Since it looks and works much like the Find box in most word processing programs (see Figure B-14, on the next page), some folks find it easier to use than learning the ins and outs of sorting, filtering, and querying.

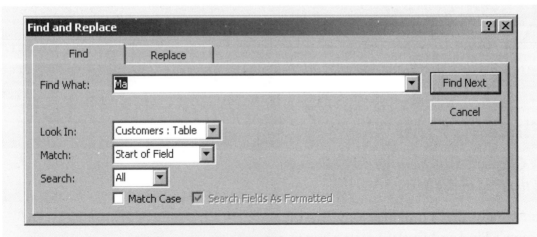

Figure B-13. Access's filtering and querying features are orders of magnitude more powerful than its Find dialog box, but it's there if you insist on using it.

APPENDIX C:
ACCESS 2003, MENU BY MENU

▶ File Menu

▶ Edit Menu

▶ View Menu

▶ Insert Menu

▶ Format Menu

▶ Records Menu

▶ Tools Menu

▶ Window Menu

▶ Help Menu

ACCESS LETS YOU VIEW YOUR INFORMATION in so many different kinds of windows (and lets you open so many at once), that it's oddly comforting to know you can depend on one thing—the menu bar. Stretching across the top of the main Access window, it offers a standard set of command menus: File, Edit, View, Insert, Format, Tools, Window, and Help. Although these menu items undoubtedly look familiar, some of the commands you find on them are specific to Access. Moreover, the contents of a menu often change depending on what kind of Access window you're working in (Table, Form, Design view, and so on). In fact, some menus appear and disappear from the menu bar according to which window you're working in, like the Records, Query, and Pivot Table menus.

Microsoft clearly values your time as well as your screen space. You can't add records in Design view, for example, so Access doesn't clutter up your screen with that menu. Similarly, the Insert menu changes wildly whenever you switch windows to show you only those items you're likely (or allowed) to insert in that particular view. So if you can't find a menu or command you're looking for, it may be because you can't use it in the current window or view anyway. Try clicking a different window or form. Table view, in general, is likely to give you the most options.

This appendix lists all commands on Access's main menu bar and briefly describes what they do. Although the menu bar lacks the speed of toolbar buttons and the glitz of task panes (after all, it's older technology), it still offers some commands you can't find elsewhere. Nothing beats the menu bar for seeing all your options at a glance. More important (and largely overlooked), the menu bar lets you use the fastest technology of all—your fingers on the keyboard. (See the box on page 339.)

 Tip: This appendix mentions some commands that pertain to advanced features that are beyond the scope of this book. When you're ready to learn more, consult a heftier tome like *Using Access 2003* by Roger Jennings (Que).

Keep Them Fingers Movin'

You can perform almost any Access 2003 menu command right from the keyboard. For tasks that you do many times a day (or many times an hour), reaching for the mouse can actually slow you down. See how one letter of each menu on the menu bar is underlined? That means you can press Alt + [that underlined letter] to open the menu. From there, you can press the underlined letter of any menu command to choose it instantly. Or you can use the arrow keys to move up and down the menu, pressing Enter to activate the highlighted command.

Once a menu is open, you can use the right and left arrow keys to move from one menu to the next, back and forth across the menu bar. If a menu command has submenus, press the right arrow key to see it, and then you can navigate it like any other menu. Press the left arrow key to back out of submenu-land.

In addition to the Alt key technique, Access has a multitude of other keyboard shortcuts. If there's a shortcut, you'll see it on the menu, like Shift+Enter for Save Record, as

shown here. For your own personal cheat sheet, search for keyboard shortcuts in Access help. Click the link to open the Keyboard Shortcuts help page (it's probably the first thing on the list of search results), and then, at the top of that page, click Show All. Voilá! You get a chart of every single keyboard shortcut in Access. At the top of the window, click the printer icon to commit the list to paper.

Finally, if you see a colorful icon to the left of a menu command, that means the command has a corresponding toolbar button. If you look around, you may see the icon on a toolbar, the objects panel, or the task pane. Next time you're mousing around, you can click the button instead. Some Access mavens even create toolbars with just their own favorite buttons. It's not too hard, as the box on page 366 explains.

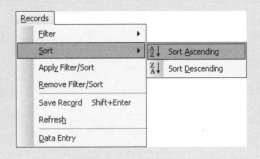

File Menu

Like others of its kind, the Access File menu is all about using and organizing the documents on your computer or network. It's where you start your database, and where you go when you're done to print, back up, and send it out to the world.

New

Opens the New File task pane, where you can choose a blank, empty database to start from, or choose one of Access's built-in templates (page 27). The pane also has links to more templates on Microsoft's Web site, as discussed in Appendix B. *Keyboard shortcut:* Ctrl+N.

Tip: To open a new *table* (or other object within your database), use the Insert menu (page 353).

Open

Opens Windows' standard Open dialog box, where you can choose an existing database file to open from anywhere on your computer or network. *Keyboard shortcut:* Ctrl+O.

Tip: For more information on navigating Windows windows, check out *Windows XP: The Missing Manual*, by David Pogue.

Get External Data

This oddly named command reveals two different options on its submenu:

▶ **Import.** Launches an Open dialog box, where you can choose a file of compatible information to bring in and use in Access. See page 314 for more detail.

▶ **Link Table.** Produces yet another Open dialog box, where you can choose a table, from within any Access database on your computer, and use it in the current database without actually adding the table to your database file.

Close

Closes the current Access window. To close Access completely, use File → Exit. Access asks if you want to save before closing.

Save

The Save command in Access works a little differently than in most other programs, in that you don't have to worry about saving *records*. Access saves each record automatically as soon as you leave it and go on to the next one. The Save command instead saves design changes that you make to database objects. That's why, when you switch from Design view to another view, or close a design window, Access asks if you want to save your changes. When you're using a form, entering records, don't bother with this command. *Keyboard shortcut:* Ctrl+S.

 Note: Because you do have to save design changes, Access has an AutoRecover feature (like other Microsoft Office programs). Your files are always safer if you save early and often.

Save As

In Access, Save As is multitalented. Instead of just letting you save the current database file under a new name, it lets you do the same thing to whatever individual object is in the front-most window—like a form. Remember that an Access database file is like a container containing tables, forms, and other database objects, so the program lets you save and copy them individually.

To save your *entire* Access database file (.mdb), see the next command.

Back Up Database

Opens a typical Windows Save As dialog box, to create an exact copy of your entire database file. Access suggests adding today's date to the file name, but you can use any naming system you choose. Since it creates a completely normal database file, you can use it any time you need a duplicate, not just as a backup.

Tip: If you don't see the Back Up Database command, you probably do see two little arrows at the bottom of the File menu. The arrows mean you're looking at an abbreviated version of the menu. Access likes to shorten its menus to save space by hiding the less commonly used commands. Click the arrows at the bottom of the menu to expand it, or just wait a moment, and the menu soon expands on its own, revealing *all* its commands. Unless you work on a tiny subnotebook screen, you can tell Access to show the entire menu every time in the Tools → Customize → Options panel.

Export

Starts the process of exporting the current table or other database object. The Export dialog box lets you choose a name, location, and file type for the exported material. For instance, you can save a table as another Access table, or as an Excel or text document, so you can use its information in another program.

File Search

Opens the task pane to the Basic File Search panel. If you can't find the database yourself in the Open dialog box, you can tell Windows to go look for it by typing some text that you know is in the desired file. The pane also lets you limit your search to certain folders, drives, and file types, and to a handy Search Tips link if you need assistance.

Page Setup

Usually used before you print a report or other Access document. The Page Setup dialog box lets you choose margins, paper size, column layout, and so on. (As with the Open dialog box, the options you see here are pretty standard to Windows.)

Print

Opens the standard Windows Print dialog box, where you can select a printer, choose which pages to print and how many, and so on. In Access, you usually print a report of your database's information (page 48). *Keyboard shortcut:* Ctrl+P.

Send To

The Send To command is Access's way of making it easy to email your database to someone. The submenu has two options, but the second one, **Mail Recipient (as Attachment)**, is usually the only one available. Choosing it creates an attachment from the current window or selection, and then opens your email program with a new message ready to address and send.

(The first option, **Mail Recipient**, places selected information right in the body of an email. Most Access windows don't lend themselves to that treatment.)

Database Properties

Opens the properties sheet for the database file, where you can view some statistical information, type a title, author, and so on. Windows and other programs, and some technical-type people, use this information to learn about your file.

[Recent Files]

At the bottom of every File menu is a list of the last few databases you've had open. Instead of using the Open dialog box, scooting down here to choose one is a much faster way to pick up where you left off in Access. You can change the number of files in this list, or eliminate the list entirely, in the Tools → Options → General panel.

Tip: If a menu command is "grayed out," that means it's not available to you at the moment. For example, if you're working in a form and the View → Subform command looks light gray instead of black, you can be pretty confident that the form doesn't have any subforms (page 132). Sure, it's frustrating if you were expecting to use subforms, but think of the unavailable command as a gentle way of alerting you to the problem. It's better than choosing a normal-looking Subform command and wondering why nothing happens.

Exit

Closes the Access window and everything in it. If you've made any database changes and not yet saved them, Access gives you a chance to do so before exiting. If you're not sure, click Cancel to stop the whole exit process and go right back to your database.

Edit Menu

The Edit Menu commands focus on editing tools, whether that means moving text around in an email message or memo, looking for a text string inside Entourage's files, managing message threads, or changing an item's category.

Undo

Takes back the last thing that you did. The wording of the command varies depending on what you just did and what window you're in. Undo can toss out the last change you made to a record, or put something you dragged in Design view back where it started. *Keyboard shortcut:* Ctrl+Z.

Undo Current Field/Record

When you're entering information into a table, datasheet, or form, this command lets you back out of any changes you've made to that record—that is, *until* you go on to another record. When you do, this command changes to **Saved Record**, giving you one last chance to return to the previous record before you made those changes. As soon as you start typing in the *new* record, however, the Undo command erases any memory of the previous record and turns back into a normal Undo command. *Keyboard shortcut for all these options:* still Ctrl+Z.

Redo

Once you've undone something, the Redo command becomes available, in case you change your mind. Again. *Keyboard shortcut:* Ctrl+Y.

 Warning: When you switch to a different view or different object in your database, Access erases its Undo memory. When you come back to a window, the menu says you Can't Undo (or Redo) what you did the last time you were there.

Cut

Cuts the selected text or object out of the document and puts it on the Clipboard, ready for pasting into a different window or program. Works on whatever you've selected—text, records, or (in the Database window) objects. *Keyboard shortcut:* Ctrl+X.

Copy

Copies the selected text or object and puts it on the Clipboard, ready for pasting into a different window or program. It works just like Cut, but duplicates instead of deleting what you've selected. *Keyboard shortcut:* Ctrl+C.

Office Clipboard

Opens the Office Clipboard in the task pane, which lists the last 24 things you've cut and copied in Access (and any other Office programs you have open). You can go back and reuse any of these clippings until you exit Access, which clears the clipboard. *Keyboard shortcut:* Press Ctrl+C twice.

Paste

Places whatever you've cut or copied where the cursor is blinking. *Keyboard shortcut:* Ctrl+V.

Paste Special

Opens the Paste Special dialog box, where you can change the format of what you're pasting. For example, you can paste the contents of a record you've copied as plain text, without all the formatting that makes Access recognize it as a record. (Expand the Edit menu if you don't see the Paste Special command.)

Tip: Adding a linked object is part of Office's Object Linking and Embedding feature (OLE for short). All Office programs use OLE. The linked object (the one in your database) updates automatically whenever you make changes to the original. For a fuller discussion of OLE, see *Excel: The Missing Manual* by Matthew MacDonald.

Paste as Hyperlink

Pastes the selected item as a link you can click to go to another file (page 355).

Paste Append

Places the cut or copied fields in a new record at the end of the table. This highly useful, but little-known, command is designed especially for pasting record information. If you try to paste that information using the standard Paste command, you get an error message.

 Tip: You can use Paste Append freely in both Excel and Access, to paste entire records or just a few selected fields. The only requirement is that the material you're pasting and the destination table or spreadsheet have the same fields.

Duplicate

(Form and Report Design views only.) Copies the selected item and puts it right there on the screen next to the original.

Create Shortcut

(Database window only.) Makes a shortcut icon of whatever you've selected in the Database window, just like a shortcut on the Windows desktop.

Delete

Completely removes the selected text, record, or object without copying it to the clipboard. Before deleting an entire record or object, Access asks for your confirmation. *Keyboard shortcut:* Del.

Rename

(Database window only.) Lets you type a new name for a table or other database object.

Groups

(Database window only.) Lets you create groups of tables, forms, and other objects in your database. Great for reducing Database window clutter as you add objects to your database. For instance, you can create a separate group for the reports you use only at tax time, and you don't have to look at them the rest of the year. Just click the group's folder in the Objects bar when April 15 looms.

A submenu lets you Rename and Delete groups just like other database objects.

Add to Group

(Database window only.) Opens a submenu listing any groups you've created, plus a built-in group called favorites. Choose one to add the selected object to that group.

Delete Record, Delete Column

Below the Delete command, the menu may show more specific options.

Select Record

Selects whatever record you're currently in, a real convenience in Form view.

Select All

In Design and Query views, selects all the labels and fields in the current window, so you can cut or copy them.

Select All Records

Selects all records in the current table. *Keyboard shortcut:* Ctrl+A.

Select Form

In Design view, lets you select an entire form to paste (in a new design window, say).

Find, Replace

Opens the Find and Replace dialog box, as discussed in detail on page 335. *Keyboard shortcuts:* Ctrl+F to open to the Find tab, Ctrl+H to open to the Replace tab.

Go To

Opens a submenu where you can jump directly to the First, Last, Next, and Previous records. It's the menu equivalent of the buttons at the bottom of form and table windows, but may be even faster if you memorize the Alt key combinations (see the box on page 339). At the bottom of the submenu is New Record, which has its own nifty shortcut: Ctrl++.

OLE/DDE Links

Opens a window where you can see all the links in the current database. This feature is available only if you've created linked objects (page 345), or in huge, complex database systems created by network administrators or Web designers.

View Menu

As well as letting you switch between different views of the same window, this menu opens new view windows for many aspects of database creation and management.

Design View

Switches the current form to Design view, as discussed in detail in Chapter 3.

SQL View

(Query window only.) Shows the underlying SQL statement for a query (page 189).

Form View

Switches Design view back to Form view.

Datasheet View

Takes you to the Datasheet view (page 44) for whatever table you're currently working in. In other words, it lets you see your table as a table.

PivotTable View

Opens the Pivot Table view for the current form, or, if there isn't one, opens a blank pivot table screen and the Pivot Table Field List, so you can drag and drop fields to create the pivot table.

PivotChart View

Similar to Pivot Table view, it lets you drag fields onto a graph to display your information in one of those charts that make such a good impression at company meetings.

 Tip: When you're in Pivot Table or Pivot Chart view, a new menu appears by the same name, where you can do things like total and rearrange the information displayed. For full coverage of Pivot Tables, see *Excel: The Missing Manual* by Matthew MacDonald.

Table Names

(Query window only.) Shows (or hides) the names of the tables that each query field comes from. You may want to hide names if they're all in the same table.

Totals

(Query window only.) Adds a Total row to your query form (page 240).

Subform in New Window

(Design view only.) Lets you add a subform to your form, as discussed on page 144.

Database Objects

(Database window only.) Lists the same things as in the Objects bar: Tables, Queries, Forms, Reports, Pages, Macros, Modules, and any Group folders (page 17). Choose one to go to that panel of the Database window.

Large Icons, Small Icons

(Database window only.) Lets you choose the size of the icons displayed in the Database window.

List

(Database window only.) Switches the Database window to a list view.

Details

(Database window only.) Similar to list view, has columns that display information about each object in addition to the name, like a description, and the date you last modified it.

Arrange Icons

(Database window only.) *Sort* would be a better name for this command. It lets you choose how to sort the icons in the Database window—alphabetically by name, chronologically by the date you created them, and so on. Turning on AutoArrange keeps them in that order automatically whenever you move, add, or delete objects.

Line Up Icons

(Database window only.) If you've dragged objects around (which you can do in an icon view), this command puts them back into neat rows.

Properties

Opens the Properties sheet (page 95) for the current window or selected object. *Keyboard shortcut:* Alt+Enter.

Field List

(Design view only.) Opens a separate window listing all the fields in the current table, so you can drag them onto a form or report you're creating.

Code

(Design view only.) Opens the current form in Microsoft Visual Basic Editor. In this window, you can create and modify macros using the Visual Basic programming language. The tools in this window make Visual Basic easier to use than most programming languages, but you'll need a little instruction first. (If you end up in Code view by mistake, in the upper-left corner, click the little Access icon to return to Access.)

 Tip: A fine primer on Visual Basic is *Now Playing: Visual Basic 2005 Express* by Wallace Wang (No Starch Press). *Excel: The Missing Manual*, mentioned in the Tip on page 349, also has good basic coverage.

Ruler, Grid

Displays these elements of the Design window (page 115).

Toolbox

Opens the panel of Design tools (page 111).

Page Header/Footer, Form Header/Footer

(Design view only.) Adds these elements to your layout (page 269).

Task Pane

Opens the Office task pane at the right of your screen, to whatever pane you were last looking at. *Keyboard shortcut:* Ctrl+F1.

Object Dependencies

Opens the Object Dependencies task pane, where you can see what tables, forms, queries, and reports in some way rely on what you're looking at in the current window (or vice versa). For instance, if you're looking at a form that displays customer information, you'll see the table that contains your customer records in the dependencies list. Because your form gets its information from that table, Access says the form has a *dependency* to the table.

What this dependency means to you is, if you delete the table, you're going to render the form useless. But you can delete the form without harming the table at all. It's a good idea to consult the Object Dependencies pane before you delete a table or any major object in your database.

Indexes

(Table window only.) Lets you index fields in your database (page 73).

Join Properties

(Query and Relationship windows only.) Opens the Join Properties dialog box, where you can create links between tables (page 140).

Toolbars

Opens a submenu that lists all available toolbars in Access. You have complete control over which toolbars are open, but Access usually keeps one open for you depending on the view you're in: Table Datasheet, Form view, or Form Design. This main toolbar contains the Save, Cut and Paste, Undo and Redo, and other commands you're most likely to use. Other options are:

▶ **Formatting.** Shows various options for formatting text, same as the Format menu.

▶ **Task Pane.** Does the same as selecting View → Task Pane.

▶ **Toolbox.** Opens a panel of buttons for editing and creating onscreen items in Design view (page 111). It's the same as choosing View → Toolbox.

▶ **Web.** Lets you create, follow, and edit hyperlinks in Access, and open Web pages (in your Web browser).

▶ **Customize.** Lets you create your own toolbars, as described in the box on page 366. It's the same as the Tools → Customize command.

Zoom

Lets you choose how big to see the page on your screen, from 1000% all the way down to 10%. You can also Fit to Window. Zoom is usually available only in Report view.

Pages

Lets you choose how many pages to display onscreen at the same time, and is mostly useful for getting an overview of a report.

Refresh

Access lets multiple people use a database simultaneously on a network. Choosing Refresh tells Access to update your window with changes others have made.

Note: Refresh doesn't recognize added or deleted records unless you're working in a special kind of shared database called an Access Data Project (ADP). Network administrators can set these up on a SQL server.

Insert Menu

Lets you add all sorts of objects into your database. Depending on the view you're in, you can add records or fields to a table, or various layout features to a form.

Tip: If you're in the Database window, the Insert menu contains none of the commands listed here. Instead, it lets you add *objects* to your database, like tables and forms.

New Record

Adds a new record to your database, ready to fill in. *Keyboard shortcut:* Ctrl++.

Column, Row

Adds a new field to the current table. In Datasheet view, a new field is a column. In Table Design view (page 45), it's called a row, since fields in that window are arranged in rows. Fortunately, you don't have to worry about choosing the right one—Access shows only the appropriate command for the view you're in.

Lookup Column/Lookup Field

Starts the Lookup Wizard, which lets you add a lookup field to your table. You can create a column of new values, or utilize information in a field that actually belongs to another table (page 333). It's a way of keeping these values separate from your main table, without creating a relational database as discussed in Chapter 4.

Subdatasheet

Opens the Insert Subdatasheet dialog box, where you can choose a table or query to become a subdatasheet to the datasheet you're currently working in (page 132).

Page Numbers, Date and Time

(Design view only.) Lets you add page numbers and the current date and time to the header or footer of a form, query, or report.

Chart

(Design view only.) Launches the Chart Wizard, where you can choose information from any table in your database and format it as a chart. The chart form updates automatically as you add and edit information in your database. Charts in Access work just like charts in Microsoft Excel, and you can learn all about them in *Excel: The Missing Manual* by Matthew MacDonald.

Object

In Design view, lets you add an Office object to your form, which can be an Excel chart or worksheet, a Word document, a picture, and so on. It gives you a way of using, say, Word's powerful text formatting tools in your database.

ActiveX Control

(Design view only.) Places an ActiveX control on your form. ActiveX controls are part of Microsoft's Visual Basic scripting system (page 351). For one very simple example, they let database gurus create buttons that launch a script when clicked. To learn more, *Access Database Design and Programming, 3rd Edition,* by Steven Roman (O'Reilly) is a great reference.

Hyperlink

(Design view only.) Opens the Insert Hyperlink dialog box, where you can navigate to and select the thing you want to link to, be it a Web page, another part of your database, a document on your computer, or an email address.

Hyperlink Column

(Table window only.) Adds a new column to your table that's specially formatted to link to records in another table (page 79).

Tab Control Page

(Design view only.) This command adds a new tab page like the one you can see in Figure 1-3 to your form. Once you've got the tab, you can drag fields onto it just like any other form.

Format Menu

This menu offers commands that let you adjust the appearance of your onscreen information. The Database window doesn't show this menu, since there's nothing to format. To format a Report, switch it to Design view; otherwise, you won't see a Format menu either.

Font

Opens the Font dialog box, where you can choose any of the fonts installed on your PC, as well as size, bold or italic, and other effects.

Datasheet

Opens the Datasheet Formatting dialog box, where you can choose colors for the sheet's background and its cell borders. You can also add sophisticated-looking effects like a 3-D raised or sunken look to each cell.

Row Height, Column Width

Opens a small dialog box where you can type the desired dimensions in points.

Hide Columns, Unhide Columns

Controls the clutter factor by choosing which columns to show in Datasheet view. (This command doesn't actually delete columns.)

Freeze Columns, Unfreeze All Columns

Lets you freeze a column (usually the left-most one, containing record numbers or names), so that it stays in place as you scroll to the right to view the rest of the columns.

Subdatasheet

This submenu lets you control the display of a subdatasheet: You can expand all the child items or remove the subdatasheet. (This command is available only after you've inserted a subdatasheet.)

AutoFormat

(Form/Report design views.) Lets you choose one of Access's built-in themes, like Blends or Ricepaper for forms, or Casual or Corporate for reports. When you're in a hurry, they're fine, if a little bland. When you choose one in the AutoFormat window and click OK, Access instantly applies it to your entire layout.

Conditional Formatting

(Form/Report design views.) When you choose this command after clicking one of the fields or controls on your form, it opens the Conditional Formatting dialog box.

This window lets you select a different appearance for the field when certain conditions are met—like making negative numbers appear "in the red."

Align

(Form/Report design views.) When you're designing your own form, this submenu helps you get the fields and/or labels lined up. You can line them up by their left edges, or choose Right, Top, or Bottom. The To Grid option neatens up your form by sticking your fields or labels to the nearest gridline (page 117).

Size

(Form/Report design views.) Oddly, this submenu doesn't let you specify size, as you would when formatting text. Instead, it's a smoother-outer, like the Align submenu above. You can choose:

▸ **To Fit.** Makes the selected field or label grow or shrink to just hold its contents.

▸ **To Grid.** Snaps items to the nearest gridline.

▸ **To Tallest, Shortest, Widest, Narrowest.** When you select multiple fields or labels, choosing one of these dimensions resizes all of them to match. For example, if you choose tallest, Access finds the tallest one you've selected and makes the rest of them equally tall.

Horizontal Spacing

(Form/Report design views.) Available only when you've selected multiple fields, this command offers three options for quickly regularizing their arrangement. To use it, select only fields across from each other, not one beneath the other, and don't select labels. Otherwise, the command doesn't work properly. Then select one of the following options from the submenu:

▸ **Make Equal.** Keeps the right-most and left-most fields in place and evenly spaces the ones in between them.

- **Increase.** Keeps the left-most field in place and spreads the rest of the selected fields as far to the right as possible, but with even spacing and without letting them bump into other form objects.

- **Decrease.** Keeps the left-most field in place and pulls all the other selected fields in closer.

Vertical Spacing

(Form/Report design views.) Does the same thing as Horizontal Spacing, but works on selected fields stacked on top of one another. The Increase and Decrease options keep the *top-most* field in place and realign all the others.

Group

(Form/Report design views.) When you select multiple fields and/or labels and then choose this command, Access considers them as a group and shows a thick black border all the way around them to indicate as much. Dragging, cutting, pasting, and aligning all work on the group as a whole.

Ungroup

(Form/Report design views.) Removes the groupness from the selected group, returning objects to their individual state.

Bring To Front, Send to Back

(Form/Report design views.) When layout objects overlap (intentionally), you can choose which one goes in the foreground or background.

Records Menu

The commands on this menu all have to do with sorting and filtering records, so you see it in the menu bar only when you're in a Table, Form, or Query window. If you want to work with your records and can't see this menu, you probably need to switch out of the Database window or out of Design view.

Tip: The commands in this menu are covered in much greater detail in Chapter 5.

Filter

This submenu gives you four options:

▶ **Filter By Form.** Opens a special, blank view of the current datasheet or form, where you can choose the fields to filter by (page 171).

▶ **Filter By Selection.** Filters out (hides) all but the currently selected records. Also filters for text you've selected in *part* of a field (page 168).

▶ **Filter Excluding Selection.** Hides all records that meet the selected criteria.

▶ **Advanced Filter/Sort.** Opens the Filter dialog box (page 178).

Tip: Click the Filter (funnel) button on the toolbar to undo any of these filters.

Sort

Offers a submenu with two options, Ascending and Descending. Works on whatever field your cursor's currently in. (Doesn't appear in Form view.)

Apply Filter/Sort, Remove Filter/Sort

Toggles between sorted/filtered records and unsorted/unfiltered records (whichever you did last).

Save Record

Saves the record you're currently working in. *Keyboard shortcut:* Shift+Enter.

Refresh

Updates what's in the current database window with changes other people have made (page 353).

Data Entry

Switches the form, datasheet, or query to a special, blank form, ready for you to add a new record to your database. On the toolbar, click the Filter button, or choose Records → Remove Filter/Sort to return to the normal view.

Tools Menu

The items on this menu are features that generally apply to Access as a whole. For instance, it's how you get to the all-powerful Options dialog box and the Relationships window.

Spelling

Checks the spelling of the text in the current record or table, and doesn't work in Design view.

Office Links

The three options on this submenu open wizards that help you connect your database information to another Office program (Word or Excel). For example, for mass mailings, you can merge address information in Access with a letter written in Word.

Online Collaboration

Choosing the Meet Now option launches Microsoft Net Meeting.

Speech

Launches Office's Speech Recognition feature, which lets you say commands instead of choosing them. When you choose Speech for the first time, a wizard, complete with video, opens to guide you through the process of training Access to recognize your voice.

Relationships

Opens Access's Relationships window (page 129).

Tip: When the Relationships window is open, a Relationships menu appears in the menu bar. Its commands are covered in Chapter 4.

Analyze

Lets you check for possible problems in your database, or just learn more about how it works. You have three options:

▶ **Table.** The Table Analyzer Wizard points out duplicate records and misspelled or inconsistently spelled data. Buttons called "Show me an example" open explanatory messages in a separate window. As you click Next, the wizard shows you each problem it detects and offers to walk you through the solution. (You can say No, or click Cancel to back out any time.)

▶ **Performance.** The Performance Analyzer options a tabbed dialog box listing every single object, down to the most minute, in your database,. You select one at a time for Access to check. Access either reports that it found no problems or opens a dialog box where you can read about the problem and choose whether or not to let Access fix it.

▶ **Documenter.** After choosing an object from a dialog box exactly as in the Performance Analyzer, Access prepares a written report listing every single detail about that object. You can print this page like any Access report. (Much of the information comes from the Properties sheet; see page 95.)

Database Utilities

The options on this submenu let you work with your database file as a whole:

▶ **Convert Database.** Opens a sub-submenu where you can choose to save your database formatted for an earlier version of Access.

▶ **Compact and Repair Database.** Access performs a repair on any corruption it finds, reduces file size, and then reopens your database. It's a good maintenance routine.

- **Back Up Database.** Similar to the Save As command, lets you save your database under a new name, as a backup copy.

- **Linked Table Manager.** If you've created links to tables outside your database (page 79), this command opens a window where you can view, edit, and delete them.

- **Switchboard Manager.** Opens a dialog box listing all switchboards (page 40) in your database. If you haven't created one, a message box offers you the chance to do so now. The Switchboard Manager window lets you add, delete, and edit all your switchboards from one convenient location.

- **Make MDE File.** Converts your database into a special format (with an .mde, not .mdb, extension). Unlike a normal database, in an MDE file you can't switch to Design view, create new queries, and so on. It's the way to go if you've worked hard on a database and don't want anyone messing with it.

 Warning: Be sure to create a backup before converting to an MDE file. You can't convert an MDE file back into an MDB file.

Security

This command opens a submenu with options that let you control who has access to your database.

- **Set Database Password.** Opens a dialog box where you can type the password. Assigning a password to open your database is the simplest form of security. (Write it down in a safe place, too, or you may never be able to open the database again!)

- **Workgroup Administrator.** If it appears, shows who owns the copy of Access and is in charge of letting others log into it.

- **User and Group Permissions.** Opens a dialog box where you (the Administrator) can choose other people with accounts (see below) and select which database objects they have access to and what they can do to them (Read Data, Modify Design, and so on).

- **User and Group Accounts.** Where you select the names of people with accounts on your computer or network and give them User or Group accounts for your database.

- **User-Level Security Wizard.** Opens a wizard that walks you through the process of setting accounts and passwords for your database, and then creates a report of the settings you've made.

- **Encode/Decode Database.** Less secure than it sounds, this command simply saves a copy of the database file in a format that only Access can read. No one with, say, a word processor or Excel can sneak into your information. It also shrinks the file size, so it's a good option for emailing or saving the database file to a disk.

 Tip: For all the details on security features, consult a book like *Using Access 2003* by Roger Jennings (Que).

Replication

This advanced feature lets you add a copy of a table from one database to another and keep the information updated in both places. It's network administrator territory.

Startup

Once you've set security options like accounts and permissions, you can use this dialog box to control what happens when your database folks open the file. For instance, you may want to hide the database window from data entry people, so they have to use your switchboard (page 39), which shows only the forms they're supposed to use.

Macro

Opens the Visual Basic Editor (page 351). The submenu also lets you run macros that you or someone else has written into the database. The Security option lets you turn some or all macros off, since macros can be a vehicle for computer viruses.

Add-Ins

Opens the Add-In Manager, a wizard that lets you install add-ins to your copy of Access (the add-in must be on your computer first). Add-ins are mini-programs that add supplementary features to Access. (The Add-In Manager itself is, in fact, an add-in.) Usually, you get add-ins by downloading them from Microsoft's Web site (page 297) or a third-party resource like *www.softwareaddins.com*.

ActiveX Controls

See page 354 earlier in this appendix.

AutoCorrect Options

Opens the AutoCorrect dialog box. If you've used Microsoft Word, this window may look familiar. Like Word, Access automatically corrects your typing if you forget to capitalize the first letter of a sentence, hit Caps Lock by mistake, and so on. In this window, you can tell Access to stop trying to fix things for you.

Customize

Access is a very customizable program: You can add and remove commands from menus, create your own toolbars, and more. This dialog box has three tabs—Toolbar, Customize, and Options.

▶ **Toolbars.** This panel lists all Access toolbars. Turning the checkboxes on and off controls which ones appear automatically. For instance, if you filter and sort a lot, turn on the Filter/Sort toolbar so it's always there—no need to go to the View → Toolbars menu every time (Figure C-1).

▶ **Commands.** This panel lists all Access commands, and it's more exciting than it looks. When it's open, you can drag these commands to add them to any toolbar or menu onscreen. You can even create new menus and toolbars of your own invention (see the box on page 366).

▶ **Options.** This panel controls some simple menu and toolbar settings, like whether to show all commands on a menu every time (or only expand it fully after a couple seconds, as described in the Tip on page 342).

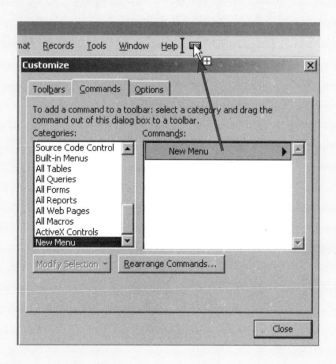

Figure C-1. The last item on the Categories list is called New Menu. When you click it, you can drag New Menu to the menu bar. Click Modify Selection (or right-click the New Menu) to name it. For example, create a new menu named Reports. Click All Reports in the Categories list, and drag the report icons, one by one, up to the menu. Wait until the I-beam appears before releasing the mouse.

Options

The Options dialog box offers 12 tabs, each of which lets you control how a different feature of Access looks and acts. Most of the time, you won't need to adjust any of these, although the General tab is worth a visit. This panel lets you set up some useful features like the following:

Modding Toolbars and Menus

The Customize dialog box is like no other in Access. When it's open, your whole Access window becomes a dialog box. The toolbars and menus look the same as always, but now you can move and edit them at will.

The Toolbars tab lists all toolbars in Access. You can turn these toolbars on and off, to control which ones appear automatically, as explained on page 364. When you turn one on, it immediately appears at the top of your screen.

When the Customize dialog box is open, you can remove toolbar buttons by dragging them off the toolbar. When you see the X icon at your pointer, let go. Poof—it's gone. Click Reset to restore customized toolbars to original condition at any time.

You can also reposition toolbar buttons by dragging them to the new position—indicated by a thick, black I-beam. (If you click Undo a lot, you

may want to put that button at the far left or far right of the toolbar, so you have an easier time spotting it.)

The Commands tab lists all Access commands. Drag them from the list onto any onscreen toolbar to add those command to the toolbar. If the command has a button, the button appears on the toolbar. If there's no button, the wording of the command appears instead.

Just like toolbar buttons, you can also drag the menus in the menu bar to delete and rearrange them. Also, when you open a menu, you can drag commands on and off it from the Commands panel.

▶ **Recently used file list.** Usually, the bottom of the File menu shows the last four files you've visited to make it easier to reopen them. You can increase that number here, or take it all the way down to zero to conceal your tracks.

- **Default database folder.** Choose the folder on your computer where you want to store most of your databases. Access offers it as the first choice in the Save dialog box.

- **Print margins.** No matter what you're printing, set the page margins here. They come factory-set to 1 inch on all sides, but big reports need to crowd more information on the page.

Window Menu

This menu has just a few commands, and they all have to do with the appearance of Access windows on your screen. Since you can easily have so many windows open at once that you can't find your way, this menu can help you get organized quickly.

Tile Horizontally, Tile Vertically

Shrinks all your open windows so they fit on the screen at once, so you can see them all with no overlap. Horizontally creates wide, short windows, and Vertically crates tall, skinny ones. For example, if you have five windows open and choose Tile Vertically, you get five skinny windows lined up across your screen. Next, you can resize them any way you like.

Cascade

If you have lots of open windows, the previous two commands may make them too small to recognize. The Cascade option overlaps them in a stack, with just the title bars showing. You can use the title bar to identify the window you're looking for.

Hide

Hides the front-most window. Unhide makes *all* hidden windows visible again.

Arrange Icons

Places the bars for minimized windows in a neat line along the bottom of your Access window. It's a cousin to the View → Arrange Icons command in the Database window, except it works on the "icons" for open windows, not closed ones.

[Window Names]

Just like the list of files at the bottom of the File menu, the Window menu lists all open windows. Just choose the one you want to bring to the front.

Help Menu

As discussed in Appendix A, this menu is your ticket to all forms of Access help.

INDEX

Symbols

- (hyphen)
range wildcard, 174
- (minus) sign, linked tables, 133
 # (pound sign)
dates in Access, 227
wildcard symbol, 174
( ) (parentheses), grouping in expressions, 238
* (asterisk)
multiplication symbol, 238
wildcard symbol, 174
using in a filter, 176
+ (plus) sign, linked tables, 133
< (less than) operator, 175
= (equal to) operator, 175
> (greater than) operator, 175
? (question mark)
wildcard symbol, 174
using in a filter, 176
[ ] (brackets), in expressions, 238, 250

A

Access
installing, 288-290
launching, 23
Northwind database (example), 200

Access 2003 Assistance page, 299-302
Access Database Wizard, 24-38
adding title and picture, 34-38
choosing a template, 25-29
choosing styles for forms and reports, 33-34
choosing table fields, 29-33
Access window, 16
Action queries, 187
adding, 240-245
Advanced Filter/Sort, 164, 178-181
adding criteria, 178-180
applying and removing, 181
saving as a query, 181
AND operator, 175, 177
antivirus software, 39
ascending sorts
database records, 155
report data, 275
Asset Tracking template, 27
Autoforms, 90, 97-100
Autolookup queries, 187
AutoReport: Columnar, 272
AutoReport: Tabular, 272
averages, calculating, 233-235

B

BETWEEN operator, 175
billing clients (database template), 27
blank database, creating, 49
bound controls, forms, 94

C

calculated controls, forms, 94
calculations
    averages, 233-235
    Expression Builder, 245-256
    expression syntax, 238
    getting sums, totals, and averages
        from database, 231
    subtotal, total, or grand total, 240-245
    total sales for a specific date, 252-256
    using numbers in two columns to
        create a third, 236
Chart Wizard, 272
Charts reports, 262
checkbox controls, forms, 95
    dragging, 114
clicking the mouse, 8
columnar forms, 91
Columnar reports, 259, 272
columns, 17
    moving for multiple field sorts,
        159-160
    (see also fields)
Combo box controls (forms), 95

commands, adding to toolbars, 366
common field, 131
comparative expressions, 176
computer viruses, 39
Contact Management template, 27
controls (form), 94
    dragging, 114
CreatingForms database, 97
criteria (in queries), 221-223
Crosstab queries, 186
Crosstab Query Wizard, 190, 200-203
Ctrl+Break, stopping a query, 215
Ctrl+P, printing queries, 216
currency format, 243, 249
Customize dialog box, 366

D

Data access pages, 328
data source
    choosing for reports, 273
Data view, 46
database management software, 3
    when not to use, 5, 9
database objects
    defined, 17
    determining database design, 21
    getting into a database, with
        switchboard, 41
Database window, 5
**Database Wizard (see Access Database
    Wizard)**

expressions (*continued*)

    using in filters, 175

    viewing in Zoom window, 231

Extensible Markup Language (XML), 328

F

FAQs (frequently asked questions), 314–336

    importing and exporting, 314–329

    validation, 329–334

fields, 17

    adding to forms in Design view, 118

    changing properties and deleting, 42–46

    choosing for a form, 102

    choosing for reports, 273

    choosing for table, 29–33

    common field in linked tables, 131

    form field, 24

    Select queries, 186

    selecting for filtering/sorting, 178

    sorting on multiple, 157–160

        moving columns for, 159–160

    validation, 329

File menu, 340–344

Filter by Form menu, 164

Filter by Selection menu, 164

Filter Excluding Selection menu, 164

Filter for shortcut menu, 164

filters, 163–181

    Advanced Filter/Sort, 178–181

        adding criteria, 178–180

        saving as query, 181

    applying and removing, 176–177

        Advanced Filter/Sort, 181

    applying in a query, 198–199

    expressions in, 175

    Filter by Exclusion, 170

    Filter by Form, 171

    Filter by Selection, 168–169

    Filters menu, 359

    finding all variations of an entry, 173

    operators in, 175

    queries vs., 185

    saving or discarding, 165

    wildcards, 174

    wildcards, operators, and expressions, 172

Find and Replace dialog box, 335

Find Duplicates Query Wizard, 191, 203–210

Find Unmatched Query Wizard, 191, 211–215

flat databases, situations for use, 126

footers

    adding to forms in Design view, 116

    report, 267

        Group Header/Footer, 269

        page footer, 269

form fields, 24

W

Web data format (XML), 328
wildcards
  defined, 173
  using * in a filter, 176
  using in filters, 174
Window menu, 367

X

XML (Extensible Markup Language), 328

COLOPHON

Matt Hutchinson was the production editor for *Access 2003 for Starters: The Missing Manual*. Chris Downey proofread the book. Marlowe Shaeffer and Claire Cloutier provided quality control. Ellen Troutman wrote the index.

Nicole Skillern created the series cover design. Linda Palo produced the cover. Marcia Friedman designed the hand lettering on the cover.

Tom Ingalls designed the interior layout. Keith Fahlgren converted the text and prepared it for layout. Robert Romano, Jessamyn Read, and Lesley Borash produced the illustrations.

Better than e-books

Buy *Access 2003 for Starters: The Missing Manual* and access the digital edition FREE on Safari for 45 days.

Go to www.oreilly.com/go/safarienabled
and type in coupon code 3HR6-KHQQ-NM5H-JUQ1-KHEL

Search
thousands of
top tech books

Download
whole chapters

Cut and Paste
code examples

Find
answers fast

Search Safari! The premier electronic reference
library for programmers and IT professionals.

Related Titles from O'Reilly

Windows Users

Access Cookbook, *2nd Edition*

Access 2003 Personal Trainer

Access Database Design & Programming, *3rd Edition*

Excel Annoyances

Excel Hacks

Excel Pocket Guide

Excel 2003 Personal Trainer

Excel: The Missing Manual

Outlook 2000 in a Nutshell

Outlook Pocket Guide

PC Annoyances, *2nd Edition*

PowerPoint 2003 Personal Trainer

QuickBooks 2005: The Missing Manual

Windows XP Annoyances For Geeks

Windows XP Cookbook

Windows XP Hacks, *2nd Edition*

Windows XP Home Edition: The Missing Manual, *2nd Edition*

Windows XP in a Nutshell, *2nd Edition*

Windows XP Personal Trainer

Windows XP Pocket Guide

Windows XP Power Hound

Windows XP Pro: The Missing Manual, *2nd Edition*

Windows XP Unwired

Word Annoyances

Word Hacks

Word Pocket Guide, *2nd Edition*

Word 2003 Personal Trainer

Our books are available at most retail and online bookstores.

To order direct: 1-800-998-9938 • *order@oreilly.com* • *www.oreilly.com*

Online editions of most O'Reilly titles are available by subscription at *safari.oreilly.com*

Keep in touch with O'Reilly

Download examples from our books

To find example files from a book, go to: *www.oreilly.com/catalog* select the book, and follow the "Examples" link.

Register your O'Reilly books

Register your book at *register.oreilly.com* Why register your books? Once you've registered your O'Reilly books you can:

- Win O'Reilly books, T-shirts or discount coupons in our monthly drawing.
- Get special offers available only to registered O'Reilly customers.
- Get catalogs announcing new books (US and UK only).
- Get email notification of new editions of the O'Reilly books you own.

Join our email lists

Sign up to get topic-specific email announcements of new books and conferences, special offers, and O'Reilly Network technology newsletters at:

elists.oreilly.com

It's easy to customize your free elists subscription so you'll get exactly the O'Reilly news you want.

Get the latest news, tips, and tools

www.oreilly.com

- "Top 100 Sites on the Web"—PC Magazine
- CIO Magazine's Web Business 50 Awards

Our web site contains a library of comprehensive product information (including book excerpts and tables of contents), downloadable software, background articles, interviews with technology leaders, links to relevant sites, book cover art, and more.

Work for O'Reilly

Check out our web site for current employment opportunities:

jobs.oreilly.com

Contact us

O'Reilly Media, Inc.
1005 Gravenstein Hwy North
Sebastopol, CA 95472 USA
Tel: 707-827-7000 or 800-998-9938
(6am to 5pm PST)
Fax: 707-829-0104

Contact us by email

For answers to problems regarding your order or our products:
order@oreilly.com

To request a copy of our latest catalog:
catalog@oreilly.com

For book content technical questions or corrections: **booktech@oreilly.com**

For educational, library, government, and corporate sales: **corporate@oreilly.com**

To submit new book proposals to our editors and product managers:
proposals@oreilly.com

For information about our international distributors or translation queries:
international@oreilly.com

For information about academic use of O'Reilly books:
adoption@oreilly.com
or visit:
academic.oreilly.com

For a list of our distributors outside of North America check out:
international.oreilly.com/distributors.html

Order a book online

www.oreilly.com/order_new

 **O'REILLY**®

Our books are available at most retail and online bookstores.
To order direct: 1-800-998-9938 • *order@oreilly.com* • *www.oreilly.com*
Online editions of most O'Reilly titles are available by subscription at *safari.oreilly.com*